THE LAND WITHIN

THE LAND WITHIN

The Process of Possessing and Being Possessed by God According to the Mystic Jan van Ruysbroeck

by

PAUL MOMMAERS

Translated by

DAVID N. SMITH

FRANCISCAN HERALD PRESS
1434 West 51st St. • Chicago, Ill. 60609

247.22
RUH(MO)

The Land Within: The Process of Possessing and Being Possessed by God According to the Mystic Jan van Ruysbroeck by Paul Mommaers, translated by David N. Smith from the Dutch, *Waar Naartoe Is Nu De Gloed Van De Liefde?:* Fenomenologie van de liefdegemeenschap volgens de mysticus Ruusbroec, Patmos Verlag, Antwerp/Utrecht, 1973. Copyright ©1975 by Franciscan Herald Press, 1434 West 51st Street, Chicago, Illinois, U.S.A. No part of this book may be reproduced in any form by print, photoprint or any other means without written permission from the publisher.

Library of Congress Cataloging in Publication Data:

Mommaers, Paul, 1935 -
    The Land Within.
    Translation of Waar naartoe is nu de gloed van de liefde?
    Includes bibliographical references and index.
    1. Jan van Ruysbroeck, 1293-1381. 2. Mysticism—
Middle Ages, 600-1500. I. Title.
BV5095.J3M6513   248'.22'0924   75-19472
ISBN 0-8199-0583-6

NIHIL OBSTAT:
  Mark Hegener O.F.M.
  Censor Deputatus

IMPRIMATUR:
  Msgr. Richard A. Rosemeyer, J.D.
  Vicar General, Archdiocese of Chicago

"The Nihil Obstat and Imprimatur are official declarations that a book or pamphlet is free of doctrinal or moral error. No indication is contained therein that those who have granted the Nihil Obstat and Imprimatur agree with the contents, opinions, or statements expressed."

248
.22
mol

MADE IN THE UNITED STATES OF AMERICA

Contents

Foreword

This presentation of Ruysbroeck is the direct result of a scientific investigation of his works. I began by suspecting that what the master of mysticism in the Low Countries had provided was above all a phenomenology of the community of love and that his language was descriptive. This formed the basis of my working hypothesis and as I continued with my study of the whole body of Ruysbroeck's writings, using the now familiar methods of literary criticism, this initial supposition was gradually confirmed.

I have, however, also attempted to do something else in this book, although this may cause some consternation among readers of a more philosophical turn of mind. I have tried to make this early author accessible to people living today by conveying something of the splendour of his writing in present-day language. In the second part of this book, then, I have interpreted and reproduced as faithfully as I could some of the most important passages in his works.

Finally, I have to offer my sincere thanks to all those who have helped or encouraged me to write this book and especially to Professor A. Deblaere S.J., without whose help the work would never have been completed.

PART I

INTRODUCTORY QUESTIONS

It would at first sight seem to be a rather remarkable and indeed doubtful undertaking to publish a book about Jan van Ruysbroeck (1293-1381) today. It is certainly no longer a very popular practice to return to the past if one's interest is not purely antiquarian. Above all, we have to be up-to-date, begin every day with a clean sheet and, like modern magicians, do everything spontaneously. What, then, can be gained nowadays in real "existential" experience from digging up the remote past, in this case the writings of a remote fourteenth century mystic, especially when there are few things more controversial than mysticism?

There is, of course, a great deal of interest in mysticism now, but the wind is blowing from the East and not so much from the West, where the Christian mystics tend to be ignored. This certainly applies to men like Ruysbroeck, who left behind an account of his sixty or so years of personal religious life in unparalleled prose and who never lost the sound common sense of his native Brabant even in the loftiest contemplation. It is moreover true that even the most passionate supporters of mysticism provide us with very few precise data about what really happens in meditation.

It is difficult nowadays to find concrete examples of the practice of mystical commitment and it is also striking how seldom the demands of purposeful activity are

3

met by mystical means. The consequence of this is that mysticism almost entirely fails to touch the great mass of sober, cool-headed believers. These are able calmly to waive aside all new experiences of a mystical kind and, in their compassion, leave them to the so-called social misfits, who are free to look for security in the purely subjective refuge of mystical "feeling."

Yet there is undoubtedly great interest in mysticism today and, even though this may be no more than a contemporary fashion, it does point to a real need. We know that clothes do not make the man and that not everyone who wears a cowl is a monk, but it is equally true to say that we also express something of ourselves in our fashions. We may truthfully say that there is among the present generation a great desire to experience something that does not belong strictly to the scientifically calculable world, something not directly useful, measurable and therefore ultimately boring.

One has the impression that everything that goes on around us can be predicted by experts — every aspect of reality is covered by a specialist. Even before anything can happen, the glow of astonishment is overshadowed and all that is left is an object that can be dealt with. Some people are almost afraid to see the fresh green of spring or the red shades of autumn, because they have been taught that it is simply a question of light waves. The miracle that something is there grows stale almost before it is experienced because we are told by science what it is.

We may go further and say that what takes place within us, that continuous happening in the realm of what we call the soul, is similarly affected — it is only worth considering if it can be fitted somewhere into the pattern of our established knowledge. There is, however, also that great mystery of our inner life which can never be fully expressed or explained, the dark side of the moon that will never be seen on our television screens, but this is of secondary importance. It is even regarded with suspicion, although the experts tell us that they will, in time, be able to offer a complete explanation. So we are scientifically reassured, but at the same time hopelessly bored.

The main character in a recent book by Saul Bellow is a man who is especially, if not completely weighed down by this narrowness perfected by science. He had come to the conclusion that "intellectual man had become an explaining creature. Fathers to children, wives to husbands, lecturers to listeners, experts to laymen, colleagues to colleagues, doctors to patients, man to his own soul, explained. The roots of this, the causes of the other, the source of events, the history, the structure, the reasons why. For the most part, in one ear out the other. The soul wanted what it wanted. It had its own natural knowledge. It sat unhappily on the superstructures of explanation, poor bird, not knowing which way to fly."[1]

"Life, when it was like this, all question-and-answer from the top of the intellect to the very bottom, was really a state of singular dirty misery." Mr. Sammler came to believe. "When it was all question-and-answer it had no charm. Life when it had no charm was entirely question-and-answer. The thing worked both ways. Also, the questions were bad. Also, the answers were horrible. This poverty of the soul, its abstract state, you could see in faces on the street. And he too had a touch of the same disease — the disease of the single self explaining what was what and who was who. The results could be foreseen, foretold."[2]

What is particularly striking, however — not as an argument for or against mysticism or the reading of mystical works, but simply as a symbolic reaction — is that Mr. Sammler, after having read historians of civilization, with "side excursions" into modern philosophy and taking on Doctor Faustus and "essays on history and politics," changed his diet of reading. "After four or five years of this diet," the author tells us, "he wished to read only certain religious writers of the thirteenth century — Suso, Tauler, and Meister Eckhardt. In his seventies he was interested in little more than Meister Eckhardt and the Bible. . . . He read Eckhardt's Latin at the public library from microfilm. He read the Sermons and the Talks of Instruction — a few sentences at a time — a paragraph of Old German — presented to his good eye at close range."[3]

There are also signs that psychologists are beginning to realize that modern man is above all frustrated in the sphere of experience. In his book *The Politics of Experience,* R. D. Laing devoted several pages to what he called the "almost unbelievable devastation" that we have made of our experience and no one will deny that he has put his finger on a very sore spot: "As for our bodies, we retain just sufficient proprioceptive sensations to coordinate our movements and to ensure the minimal requirements for biosocial survival — to register fatigue, signals for food, sex, defecation, sleep; beyond that, little or nothing. Our capacity to think, except in the service of what we are dangerously deluded in supposing is our self-interest, and in conformity with common sense, is pitifully limited: our capacity even to see, hear, touch, taste and smell is so shrouded in veils of mystification that an intensive discipline of un-learning is necessary for *anyone* before one can begin to experience the world afresh, with innocence, truth and love. And immediate experience of, in contrast to belief or faith in, a spiritual realm of demons, spirits, Powers, Dominions, Principalities, Seraphim and Cherubim, the Light, is even more remote. As domains of experience become more alien to us, we need greater and greater open-mindedness even to conceive of their existence."[4]

Professor J. H. van den Berg[5] has also conducted an inquiry into the precise nature of the spiritual disease or at least the need of our times. Until recently, the psycho-therapist would have been principally concerned with unconscious sexuality and aggression and he would have tried to cure his patients by bringing these to light. Now, however, he is increasingly required to help his patients to become conscious of another banished sector of their psyche — their "spirituality." He describes this as follows: "The realm of the spirit has in recent years been seriously neglected. Yet it exists. Everyone has his own ideas, his reflections, his 'philosohy.' Whenever he thinks in this way, he is already in the realm of the spirit. It is even possible for him to cherish an ideal. . . . This enables us to transcend ourselves. We are there, above ourselves, when we admit to ourselves that we are mortal. Whoever lives to his heart's content sexually or to the utmost of his ability aggressively may ask himself the question: 'what ought I to think about my life when I am old?' The question is discredited . . . but it is still meaningful. Of all living organisms, man is the only one who knows that his life must come to an end. Does that play an important part? Anyone who thinks of that part is already in the highest compartment (that is, of spirituality), where there are all kinds of things, including *one thing and another*. This is as impenetrable and as fundamental as the deepest ground of the lowest compartment, which has been given the name *vitality*. That one thing and another has, since time immemorial, been given the name of *God*.

"This last sentence does not really work any more. But we are at least bound to say this about it: everyone knows it. If we try to penetrate into the realm of the spirit, into our own ideals, shall we say, and sooner or later we shall reach what is impenetrable, but this will not be without meaning. There is an unknown vitality that stimulates us and enables us to live from the earth. In the same way, there is also something unknown and of a different kind which makes us think, reflect, desire and, in a word, transcend our own individual, self-seeking *vital* existence."

Within the context of the general decline of experience, a specific problem of Christian life is highlighted — the simple but earnest complaint so often made by believers that they are not conscious of God's grace and redemption. The source of living water is not only very deep, it is also hopelessly well concealed, so well that it is almost impossible for the Christian to feel really, rich, let alone happy. Where is that promise of abundant life? This difficulty can, of course, often be set aside by making an appeal to pure faith (pure in this case suddenly coming to mean blind). It is also possible to repress the question, which is based on empirical experience, with the help of answers drawn from theory. But neither of these solutions will satisfy the believer's longing for personal experience of God or answer his cry: "Where is my God here and now?" and "Help me to taste the sweetness of his yoke." Instead of bread, he is given brilliant stones — a theology adapted and re-adapted to the modern world-view, a more humane morality, a liturgy which catches on more easily and a way of preaching the Word of God that gets across at once. Everything, in other words, directed towards conviction and justification, but nothing to stimulate personal spiritual perception. A great deal of visible structure, but practically no inner experience.

All these expressions of Christian life are absolutely necessary. There has to be reflection, organization and continuous adaptation. As soon as Christianity retreats into pietism, it ceases to exist. On the other hand, however, it is equally certain that any form of Christianity which does not communicate God tangibly and lead the believer to experience the one who is "Quite Other" has already lost its soul.

Two examples taken from the history of the Church can enable us to understand this. The first is that almost all the great reformers were practical and efficient men who set off — in the literal sense of the term — from the point of personal experience. The Christian who is really up-to-date and contemporary in his attitude has never been purely active, restless or agitated or characterized by the conviction firstly that his own behavior is out-of-date and reflects that of his limited environment and secondly that he has to adapt his way of acting as sensibly as possible, so that his own ideal and his conviction will perhaps have a chance of success. On the contrary, authentic renewal is always the result of a renewed inspiration in men who have previously had direct experience of God. Ruysbroeck's comment about the founders of the mendicant orders is, to some extent at least, a universally valid law: "The men who founded the mendicant orders possessed God in loneliness of spirit. Inwardly impelled by God and love of the brethren, they went out to the people and filled the whole world with holy living and salutary teaching. . . . All they sought were God's honor and the general well-being of the whole world."[6]

Being and doing, praying and working, experiencing and thinking — these have always gone together in all great Christians. This has always been so, despite the inclination on the part of so many of the Church's theologians to explain faith in abstract terms without reference to man's psyche and his experience.

The second example from the history of Christianity is this. The Church has never — through indifference or because of a Stoic attitude — been able to accept "pure" faith as sufficient. Again and again men have arisen in the Church who have claimed that they have experienced God and his grace and redemption personally. The Church's tradition, which covers almost twenty centuries of Christian existence, includes not only many dogmatic pronouncements and theological treatises as well as practical applications of these in everyday life, but also an inexhaustible source of living witnesses, who have frequently written down their experience of God. Many of these Christians have possessed the exceptional gift of a deep consciousness of the presence of God within them and the ability to describe this presence in words. The most interesting of these spiritual writers are known as the mystics.

In order to give some insight into what mysticism really is, we will now go on to provide an outline of some of its most important elements. This may at the same time help to make the situation clear enough for the reader to be able to approach Ruysbroeck's work in a critical spirit. In this outline, we shall confine ourselves to those data in the Christian texts which most call for attention.[7]

1. What is Mysticism?

At the very beginning it has to be emphasized that, although the mystic is exceptional, he is not a man set aside. He is extraordinary and inevitably arouses either envy or admiration, but he is not an anomaly. He forms quite an ordinary part of the objective reality of Christian life and thought, insofar as this can be described, compared and defined and insofar as it is possible to mark off limits between one aspect and another. He does not belong to any special category of being and there is certainly no need to explore and throw light on any unusually deep levels of objective experience in order to find a suitable place for the mystic in the world. Like every other man or woman, he is a creature and has received his life from God, who preserves him in that life. Like every other Christian, he has the Three Divine Persons abiding in him. As far as his objective relationship with God is concerned, then, there is nothing out of the way.

The distinction between the mystic and the non-mystic, however, is to be found in the way in which the former experiences "ordinary" data. Whereas, in the case of most non-mystical Christians, union with God and his creation and redemption — or at least many aspects of this — remain points of faith, a conviction or a philosophical conclusion, in the mystic's experience they become fully conscious psychological realities. He is, in other words, able to perceive what normally remains hidden and, if his development is uninterrupted, he can also realize this in his life and it ceases to be abstract and becomes for him a concrete reality. As the fourteenth century English mystic Walter Hilton said, he not only receives "reform in faith only," but also experiences "reform in faith and feeling."[8] He is not the recipient of any special kind of "sanctifying" grace, but he certainly becomes conscious of the presence of grace:

This tasting of manna is an awareness of the life of grace, which comes from the opening of the soul's eyes. And this grace does not differ from the grace that the elect soul feels at the beginning of its conversion; it is the same grace but experienced in another way.

Many of the mystics have declared that they were different from other Christians only insofar as their experience was concerned and none has expressed this conviction more clearly than Ruysbroeck. This revealing remark can be found in his "Spiritual Espousals" (*Die Gheestelike Brulocht*) at the precise place where he describes the mystical experience:

This is common to all good men. But how that may come about remains hidden from them all their lives if it be that they are not inward and untrammelled by any creature.[9]

The "good man" who remains "external," that is, whose attention is exclusively or excessively fixed on virtues and an external way of life, certainly possesses God, but he is not conscious of this — "And therefore he possesses that of which he knows nothing."[10]

How, then, can we define the mystic? He is a man who experiences the presence of God. But of course we have to go a little further into the precise meaning of this "experience" in this context. First and foremost, what we have here is a knowledge of God, the invisible one, without any "means" being involved. (The word "means" is used here in the way in which it was employed by the mystical writers of the Netherlands and its meaning can perhaps best be sensed if we think of the modern terms "intermediary," "mediation" or "coming between." The seventeenth century French mystics translated this phrase "without means" by *sans entre-deux*.)

As a rule, man is so closely associated with the world of the senses that he can only approach God consciously by "means" of ideas, images and concepts. He is able to know God, but only in and through something that is not God himself. He has to be content with references to God. However subtle the mirror in which he is able to see God may be and however authentic the signs may be, the distance between him and God remains and with it the indirectness, the lack of immediacy, the fact that there is an intermediary.

The average Christian undoubtedly feels God from time to time, but this contact is quickly hidden again and is known to be indirect. On closer inspection, it is usually found to be having some kind of feeling for God rather than really touching and tasting the Other. All of us have, at some time or other in our lives, become aware of the presence in us of certain surprising qualities, a peace and joy coming from an unknown source or an unpremeditated goodness. All these are undoubtedly given by God, but are they really anything more than a distant echo in non-mystical people of our being after all of what God himself is, a reflection from which we can, by "means" of reasoning, conclude that God is present. We cannot feel God himself "without means" and always remain at the level of references.

In the case of the mystic, however, the veil is —
suddenly and usually unexpectedly — lifted. The wall
of ideas and affections, which is usually impenetrable,
falls and the mystic sees and feels God with a certainty
and a directness that is paralleled only in sensory perception. He comes into direct contact with God, the invisible
one. The Other is indisputably present for him. The following passage in the journal of Dag Hammarskjöld
points clearly to this sudden coming to direct knowledge
of God:

Then I saw that the wall had never been there, that the "unheard-
of" is here and this, not something and somewhere else,
    that the "offering" is here and now, always and everywhere —
"surrendered" to *be* what, in me, God gives of himself to himself.[11]

Teresa of Avila has borne witness in a particularly
interesting way to this direct experience of the presence
of God. She experienced his presence not only "in all
things," but also, as a threefold presence, "in the soul."
In both cases, she was unable to accept — the evidence
was clearly more powerful than the extremely weighty
interpretation of "men without knowledge" — that this
was simply an indirect presence "only through grace":

In the beginning it happened to me that I was ignorant of one
thing — I did not know that God was in all things: and when he
seemed to me to be so near, I thought it impossible. Not to believe
that he was present was not in my power; for it seemed to me, as
it were, evident that I felt there his very presence.
    Some unlearned men used to say to me, that he was present only
by his grace. I could not believe that, because, as I am saying, he
seemed to me to be present himself: so I was distressed. A most
learned man, of the Order of the glorious Patriarch St. Dominic,
delivered me from this doubt; for he told me that he was present,
and how he communed with us: this was a great comfort to me.
    An interior peace, and the little strength which either pleasures

or displeasures have to remove this presence (during the time it lasts) of the Three Persons, and that without the power to doubt it, continue in such a manner that I clearly seem to experience what St. John says, "That he will dwell in the soul," and this is not only by grace, but that he will also make her perceive this presence.

This brings so much good that it is unspeakable and especially this — that it is no longer necessary to look for visions to know that God is there.[12]

Another well-known description of this mystical experience can be found in the works of Bernard of Clairvaux, who tells us that God does not come to us by any of the ways that are normally known to us and that his presence cannot be classified under any of the usual headings of human experience:

I confess, then, though I say it in my foolishness, that the Word has visited me, and even very often. But although he has frequently entered my soul, I have never at any time been sensible of the precise moment of his coming. I have felt that he was present. I remember that he was with me; I have sometimes even been able to have a presentiment that he would come; but never to feel his coming nor his departure. For whence he came to enter my soul, or whither he went on quitting it, by what means he has made entrance or departure, I confess that I know not even to this day. . . . It is not by the eyes that he enters, for he is without form or color that they can discern; nor by the ears, for his coming is without sound; nor by the nostrils, for it is not with the air but with the mind that he is blended. . . . By what avenue, then, has he entered? Or perhaps the fact may be that he has not entered at all, nor indeed come at all from outside. For not one of these things belongs to outside. Yet it has not come from within me, for it is good, and I know that nothing good dwells within me (Rom 7: 18). I have ascended higher than myself and lo! I have found the Word above me still. My curiosity led me to descend below myself also, and yet I have found him still at a lower depth. If I have looked without myself, I have found that he is beyond that which is outside me; and if within, he was at an

inner depth still. And thus I have learned the truth of the words
I had read: "In him we live and move and have our being" (Acts
17: 28).[13]

Bernard is speaking here of a knowledge of God
gained in human experience, a direct perception of his
presence. Gerson called this a *cognitio experimentalis*
and Augustine Baker an "experimental knowledge." It
is the first specific gift received by the mystic. The
immediacy of this experience must not, however, be
confused with clarity or completeness. Mystics are fond
of comparing their contact with God to the togetherness
of two friends in a dark room and they prefer to speak,
not so much of seeing or looking, as of feeling, touching
and being touched. They are very conscious of the inexhaustible nature of the presence of God, which is too
great to measure. They also always affirm again and
again that faith is not as it were placed in parenthesis
or made superfluous by mystical experience. On the contrary, such experience throws light on faith. They insist
too that man's experience of God is always obstructed
so long as he remains in the body.

Man does not make — he receives. This is another
very important aspect of mystical experience, which is
always given and never seized. Whether he is urged on
or supported by grace or not, a man can achieve a great
deal. He can acquire a deep knowledge of God and he
can produce ardent feelings. He can learn to live ex-
cellently. But he can only undergo the presence of God.
It is only when he is passive in the presence of the Other,
who as it were intrudes upon him, that he will be led
into mystical experience. The mystic, then, is always
long-suffering and never excessively — or exaggerated-
ly — active in his intellect or his emotions.

It is surely true to say that our association with others — especially as soon as we begin to know them as persons — gives us moments of long-suffering and that this experience is a distant foreshadowing of the passivity of the mystic. The person who has never experienced this is indeed empoverished, since it is an essential aspect that is latent in every encounter. It can be recognized by a sudden loss of power and an unexpected collapse of all our carefully prepared approach to the other, all our ideas, longings and fears imperceptibly receding, so that we are left in silent admiration of what *is* there before us. This happens above all in the encounter with God and, in an important passage in his "Rule of Perfection," Benedict of Canfield[14] has described his own personal experience of this total mystical impotence:

It will therefore be clear from everything that has been said so far that no lamentations, reflections or exercises of the intellect can contribute to this kind of unity with God. All our senses, all our judgments and all our human arguments must bow here before God's glory. Finally, all intellectual activity must be set aside. I am bound to conclude that there is no single human or active means of achieving this unity with God or the essential Will. And it is therefore true that this Being cannot be understood unless it allows itself to be understood, cannot be comprehended unless it allows itself to be comprehended, cannot be seen unless it gives itself to be contemplated, cannot be tasted, known or possessed unless it wants to be tasted, known or possessed. The divine Being allows itself to be understood when, how and by whom it wants. It allows itself to be tasted and possessed when, how and by whom it wishes. In ourselves, we can do *nothing*.

In his description of this mystical "touching," Ruysbroeck emphasizes that:

The creature suffers and endures this touching, for here there is a uniting of the highest powers in the unity of the spirit, above the multiplicity of all virtues. And in this there is no person operative but God alone, out of his free liberality, who is the sole cause of all our virtue and all our blessedness.[15]

Anyone who knows anything about the history of religion in Europe will at once look for the spectre of "quietism" behind this passivity of the mystic. It is therefore important to stress that this "suffering and enduring" described by Ruysbroeck does not mean the end of all spiritual activity. On the contrary, what the mystic has to allow to become quiet is his *own* activity. He must allow his own faculties to rest, but only insofar as they are governed by his own will and are the expression of himself, who is concerned with acquisition and knows what he wants, has his own way in everything, is capable, masterful and determined. Passivity in the mystical sense means above all leaving the initiative and the leadership entirely to the Other. It is not in any way laziness, extinction or simple *laisser-faire*. On the contrary, the mystic has to make himself open to the overwhelming influence of God which goes far beyond his own efforts, calls for a sharpened degree of attentiveness and requires total receptivity on his part. All the great mystics have declared again and again that they have never lived more intensely or done more than when they gave up all personal power. This principle is very clearly expressed in the passage in Ruysbroeck's "Spiritual Espousals" which follows the text quoted above. Before we examine this passage, however, we must analyze Ruysbroeck's understanding of the psychological structure of man.

Most of the spiritual writers of the Netherlands and the Rhineland follow Augustine in their view of the human psyche as consisting of two great aspects. On the one hand, they distinguished the "ego" or everyday consciousness. The various human faculties reside in this conscious ego and are subdivided into the higher and the lower powers, the first including everything concerned with sensibility, the second consisting above all of the intellect and the will. These faculties are the instruments of the ego, which is always striving to appropriate reality, to know and to possess. On the other hand, there is the great sphere or territory — these terms are, of course, used figuratively in this context — of the most profound self; and the ordinary ego or consciousness usually has no knowledge of this level, which is manifested above all in mystical experience.

This is the level of the "unity of the spirit" and of the "being." It lies outside the sphere of the faculties and is untouched by the ego. It is here that is found, both at the psychological and at the purely objective level, man's most profound and definitive essence, his "ground." Whoever — like the mystic — is permitted to descend into this most distinctive center of man's being, however, inevitably discovers that this "being" is in no sense an independent, closed or limited reality. It is, on the contrary, an openness that cannot be defined or restricted, the "wilderness" in which man "depends on God." It is here that the Creator keeps his creature in being. It is also here that the Trinity dwells. It is from here that God — and God alone — can work "outwards from within."

It ought, then, to be clearer to the reader what is meant by mystical "passivity" and we can now go on to consider the significance of the mystical "touching" which, according to Ruysbroeck's text, takes place in the "unity of the spirit," in other words, outside the sphere of the faculties which seek to possess. Even the intellect and the will, which are the most subtle and spiritual of all, are usually not equal to this presence. This does not mean, however, that they are consequently condemned to extinction. They have more to do than ever, but the task is beyond their powers. They are stimulated more than they have ever been by something that is greater than themselves and cannot be included within any known framework of their own. As Ruysbroeck says:

In the unity of the spirit, where this spring (of touching) flows, man is above working and above reason, but he is not without reason, for the enlightened reason and in particular the power of the soul to love feels this touching, yet reason can never understand or comprehend the manner nor the fashion of it, nor how nor why that touching came about.[16]

This passivity is usually expressed very sharply in the sudden and unexpected character of the mystical experience. The Christian does what he can, but reaches the limit of his possibilities. Despite all his courage, faithfulness and good will, he cannot force God to be or to remain tangibly present. His meditation then probably becomes a tiresome labor and is eventually exhausted All his good and precious feelings become dry and barren and the practice of virtue loses its happiness and becomes hard and joyless. Ruysbroeck has vividly described the situation of the man who is on the threshold of mystical experience, using the parable of the maidens and the bridegroom.

The prudent virgin, that is, the pure soul, who has abandoned earthly things and lives with God in virtues, she has taken into the vessel of her heart the oil of charity and virtuous works, by the light of the lamp of an unsullied conscience; but when Christ the Bridegroom tarries in trust and in fresh inpouring of gifts, the soul becomes sleepy and weary and slumbers. In the middle of the night, that is, when men least expect it and watch for it, a cry is raised in the soul, a cry not of the senses: "See, the Bridegroom comes; go out to meet him" (Mt 25: 6).[17]

God's coming, then, is purely gratuitous, but this does not mean that it is either meaningless or unnecessary to prepare for it. It is true that there may be no causal connection between man's striving in prayer and God's bestowing of mystical grace. There is no guarantee that the man who prays constantly will experience God's presence. It is not the Lord's habit simply to scatter the seed of his grace at random on any fallow ground that happens to be at hand. He may, however, come to someone who is unprepared or even unwilling and he may mystically touch someone who is only in the first stages of prayer. William of St. Thierry wrote:

It may happen that the experience of pure prayer and that sweet taste of love are not found, but that they come and find us. Grace may be ahead of the man who is, as it were, not prepared for it, the man who does not ask, does not seek and does not knock. Just as a slave is admitted to his master's table, so too is the uneducated spirit raised up to this kind of experience of prayer, which is otherwise usually given as a reward for services rendered by perfect souls.[18]

God, then is free. He may come by any way. Usually, however, mystical experience is the crowning — not the fruit — of a persistent longing and perhaps a reward — not a prize — for constant practice. Ruysbroeck has indicated how complex the process of preparation can be:

When a man by means of charity and an intention towards God offers himself up to God in all his works and in all his living, to his honor and praise, and seeks rest in God beyond all things, then he must, with humility and patience and forgetfulness of himself, still await new riches and new gifts, with certain confidence: and still he must be untroubled, whether God gives to him or does not give. Thus a man makes himself ready and pleasing, so that he may receive the interior life of yearning for God. When the vessel is prepared, one pours into it the precious liquor. There is no more precious vessel than the loving soul, nor is there a more cordial drink than the grace of God.[19]

It is clear, then, that two essential aspects of mystical experience are directness and passivity. The mystic is moreover someone who is aware that God himself is present. This brings us to a third aspect of mystical experience which is perhaps the most important of all, namely that God's presence is in no sense an uncommitted spectacle. God does not appear as a Supreme Being in the coolness of his beauty and satisfied and complete in himself. On the contrary, he appears to claim man, to receive him and to unite himself with him. The essence and the culmination of mystical experience is unity with God. Its deepest and most powerful motivation is the Love which unites what is separated and different. In this experience, all feeling and knowing amounts to a sense of union with the Other. Dag Hammarskjöld, who, as we noted above, saw that "the wall had never been there" and spoke of being "surrendered to be," also wrote:

I don't know who — or what — put the question, I don't know when it was put. I don't even remember answering. But at some moment I did answer Yes to Someone — or Something — and from that hour I was certain that existence is meaningful and that, therefore, my life, in self-surrender, had a goal.[20]

Thus the "touching" that Ruysbroeck discusses in his "Spiritual Espousals" is not simply an interesting or even an instructive phenomenon, a revelation, without any consequences for man, of a God who afterwards quietly withdraws again. To think this is to forget that this

mystical "touching" comes above all from the unity
which exists between God and the soul in "all good
men," but which has in most cases still to be realized:

And above this touching in the silent existence of the spirit there
hovers an incomprehensible clarity, and that is the exalted Trinity
whence this touching proceeds. There God lives and reigns in the
spirit and the spirit in God.[21]

What, then, is this "touching," if we examine it more
closely, but a creative and irresistible invitation to being
one with God? This "touching" brings with it a "tempest
of love" and leads to "one single love":

In this tempest of love two spirits contend, the Spirit of God and
our spirit. God, by means of the Holy Spirit, inclines himself
towards us and through this we are touched in love. And our
spirit, through the operation of God and its capacity for love,
hastens and inclines itself into God and through this is God
touched. From these two there rises the contention of love: there
where deepest in it they meet and where it is most inwardly and
piercingly visited, each spirit is wounded by love. These two
spirits, that is to say our spirit and the Spirit of God, shine and
illumine each the other, and each shows to the other its counten-
ance. This constantly makes the one spirit in love to strive after
the other. Each demands of the other that which the other is and
each offers and forces on the other that which it itself is. This
makes the lover flow away to nothing. God's touching and his
giving, our loving striving and our giving back to God, this holds
love steadfast. This flowing out and flowing back again makes the
well of love overflow. In this way God's touching and our loving
striving become one single love. Here man is possessed by love,
so that he is able to forget himself and God, and know of nothing
else but love.[22]

The experience of God's presence is therefore, for the
mystic, always an experience of union with God. In the
passage that we quoted above, Bernard of Clairvaux

observed that the Word who visited him was blended with the spirit and Angela of Foligno said: "If the soul has this feeling, making it certain of the presence of God . . . it becomes aware of the infinite God being blended with it and keeping it company." A masterly description of the way in which God's becoming visible to the mystic is at the same time an experience of mutual possession has been provided by Benedict of Canfield, for whom God's presence — this is a key-word in Benedict's vocabulary of mysticism — is union; and seeing God is love:

Happy is the soul who in herself perceives the Bridegroom visibly, who is completely filled with this vision and who lets her longings and her many activities flow away in him. Such a soul is very fortunate because she sees him in this revelation and she also sees where and how he rests in her. . . . In this fulfilment, she sees that she is entirely grasped and possessed by her Bridegroom, who makes himself so completely her master that from that time onwards all her powers are concentrated on the task of receiving him and entertaining him and she is full of him, like a pregnant spouse.[24]

This third aspect of mystical experience, God's possession of the soul in loving union, can be illustrated by a twentieth century example. Dom Cuthbert Butler[25] quoted a passage from the diary of a Carmelite, who described her experience of God's presence and of her being "plunged" in him:

During prayer on the evening of the third day I entered the interior of my soul, and seemed to descend into the giddy depths of an abyss where I had the impression of being surrounded by limitless space. Then I felt the presence of the Blessed Trinity, realizing my own nothingness, which I understood better than ever before, and the knowledge was very sweet. The divine Immensity in which I was plunged and which filled me had the same sweetness. . . .

Without seeing anything with the eyes either of the body or the soul, I realized that God was present, I felt his gaze bent on me full of gentleness and affection, and that he smiled kindly upon me. I seemed plunged in God. My imagination was submissive and did not act. I did not hear any noise that might be going on around me. My soul looked fixedly into the gaze invisibly bent on me, and my heart repeated untiringly: "My God, I love thee!"

This is, of course, altogether too rough and ready an outline of what the mystic is — there is no more difficult subject to describe in a brief sketch than the mystic. But it should by now be clear at least that, even though he may also be a theologian or a diplomat if he is a man and a Carmelite with a gift for writing or a mother of four children if she is a woman, the mystic is above all someone who experiences God by being conscious of God's presence in a direct, passive and uniting way.

In order to prevent further misunderstandings that may arise, we must now try to define more precisely what is meant by "experience" in the case of the great mystics. This is all the more important, since "experience" has nowadays become not only a fashion, but also a fashionable product. In the first place, mystical experience must be clearly distinguished from the luxuriant growth of phenomena that take place outside the normal pattern of nature — levitations, visions, voices and so on as well as various stunts of a highly suspicious nature. These psycho-physical phenomena are still often described as "mystical" but they have, in themselves, nothing to do with the mystic's experience of God.

A great deal of light has been thrown on this question of mystical experience and paranormal phenomena by specialists in what are known as the "positive" sciences, in this case above all biologists, physiologists and psychologists. What is more, research into the whole question was already producing results quite a long time ago. William James, for instance, gave his Gifford Lectures on "Varieties of Religious Experience" at the very beginning of this century, in 1901-1902. (From the purely historical point of view, these lectures are very revealing, showing the independent scientific investigator in the best possible light.) Another prominent early research-worker, J. Maréchal, published the first volume of his *Études sur la Psychologie des Mystiques* in 1924. It was, however, only very slowly that their conclusions became fully accepted.

The main conclusion is this: none of the sensational or spectacular psychological or physiological manifestations have ever been taken seriously as forming an integral part of mystical experience, either by mystics themselves or in mystical teaching. There is no record of paranormal phenomena having taken place in the experience of such important mystics as Bernard or Gregory. It is even possible to say, without exaggerating in the cause of apologetics, that no mystic of any stature has ever been concerned with parapsychology. Whenever mystics have experienced anything strange or extraordinary, they have usually found it embarrassing and tiresome and have implored God to free them from it. Very often, however, they have eventually discovered that it was no more than a passing reaction of the soul in the body unused to conscious encounter with God.

Ruysbroeck is one of the many mystics who experienced such phenomena. He has, moreover, described them accurately and has situated them infallibly at the very beginning of the mystical life. In his view, they were crises in the growth of earthly man who has to learn how to accept them patiently and with a certain amount of humor. The pages of the "Spiritual Espousals" dealing with Christ's "first coming into man's heart" are psychologically sound and critically stimulating. Once the initial shocks have been absorbed, Ruysbroeck leaves these epiphenomena of the mystical life and mentions them no more. At the end of the mystical way, he points, not to some sensational figure, (who might attract and hold the attention of the great mass of the people), but the "ordinary" man who can pray and work freely and who can go out with quiet efficiency to meet the needs of all his fellow-men. Teresa of Ávila, Marie of the Incarnation, the apostle of Canada, Madame Acarie — these are only a few of the many examples of mystics who, after a disconcerting experience, have led exceptionally well balanced and practical lives.

Finally, it is worth mentioning that mystics are, generally speaking, very sensitive people. But, then, is it not true to say that everyone who is able to experience, everyone who really lives, is fragile and vulnerable? And mystics are people who above all have the openness and receptivity, the refined feelings of genius. If it did not sound too pejorative, we could say that they were grateful mediums. What is more, the borderline between normal and pathological is not always completely clear in them and some mystics undoubtedly display abnormal characteristics, having a tendency for hallucinations, obsessions and so on. Although there are such cases, however, there is no justification for regarding all mysticism as a morbid phenomenon or all mystics as hysterical or obsessed people. There is, after all, a considerable difference between the two in mentality and consciousness. Finally, there is also the empirical criterion, which is traditionally respected, but by no means out of date, of the influence that mystical experience has always had on everyday behavior.

No less important is a second aspect of mystical experience in the best sense of the word. Mature mysticism has nothing whatever to do with experience for the sake of experience. Or perhaps it would be more true to say — since almost all the mystics have known what it is to be on Circe's island — this experience goes far beyond anything that happens in the ordinary human sphere. The mystic is driven without pity away from any attachment — however subtle this may be — to what he has ever known in his own, human experience and he is unable to look back in self-satisfaction to any such experience that he might call his own. As a result of this, the ambiguity and inadequacy of this personal experience, which attracts our sympathetic interest so much these days, is brought very clearly and dramatically to light in the writings of the great mystics, more perhaps than in any other kind of document. What the mystic's persistent, sincere experience reveals, after all, is that, if the Other can only become a conscious, living reality in such experience, by no means all human experience is necessarily a pure and unadulterated experience of that Other. Although the mystic's most rich and sublime experience goes beyond the ordinary experience of every day, it is in no sense a definitive and radical break with it. On the contrary, what this mystical experience exposes, because of its unsuspected and particular refinement, are the limits and the shortcomings of everyday experience. What is moreover banished from it is the self-seeking that is concealed somewhere, like a cunning germ, in almost every ordinary human experience.

Let us for a moment look at the mystical way in the concrete. What Dag Hammarskjöld called the "wall" — of ideas, concepts, images and affections — is broken through and God gives to the mystic, who then passively experiences, a clear Presence. He feels that he forgets himself and that the presence of the Other is everything. He is happy — is he not, after all, in possession of the one who is without parallel? Sooner or later, however, with a certain sense of inevitability, the mystic experiences something quite incomprehensible. This incomprehensible experience befalls him — he does not in any way, it should be noted, leave the sphere of experience. What happens is that the Presence disappears. There is no way of recalling it and it leaves no comfort behind. It goes with the same freedom as it came and the mystic who once possessed everything is left with nothing. God, who was present, is now absent (to human experience) and, even more than before, all the obstacles separating man from God are there again. The mystic himself is plunged into misery and becomes the victim of unbelief, boredom, temptation, an aversion to prayer and above all perhaps is most severely put to the test both in his own body and in his life in the society of other men. Whereas there was, before this mystical experience, a screen between him and God, with at least a chink of light showing through here and there, now there is one single impenetrable wall between them — a wall that has been called a "wall of steel." There is, however, one positive aspect, although the mystic derives no comfort or sense of freedom from it, so that it only exists objectively. This is that he is unable to return to the everyday pleasures of an existence without the presence of God.

The literature of mysticism contains many — often extremely moving — descriptions of this "dark night of the soul" and Ruysbroeck has devoted several very striking pages to this phenomenon in his "Spiritual Espousals,"[26] written, as we would expect, in his usual sober and restrained style. He tells us how Christ first comes into man's heart by "enkindling it with the inward heat of his coming," by the "rain of inward consolation" and by drawing it up and how he then comes by the fourth manner, the experience of "forsakeness." Ruysbroeck tells us clearly: "The first work and the new coming of Christ in this manner is that he hides himself and withdraws the radiance of his light and his heat."[27]

What is particularly striking here is that this very absence is a new coming. It forms an integral part of the complete mystical experience. The person who cannot experience this cross, which is impressed on the mystical experience, cannot become a mature mystic. Ruysbroeck describes the painful situation in which man is placed in this fourth manner of Christ's coming:

So man goes out and finds himself poor, exiled, forsaken. All the storm and violence and impatience of love is now cooled and after the hot summer comes an autumn after all riches great poverty. So man begins to complain, lamenting his lot: where has the heat of love departed, with inwardness, thankfulness, praise and satisfaction? Inward consolation, inward joy and sensible savor, where are they hiding? The violent tempest of love and all the gifts that he ever felt, how is it that they are dead to him? . . . Sometimes these wretched persons . . . are despised and rejected by all those who are near them. And sometimes they fall into various plagues and sicknesses. And such men fall into temptations of the body or of the soul, which is worst of all. Out of this poverty comes a dread lest one should fall and doubt on this account. This is the furthest point to which man can go without despairing.[28]

This desolation may, of course, last several years. When, however, it comes to an end — usually with a gradual but often irritating breaking of the new dawn — the mystic discovers, still as a man who experiences, that he has learnt something essential. He has been through and passed a most decisive test. "Here a man should observe with a humble heart," Ruysbroeck says in this context, "that he of himself has nothing but want and in patience and in abandonment of himself he shall say the words which Job, that holy man, spoke: 'God gave, God took away.' "[29]

What had happened? What fault had been committed? In what way had he deviated from the true path of mysticism? The man who had experienced the overwhelming Presence knew that he had not made God present himself — he knew that it was a totally unmerited gift. And yet he had apparently appropriated this gift. What is always entirely the gift of the Other had gradually and imperceptibly become part of himself. In a completely concealed way, he had become infinitely richer and had begun to grasp and comprehend the one who is quite incomprehensible. In every human experience there is an element of self-consciousness and this had come unnoticed to the fore. He had been conscious of God's Presence and had been completely open to the Other. Gradually, he had come to experience this Presence more and more as "*my* Presence."

The mystic can only become conscious of this secret merging from "Thou" to "Me," from what God is to what I can grasp, only when God himself drastically intervenes. If it were not for this purifying intervention of the Other, who allows himself to be experienced as absent, then God would, in the long run, only exist in man's experience at least insofar as he is interesting and he would more and more be reduced to the measure of mere man.

Most mystics have pointed out that this fatal change is most clearly expressed in the way in which man reacts

to God's gifts. These gifts — loving, praising and thank-
ing God, the different virtues and so on — are really the
effect in man of God's presence. They are translucent
and, in a sense, they are God himself, but only insofar
as man does not claim them as his own. As soon as he
claims these gifts and dwells in them, no matter how
little or how fleetingly, then the Giver disappears and
he, man, becomes once more the center. When that happens, loneliness is there before he is even aware of it.
All of us have known this at some time or other in our
own, non-mystical experience — for example, if we begin to look for happiness ourselves and try to possess
it, it is at once impossible to be really happy.

Ought the mystic, then, simply to return to the ordinary way of life? Would he not be safer there and
would he not avoid a number of completely useless
tests so long as he confined himself to blind faith? Would
it not be better for him simply to listen to the voice of
common sense or to those counsellors of the "spiritual"
life who prescribe a life without feeling? In this context,
the diary of Ignatius of Loyola is a very helpful document. There is no clearer statement in the whole body of
spiritual writing as to its being fundamentally wrong to
ignore or mistrust feelings resulting from God's presence.
This extremely sober saint records, after all, in some detail how, at the height of his mystical career, he shed
"tears of devotion."

What, then, is it that the mystic learns? Not to abandon the experience, but to let it progress to a new level.
He is not driven back from this experience to the stone
age of cold duty and asceticism, but rather taken forward
to an unsuspected quality of experience. Still writing in
the same section of the "Spiritual Espousals" and describing the attitude of the man who denies himself like

Job and remains faithful in his great forsakenness, the state in which he is no longer aware of God's presence, Ruysbroeck says most tellingly:

If he prospers in this manner (of desolation), he will never yet have tasted so great an inward joy; for there is nothing so satisfactory to God's lover as that he feels that he is his Beloved's own.[30]

The most surprising word in this passage is "taste," which can only be meaningful in this context if by it is meant another kind of tasting, a mode of experience that is more subtle than that which has just been described by Ruysbroeck as having been obscured by forsakenness. How, then, does the mystic come to this new aspect of mystical experience?

Above all, he has to abandon himself. But surely every Christian has to do this? That is, of course, true and to lose or surrender oneself is always the basis of the Christian life as such. Wherever a man may be in the kingdom of God, there is no stage higher than the universal law of the Cross. In the last chapter of his *Holy Wisdom,* Augustine Baker[31] asks "for what end" are all the joys and sufferings of the mystical life? (He has just given a remarkable description of the "great desolation.") The end is that we should learn Love and discover that "our supreme happiness is not receiving but loving." He adds:

There are, therefore, in a spiritual life no strange novelties or wonders pretended to. Divine love is all; it begins with love and resignation, and there it ends likewise. All the difference is in the degrees and lustre of it; love, even in its most imperfect state, is most divinely beautiful, which beauty is wonderfully increased by exercise.[32]

The beginning and the end is self-surrender. The special characteristic of the mystic's losing of himself is that it also penetrates the experience of it, the self-abandonment as it were entering his experience. All consciousness of himself is taken away from his feeling. The mystic is completely deprived of the "bright side" of experience, the enviable aspect of the spiritual life, the sublime food so eagerly consumed by the sublimated ego. Augustine Baker says of the soul that has been put to the test in the "great desolation":

She exercises resignation without the least contentment to herself therein; she learns patience in the midst of impatience, and resignation in the midst of irresignation.[33]

Ruysbroeck's new "taste" and the mystic's feeling "that he is his Beloved's own" is clearly nothing but the mystic's becoming open in his experience to the very reality of the relationship of love, his perception of the reality of self-surrender and his disregarding of any effect that this reality may have on himself. The last element is important. It is entirely incidental and in no sense essential that the mystic himself should see or feel that he is giving himself to the Other, that he should know that this action is pleasing to the Other or that he should himself experience his union with the Other. Any reflection about the mystical experience is a pure epiphenomenon.

He is not rejected, but he genuinely transcends himself. Even in his own experience, it is clearly true that the mystic is nothing and the Other is everything. What will gradually be "tasted" lies outside the limitations of the individual and can never as such be part of the ego, nor can it ever supplement the individual self. What will be tasted, then, is the Other, precisely as the one who is completely different, and the naked reality of the mystic's being *de facto* entirely in the Other's hands. Before being put to the test in the "dark night," in union with God, the emphasis was above all on his possessing God. At that time, the mystic could say: "I love you." Now, however, after passing through the dark night, what is of supreme importance is that he is possessed by God. This idea can also be expressed in Christo-centric terms in the following way. Man began by imitating Christ, saying: "I want to act and be like you; I want to come close to the Son of God." Afterward, however, quite apart from his own noble aspiration and his sincere love, he is made like Christ. Without any action on his part, he is taken into the Garden of Olives and the objective Christian virtues are implanted in him.

This change is a far from enjoyable experience for the average Christian, who is bound to react by saying, for example: "I cannot go through that any more or learn anything more from it." Did not Hadewych implore God, after all, at least to be allowed to "know" that all this was his will? The most painful lesson that Madame Guyon had to learn in this school, moreover, was to die in God's arms without being able to "see" those arms.

The new taste, however, comes precisely from being deprived of everything, except the efficiency of God's pure will. This in itself results in a manifestation of unlimited freedom and new, inviolable joy. Augustine Baker has pointed to the way in which a new experience is made available to the mystic by his self-abandonment or "resignation." In his description of the "fruits" of the "great desolation," Baker has noted on the one hand that the soul "thereby learns a perfect disappropriation and transcendence even of the highest gifts and graces of God." On the other hand, he also draws attention to the

way in which the experience is taken to a deeper level
after the "great desolation," using the psychological
structure that we have already encountered in this context:

Now she (the soul) learns by experience to make a division between the supreme portion of the spirit and inferior nature, yea,
between the summity of the spirit and the faculties of the same;
for that portion of her by which she cleaves to God seems to be
another third person distinct from herself . . . Thus at last she
perceives that she can operate without any perceptible use of her
faculties.[34]

This is really the culmination of what the mystic calls
experience — non-perceptible perception. Living in that
part of the spirit, where pure experience of this kind can
take place, is not a blind leap into nothingness, as some
Christians have claimed, but it is a jump into what is
nothing-for-me, in other words, into the Other as such.
Man's faculties are impotent and his ego, however imposing a structure it may seem from without, is empty.
Insofar as he is open to receive, however, he is then
filled in his "ground." He is filled, as Ruysbroeck has
said, where he receives like an always open palm.
This kind of experience is above all a paradox, but it
would be a great pity if we were simply to reject it because of its paradoxical nature. After all, precisely what
the mystic experiences may escape us, because we are
confined within the limitations of our ego, but the paradoxical structure of his experience is not entirely strange
to us. Everyone who risks the adventure of love and goes
sufficiently far along that dangerous path is bound to end
at a point where his understanding and his experience of
happiness are quite special. At this ultimate point, he
possesses nothing and is no longer able to hold on to his

own blessed state in self-satisfaction. The affection of
the first encounter, the sympathy with its many unconscious barbs, the going out that is also a continuous and
unconscious bringing in — does this process not lead to
an uninterrupted inclination towards the other?

Let us briefly consider what two great mystics, Benedict of Canfield and Catherine of Genoa, have said
about this question. The English Capuchin, who lived in
France and wrote in French, discussed "experience" at
great length in his "Rule of Perfection." One has the
initial impression that he shamelessly contradicts himself in this matter. On the one hand, he says that one
of the imperfect aspects of contemplation which stands
in the way of complete union with God is removed as
soon as the soul "has discovered in herself and tasted
experimentally (*expérimentalement goûté*) how her
Bridegroom is more in her than she is in herself." On the
other hand, he is also aware of the "difference made
between feeling and not feeling" as a serious obstacle.
The mystic, Benedict of Canfield insists, is on the wrong
track as soon as he begins to look for "certainty" or
for an "experimental knowledge that one is united" (*con-
naissance expérimentale qu'on est uni*).

If we examine what he says more closely, however,
we are bound to recognize that he does not contradict
himself at all, but is discussing two different levels of
experience or two different ways of "knowing":

One way consists of experimental knowledge . . . and the other
of true knowledge. The second is not experimental at the level of
sense, but at the level of the intellect (*non expérimentale selon le
sens, mais selon l'intellect*).[35]

Canfield's use of the words "sense" and "intellect"
is perhaps a little unfortunate, but it is nonetheless quite

certain that the contrast between them points to the distinction between the sphere of the "ego" and that of
"being." Canfield expresses very clearly the danger in-
herent in experience insofar as this is simply a question
of human "sense" and defines this danger as the lasting
impossibility of leaving one's own country, in other
words, of getting outside oneself. On the other hand, in
the sphere of being, the highest degree of experience
is achieved when:

The soul receives a new light and a capacity that is different from
that which she has hitherto had. She is made capable of essential
and supernatural activity, outside and above herself and all human
and natural understanding.[36]

Mystical experience, then, is not an extension of man's
consciousness in the current sense of the term. Any
broadening of the mind, in whatever wonderful or de-
lightful direction, is still too narrow, since the human
consciousness still remains no more than a property with
colored doors and unstable ceilings, a prison in which
the divine reality is held captive and experienced in the
service of the ego.

The great mystic, on the other hand, loses himself.
This self-abandonment takes place *de facto* and includes
his own powers of perception and everything that per-
tains to that perceptivity and it is this that makes it
possible for him to experience inexhaustibly. Catherine
of Genoa was therefore able to say that God was her "I"
and that she would not accept an enjoyment of God
that had to "pass through the faculties." She also tried to
put into words an insight into the nature of mystical
experience:

I see without my eyes, I understand without my intellect, I become aware without any feeling, I taste without tasting . . . Nothing can be said or thought about this seeing, which is no seeing . . . Look, that is all the blessedness that the blessed possess. And yet they do not possess it . . . Even while I am speaking about these things, I reproach myself as I look at these words and expressions — they are wrong in comparison with what I (really) feel (without any feeling) and with what cannot be understood.[37]

2. Who was Ruysbroeck? In What Sense Was He a Master?

Jan van Ruysbroeck's long life (1294-1381) covered almost the whole of the fourteenth century. Whether we regard this century as the end of an age or as a time containing many signs of an entirely new era, it is nonetheless a fascinating period of history, a richly varied volcanic landscape in a state of constant eruption. Many political revolutions took place at this time. Emancipation from the authority of the pope led to the young nations becoming involved in wars with each other — the Hundred Years' War beginning in the middle of the century in 1347 and dragging on until 1453. But from this scene of conflict there also emerged an entirely new state structure. In many places in Europe and especially in Flanders and Brabant, the towns consolidated their positions with regard to the princes and the dukes; and the trades and guilds increased their power. Famine and plagues were rife — the Black Death raged over the whole continent from 1347 until 1351 — and an unstable economy was accompanied by great disorders in society. The peasants revolted in Flanders in 1332 and the French peasant uprising, the Jacquerie, took place in 1358. The Lollards rose in London in 1381.

The Church was subjected to equally powerful shocks, causing her imposing thirteenth century structure to collapse like a house of cards. Boniface VIII had to give up the "sword" of worldly power and six years after his death the successor of Peter was staying in Avignon, a Babylonian captivity lasting from 1309 until 1377 and ending in the Western Schism. Where the official Church could no longer provide any stability a variety of "mystical" Christian groups, most of them to some degree heretical and many characterized by extravagant practices, arose and flourished. Flagellants, who scourged themselves until they bled, and Dancers passed through the towns and the Brethren of the Free Spirit achieved an all too great notoriety in the fourteenth century. These Brethren, who were less of a genuine religious sect and more of a stubborn socio-religious phenomenon, achieved great success in propagating an "inner freedom" which was often accompanied by a radical turning away from all orthodoxy and distinctly amoral behavior. Marguerite Porete, a mystic who has often rather too impetuously been regarded as a leading exponent of the ideas of these Brethren, was burnt at the stake in 1310. She was the author of the earliest known mystical treatise in the French language, the "Mirror of Simple Souls." There were also many Beguines and Beghards living during this period as nuns or monastics without vows and often with remarkable sympathies. In a word, it was a hopeless situation for anyone who still dared to dream of social order and an inspired life in the Church.

It was, however, precisely during this extremely restless period in the history of the Church that some of the greatest figures in Western mysticism arose. Two of these mystics were directly concerned in the reformation of the papacy — Catherine of Siena (d. 1380) and Bridget of Sweden (d. 1373). In Germany, the three best known mystics were Meister Eckhart (d. 1327), John Tauler (d. 1361) and Henry Suso (d. 1366) and the society of the Friends of God flourished above all in Strasbourg and Basle. Towards the end of this period, several mystical authors appeared in England as well — Richard Rolle (d. 1349), Walter Hilton (d. 1396), the anonymous author of the *Cloud of Unknowing* (the second half of the fourteenth century) and Julian of Norwich (d. 1413) are among the most important English mystics. Finally, mysticism also attained a very high level in the Low Countries at this time: one great spiritual family of exceptionally high quality and great mystical depth flourishing there. This movement began in Groenendael, where Ruysbroeck and his best known disciples, John of Leeuwen (d. 1374) and John Schoonhoven (d. 1432), lived. Later, it spread to include Geert Groote (d. 1384) and his Brethren of the Common Life and those who taught and practiced the *devotio moderna,* such as Gerlach Peters (d. 1411).

Ruysbroeck's concrete, external life falls clearly into two great periods. The first of these periods he spent in Brussels, where he served the church of St. Gudule as an assistant diocesan priest from 1317 until 1343. The second period, from 1343 until 1381, was spent in the Zoniënwoud, at Groenendael, an Augustinian priory not far from Brussels. During the earlier period, Ruysbroeck wrote several important works, including the rather unbalanced "Kingdom of Lovers" (*Het Rijcke der Ghelieven*), in which he made certain statements with which he later declared himself to be dissatisfied, the perfectly constructed and clearly formulated "Spiritual Espousals" (*Die Gheestelike Brulocht*) and a short work, "The Perfection of the Sons of God" (*Vanden Blinckenden Steen*), which is perhaps the most easily approachable treatise for anyone who wishes to begin reading Ruysbroeck.

There is very little reliable information available on Ruysbroeck's life and above all there are no precise, verifiable data about why he went to Groenendael. It may be true that a canon's hoarse voice got on his nerves so much that he had to leave Brussels, but this is of liturgical rather than of historical interest. The other traditional reason for his departure from Brussels is that he ventured to denounce the teaching of Bloemardinne, a heretical female mystic. This explanation is dramatically successful, but belongs more to the sphere of hagiography than to that of pure biography. It is probably safer to accept the rather general statements made by Ruysbroeck contemporary, Brother Gheraert, who wrote that the mystic "wanted to withdraw from the multitude" in order to be able to lead a "holy and separate life," because he "preferred to remain free from all gatherings."[38]

Whatever reason he may have had for leaving Brussels, it is clear that the future prior of Groenendael was a man who sought seclusion and who therefore, at a given moment in his life, gave up his parish work in Brussels. Even as a curate, he was described as solitarius, a lonely figure, but it would be a serious mistake to regard him as a person who sought flight and refuge from the world, resting in his solitude in a state of self-satisfaction and tired idealism. In fact, it is a striking aspect of Ruysbroeck's literary talent that, far from seeking refuge from the world, he described the situation in the Church and society with unparalleled precision and audacity. He was an acute and critical observer of what was going on around him and was in no sense a remote dreamer. He was not blind to the ostentatious dress and manners of the social upstarts of the period:

You see that, when a man has a garment made for himself, it has to be pleated, with long pieces cut out and long appendages, so close-fitting and short that it barely covers his shabby under-garments. The women look at the men's clothes and have garments made for themselves that are just as tight. It is a disgrace. They line their clothes both inside and out. They invent all kinds of novelties to delight themselves and others. They pile up moun-tains of hair on their heads . . . and wear twisted horns on their faces, just like goats . . ."

What is more, he observed that money, however it was acquired or used, meant power, even in the Church. The rich, he said

notice that the whole world bows down before worldly posses-sions — popes and bishops, princes and prelates, priests and laymen. The rich man has his share of all spiritual goods — masses are sung and said for him and all the external practices of Holy Church are at his disposal. He also obtains letters guaranteeing that he will be absolved from all his sins and from purgatory.

He was above all outraged by the desperate state of the clergy and described it in detail and without pity. This quiet contemplative was at the same time an out-spoken critic and, what is more, at a time when it was dangerous to express oneself in this way in public. Even Brother Gheraert, his ardent admirer and the faithful copyist of his works, did not dare to publish everything that Ruysbroeck wrote. "With good reason," he declared, "I have left out a great complaint against all the clerical orders in Holy Church. He wanted that to be published because it caused him so much suffering that they had moved so far away and were still moving away from their first beginning."[39]

All ranks of the secular clergy, from the highest to the lowest, were, in Ruysbroeck's opinion, the slaves of money. See for yourself, he said, whether or not the princes of the Church are good shepherds. Are they not more like "ravenous wolves who bite the sheep to death in the fields"? All they are interested in is money and power, pomp and magnificence:

When a bishop or an abbot visits his people, he goes with forty horses, a great cortège and enormous expense. But he does not pay for all this himself. Business progresses, the money flows into his purse and so souls are not touched.

At the lower end of the hierarchy, things are much the same:

There are also other priests who stand in the church waiting for money, with the servility of blind beggars or cripples. . . . Those who live from the benefice of Holy Church and ought to be pure in soul and body keep — or at least some of them — their children in their own house. They do this publicly, without blushing. They are even proud of it, as though they had a legitimate spouse.

Apart from a few exceptions, the religious led equally wretched lives, dominated by the quest for money. Power was in the hands of "cunning rogues" and "everyone who comes close to them must bow and scrape." Ruysbroeck sometimes becomes almost cynical in his descriptions, as if he had a vision of the controversial monasteries of today: "Many lessons are read, and that is valuable and good, but religion is getting worse from day to day." Ruysbroeck says all this and much more in his "Spiritual Tabernacle."[40] How, then, can anyone believe that he was simply a timid "mystic," remote from the world?

The man who left Brussels in 1343 was neither a shy "mystic" nor a solitary, unapproachable "contemplative." On the one hand, he founded a thriving community in Groenendael, where he communicated, simply

and uncalculatingly, the most intimate of man's posses-
sions, the life of the spirit, to his brethren. On the other
hand, he at the same time continued to radiate the mystery of that life to others, not only in what he wrote, but
also in his personal contacts with his fellow-men. People
came to see him from far and wide, even from as far
away as Germany, both laymen and clergy, and even as
an old man he did not hesitate to travel miles through
the forests to visit his friends.

The basic reason for his having been drawn to follow
the rule of the Canons Regular of St. Victor must therefore have been that his way of life could give Christian
people what they most urgently needed — an intensifi-
cation of the inner life. He must have sensed that, however useful and indeed necessary it may have been to
the Church to engage in the direct apostolate of everyday
activity, this nonetheless remained an artificial dressing
applied to a much deeper wound, which revealed the
absence of real religious experience. Is it, after all, not
significant that he refers directly to this painful need
precisely in his bitter accusation of his fellow-Christians
in his treatise on the "Spiritual Tabernacle"? What
Christians lack, he declares, is "taste." They come to
Church and either chatter to each other or sit with
closed minds, going off at the slightest provocation and
this is because "they have no taste for the service of
the Lord." The worst disease of the religious of his own
times was their habit of going around outside their communities. What was the reason for this, Ruysbroeck
asked. "Look — for these people the monastery is a
prison and the world is a paradise. For they have no
taste for God or eternal blessedness."

Although Ruysbroeck's writings contain certain de-
vious ideas which may make the modern reader hesitant

to accept him and he often takes rather a long time to reach his point, this point is always the same and it is of fundamental importance to the life of every believer. Incessantly, in all his writings, the Master of Groenendael plays on the same basic theme, that of man's being one with God. In certain religions or philosophies of religion, this unity with God is limited, perhaps involuntarily or perhaps simply for the sake of safety, to "liberation." What is emphasized is man's need to dissociate himself from the narrow and all-to-familiar sphere of his own existence and his most urgent task to break through the limitations of being bound to that existence. But this, often heroic, liberation is never entirely without some degree of yearning for the one ultimate Reality, who is the Other. Whatever differences or variations there may be in religious ideas or attitudes, Christian faith is always explicitly oriented towards ultimate unity with God. The central message of the gospel is expressed in the words of the fourth evangelist: "If a man loves me, he will keep my word, and my Father will love him, and we will come to him and make our home with him" (Jn 14: 23) and Paul says no less when he affirms that "he who is united to the Lord becomes one spirit with him" (1 Cor 6: 17). The Christian cannot therefore escape from this fundamental truth, that God and man are to become one. The good news of the gospel stands or falls in the task of making this great gift true.

Whoever tries to understand this unity with God within the context of Christian teaching, however, finds himself at once involved in serious difficulties. If we are scrupulous in our reasoning and thinking about the life proclaimed by Christ, which is fundamentally that God is in me and I am in God, we are immediately confronted by a remarkable and even an impossible reality. In the Christian view, after all, man is not only a created being and therefore never able to be simply identified with his Creator. He is also at the same time an inviolable person. This means that anything that is offered to him by God and religion must also always be meaningful to him as a man. No explanation, however fascinating or attractive it may be, can ever be accepted by man if it does not respect his miraculous freedom as man.

It is precisely because of this need to respect man and his future that it is so difficult for the logical thinker to understand the Christian teaching about man's being one with God. It would, after all, appear to be obvious to the logical, rational mind that the Christian promise must result in an inescapable dilemma. If the unity of God and man is so strongly emphasized, then one of the two must give way to the other. Either God, the Other, becomes man's property or man, as a person, disappears into an inhuman Other. Either God or man has, it would seem, to be annihilated and, if this principle is not accepted, real unity is out of the question. If God and man, however, are regarded as independent of each other, then an unbridgeable gulf lies between them, which is a blunt denial of the Christian promise. This difference between God and man, preventing their union, need not necessarily be a great gulf. It may be no more than a slight distance, but this would in itself be sufficient to keep God and man apart for ever. Man's union with God therefore remains an irritating paradox. Two apparently irreconcilable elements, unity and independent existence, would, it would seem, have to come together, a difficulty which cannot be argued away. Are we therefore bound to conclude that what we have here is an "unintelligible" reality and assume that it is all a dream or a structure that has not been well enough thought out?

This may be the only possible conclusion unless there is something lacking in our way of thinking or unless the language that we habitually use is too inflexible or too empoverished for what we have to say here about God and man. It is in fact quite reasonable to think that our instruments have developed in too one-sided a way for us to use them to express this kind of reality, that is, unity between persons. Our choice, efficient way of thinking is perhaps inadequate for the task, because it is exclusively adapted to one particular aspect or level of the reality and therefore cannot be used to distinguish other aspects or levels of that reality.

As soon as we begin to speak scientifically about God, man and unity, "things" come to mind. We have surely all experienced the painful feeling that, in any serious discussion, for example, about Jesus Christ or about grace, the whole subject, which may be a living reality, can easily be destroyed by analysis. All kinds of imposing, new structures can be created — sufficient to make the engineering experts' mouths water — but they are no more real than a motorway for a man who has no car. Such a person may find it very impressive and hope at most that someone will be helped by it. What we do, in other words, by means of an irresistible reflex action, is to drag spiritual realities down to the level of "beings" that can be defined and conveniently surveyed, set in order and explained. God in this way becomes a being, man another being, and the unity between them a third being, a reality alongside or above the other two, but equally defined and systematized. We work, in other words, with propositions and firm definitions which can only *be* if they are *this* or *that*. With these materials we try to create a structure that will enable us and others to understand the promise that God is in me and I am in God.

A deficiency in this way of thinking which cannot be remedied is, of course, that anything that cannot be defined as a "being," anything, in other words, that is not a "thing," is inevitably reduced to the level of a secondary phenomenon. Without exaggerating, we may say that, when this takes place, the most interesting and typical aspect of man, his personal relationship with the other, is not really taken seriously, even if it is not completely suppressed. The beginning and end of everything is the sharply defined, ordered essence, being or thing and every that cannot be included within this category is regarded as secondary in status and relagated to the accidental sphere of psychological or emotional epiphenomena. It was Bérulle who remarked that, if man's relationship with the other and everything that is purely psychological is thought to be no more than what Aristotle called an accident, the Christian experience of God could never be fully expressed. It is moreover true that it is impossible to understand or to say, at the level of beings, things or objects, that, in unity, God is still really God and man is still really man.

Anyone, then, who conceives this unity as the identification of the human "being" with the divine "being" is bound to fall into pantheism and into an illusory experience in which what is called in the Gospel of John the "eternal life" which Christ came to give "abundantly" will result in man's death. Otherwise, God's being the Other may be so strictly observed that all revelations of the love between him and man and between men themselves will be no more than comforting signs above an unbridgeable gulf. It should therefore be clear by now that unity with God is a reality which completely transcends the world of clearly defined "beings" and that anyone who tries to speak about it in objective concepts is bound to do it a grave injustice, because that terminology is inadequate.

Above all, we must remember that Ruysbroeck was a mystic and, what is more, a mystic with a language of his own and a man of experience. He was not someone who began by worrying about the unity between God and man and wondering how this kind of thing was possible. He was rather a man to whom the reality of this unity happened. He experienced it himself. It was not, for him, a problem that had to be solved in a philosophical or theological treatise, nor was it a new and difficult entity, some kind of super-object, which had to be composed from two separate "beings," God and man. For him, this unity was something that happened, a phenomenon that was so intense and could make man so happy that it was a reality of the first importance. It was not simply *a* reality — it was *the* reality. His theological training had made him very familiar with the problems — some of them insoluble — encountered in the mode of thinking that took objects as its point of departure, but here his point of departure was quite different. He spoke from his own experience. .

This mystic, moreover, had his own language. He did not try to fit his mystical experience into an already accepted system or to pass it through the sieve of the language of scholasticism. He was too great an artist for this. From time to time, he spoke as a psychologist and used the familiar language of the mystical theologians. He was also able to use concepts like "substance" and "nature" for the convenience of the philosophers. But, despite these little excursions, he was in the first place writing about his own experience. Primarily, he was a phenomenologist, in the sense of someone who describes what happens without any preconceived idea of systematizing the information. He was a writer who, patiently and often with great virtuosity, tried to reproduce in his treatises a spiritual phenomenon without distorting or diminishing it and without omitting any elements which were difficult to situate. The ultimate source of what he said was therefore always his own experience and the essential core of his writing was always his subtle and sensitive personal testimony.

At the heart of Ruysbroeck's mystical experience is that unity with God is to be found in the interplay between various elements, most of which cannot be reconciled in the world of things and beings and which cannot be combined in logical, objective reasoning. What is so astonishing is that Ruysbroeck came, in his experience of unity with God, to see these apparently irreconcilable objects as complementary aspects of the one single organic whole. His mystical experience taught him that such conflicting data were both active and resting, seeking and found, themselves yet at the same time aborded in a blessed state of forgetfulness of self and above all being both one and yet different, constituting the necessary and never to be repealed aspects of the one "living life" with God. Ruysbroeck describes this situation in the following passage:

Being at the same time poor and rich, hungry and satisfied, active and passive — these things are quite contrary to each other. Yet our highest good is to be found in this, both now and in eternity. For we can never both become God and lose our created nature — that is impossible. If, however, we remain imprisoned in ourselves, separated from God, we are bound to be wretched and miserable. We must therefore be able to experience that we are both entirely in God and entirely in ourselves.[41]

In the chapters that follow, I shall therefore treat Ruysbroeck's writing primarily as a personal testimony to his own experience and as the account provided by himself of an overwhelming human phenomenon, since this is precisely what it, in the first place, is. There is no need for anyone to be philosophically or theologically trained in order for him to appreciate the language of the Master of Groenendael or to enjoy his explorations into the realm of the spirit. There is no need even for explicit Christian faith. All that is required of the reader is a sympathetic attentiveness to what is human.

PART II

THE PHENOMENOLOGY OF THE COMMUNITY OF LOVE

1. The Different Aspects of Unity with the Other

Unity between God and man is not a purely objective datum. Their coming entirely together is in no sense a deathly situation in which one being becomes absorbed in the other, resulting in an amorphous, unmoved and unmoving "primordial" being. It is also quite different from a process of merging into an ultimate and lifeless background to all being. This fact can be clearly illustrated by referring to certain passages from Ruysbroeck's writing in which he provides a general survey of what happens to the mystic in the process of becoming one with God. He does not experience one single, decisive and final moment of unity, Ruysbroeck insists, a kind of climax or end in which everything is consummated in unity. On the contrary, what the mystic experiences are different aspects, which together form the one experience of unity. The term which Ruysbroeck uses for this combination of various aspects in the mystical experience is "ordinance," in the sense of regulating or setting in order. There is a regular structure, then, but not of a mechanical kind with specific and fixed parts or of a chronological kind, an order moving more or less auto-

57

matically towards an end. By "ordinance," Ruysbroeck means above all an interaction, an action and reaction between different elements, as in the case of a living organism. For him, then, unity with God is a spiritual experience containing various aspects which never have the effect of rendering each other unnecessary, but on the contrary constantly activate each other. In his treatise *Vanden Blinckenden Steen* ("The Perfection of the Sons of God"), he says:

We should understand the ordinance in this way. In our ascent to God, we must first give him ourselves and all our works as an eternal offering to him. Then, when we come into God's presence, we must leave ourselves and all that we do, so that we can, dying in love, enter the essential riches of God. There we shall finally possess God, losing ourselves eternally in him.[1]

It is possible to distinguish four aspects in this passage — ascent, presence, union and unity. The meaning of the last two important stages and the relationship between them is something that we shall be examining in a later chapter. At present, we shall confine ourselves to the first two and related concepts.

Ascent is the stage in the experience of unity in which man is active and in which he can of himself do what he can for God. This sincere activity leads him into the presence of God. This presence, however, calls for closer inspection, since, in the context of Ruysbroeck's "ordinance," it is an ambivalent phenomenon. In the course of spiritual experience, it is an extremely important threshold, but it may also become a stumbling block. Although it is a genuine contact with God, it may not *ipso facto* be encounter with him. Why is this? It is, according to Ruysbroeck, because man's activity is, at this stage, still emphasized and therefore God is still found in what man does for him. If we say: "we must give him ourselves and all our works," we are still using a "means." It will quite certainly lead man to God and put him in the presence of God, but as long as it remains there, it will also be a screen which has still to be broken through in the encounter, where the Other can himself appear. This encounter — which we shall examine a little more closely further on in this chapter, in the context of a very striking and positive description of it by Ruysbroeck himself — has the effect of making man leave behind not only himself but also everything that belongs to him.

It is precisely because the presence of God, which man attains by his own efforts, is so authentic and good, as well as very pleasing to God himself,[2] that it can often be one of the most serious obstacles of all, at least on the mystical way. Ruysbroeck returns several times in his works to this theme — that some men remain firmly fixed in the presence of God as an aspect of the ascent to God. A good example is this passage:

However much they may practice and however deep an under-standing they may have of all the possible manners of clinging to God in love and of all the inward and ascending ways which can be followed in the presence of God, yet it remains hidden from them. . . .[3]

Presence in this sense thus clearly points to a real experience of God, but one in which there is still a distance and a distinction between the partners. This presence has to be perfected by encounter with the Other precisely as the one who is different, although this does not mean that it is not a necessary and permanent aspect of man's experience of unity with God. The mature mystic, the

"contemplative man," inevitably comes back again and
again into the presence of God:

But just as we try to understand and describe what we feel, we
have recourse to reason. We experience a distinction and a difference between ourselves and God. And then we discover that
God — the incomprehensible God — is outside us. . . . We are
confronted here with the presence of God.[4]

When the mystic tries to grasp God, then, and to understand his blessed state of being in the Other, he at
once returns in impotence to this presence. But this is not
all. It is also part of his experience of unity with God
that God himself brings man into his presence. This idea
is elaborated a little further on in Ruysbroeck's treatise:

Then he touches us with his outward flowing movement. He lets
us be ourselves and makes us free and confronts us with his presence. He teaches us how to pray in the Spirit and to ask without
restraint. He shows us his incomprehensible riches in as many
different ways as we can imagine.[5]

Ruysbroeck describes man's encounter with God more
precisely in another "ordinance," containing the same
four aspects of man's unity with God, in his "Kingdom
of Lovers." In this passage, we are shown how, after
ascending to God, man suddenly stands in fascination,
gripped by someone who is there:

The contemplative man experiences four aspects. The first is that
his mind is free, clings with love to unity and is directed with
desire towards it. The second is that man, illuminated by grace,
suddenly gazes, in surprise and outside himself, at the riches of
the threefold God and that he is — he is no longer able to feel
astonished[6] — carried away and "overformed"[7] with an immeasurable clarity. He is received into the light of unity. The
third aspect is an enjoyable inclination towards and a clinging to

God, which causes man and all his powers to flow away. He is surrounded on all sides and filled both within and without by a superabundance of riches much greater than he would ever have been able to desire for himself. The fourth aspect is that he breaks away from himself and is lost in the abyss that is the Other. No one can walk in darkness, so that man is forever lost in it. This is the highest state of blessedness.[8]

This encounter with God is the moment when mystical experience as such really begins — suddenly I am no longer confronted with the presence of God, but God himself is there, so much himself and so different that I disappear from my own experience. Even before my first movement towards God, at the stage of ascent, God himself was present in me with his "touching." Now, however, in this encounter, this presence is fully experienced: "God causes this spiritual burning in us first of all, before all gifts; yet last of all we recognize and savor it for what it is."[9]

The most complete description of this encounter with God can be found in another passage in the "Spiritual Espousals."[10] In it, Ruysbroeck gives a clear outline not only of the effect of this encounter on man, but also of the way in which God himself appears. This is preceded by a short introduction, which is very characteristic of Ruysbroeck, who always prefers, before each new stage, to give a brief summary of what he intends to discuss at greater length. In this introductory paragraph, we find statements containing the terms used for the first level of ascent and for the second aspect of presence, which is not yet fulfilled. Examples of this are: "the man who . . . has ascended with fervent exercise," "rising up," "a love rising higher and higher," "fervently impelled back to the source of love" and finally a description of man on the threshold of encounter with God:

"For God and all his gifts impel us to return into him and we through charity and virtue and our likeness to God desire to be in him." This introductory summary of the theme is followed by the description itself, which is worth quoting almost in full. Parts of it will be familiar to the reader, since they were quoted in the first chapter in this book.

Through the loving inclination of God and through his interior working in the fervor of our spirit and through our burning love and the great effort which we make with all our powers to enter into that same unity in which God dwells, there springs the coming of Christ in inward exercises. And this is an inward touching by Christ in his divine clarity upon the innermost part of our spirit. Another coming of which we have spoken we likened to a living source with three streams. But let us liken this coming to the springs that feed the sources, for there is no river without its source, nor is there source without living springs. And so, in the same way, the grace of God flows in rivers into the highest powers of the soul and impels and enkindles men in all virtues. And grace gathers in the unity of our spirit as a source and flows into that same unity whence it springs, just as a living, flowing spring from the living depths of the riches of God, where love and grace may nevermore run dry. And this is the touching which I mean. And the creature suffers and endures this touching. . . . And in this there is no person operative but God alone. . . . In the unity of the spirit, where this spring flows, man is above working and above reason, but he is not without reason; for the enlightened reason, and in particular the power of the soul to love, feels this touching, yet reason can never understand or comprehend the manner nor the fashion of it, nor how nor why that touching came about. . . . And this touching compels the understanding to acknowledge God in *his* charity and it impels and compels the capacity for love to enjoy God without any means. . . . Through an enlightened reason the spirit exalts itself in a fervent contemplation, and observes and marks in the inmost part of itself, where this touching lives. Here reason and all created light fail as the spirit advances, for the divine clarity, hovering above, which is engendered by this touching, when it encounters them dispels all created images, because it is unfathomable. And here all created understanding behaves as does the eye of the bat in the brilliance of the sunlight. Yet the spirit is ever and anew impelled and stirred, by God and by itself, to fathem these depths in which it is touched, and so to know what God and what this touching may be. And the enlightened reason is ever and anew asking whence this comes, and plunging deep to track to its source this spring of ineffable sweetness. But the reason shall never be wiser concerning this than it was at the very first. And therefore reason and all observation say: "I do not know what it is."

2. The Life of the Trinity as the Model of the Unity of Persons

One of the most surprising aspects of Ruysbroeck's work is that it reveals his unconcerned practice of taking his own experience as his point of departure. What he wishes above all to communicate to us is what he has experienced in becoming one with God and what takes place in that unity. Despite this, however, he frequently speaks about the Trinity, describing with astonishing accuracy and certainty the life that is happening in God. Did he perhaps "see" all this? Is what he says based on miraculous revelations? Or did he rather give way to the irresistible impulse, so common among Northern Europeans, to indulge in obscure speculations? (This suggestion has been made quite often and it his deterred many people from reading his works.)

The context in which many of his passages on the Trinity are placed and the style and language in which those passages are written undoubtedly call for a special interpretation. What Ruysbroeck in fact does is to use the datum of faith, that God is one in three Persons, in order to clarify and confirm what he has described as his own experience of unity with God. What the mystic experiences with his God, in other words — a complex phenomenon with many different aspects interacting — is similar to what happens in the Trinity. What Ruys-

broeck is saying, then, is this: What I am communicating
to you as human experience is intimately related to the
teaching of Christian faith about God and this can moreover help you to understand that the truth that God is
one in three Persons is not self-evident, arbitrary or impossible to accept. Life in the triune God is, as it were,
the model of our unity with God. It is the reality of faith
which enables us to appreciate definitively the essential
being of love which is the special characteristic of persons. In this chapter, then, we shall discuss some of
Ruysbroeck's passages on the Trinity. They contain in a
concise and very clear form some of the great themes of
the mystical experience of unity with God and a number
of specific terms used by Ruysbroeck himself.

When a man sinks into the light without manner which is God's
being, all God's activity and that of his creatures ceases. (For
there is in God's being no activity on the part either of God himself or of his creatures, for it is precisely where they find enjoyment of God's being that the Persons abandon their distinctive
nature.) This nature is, however, eternal and the Persons cannot
therefore ever cease to exist. And this takes place in an experience
of an enjoyable inclination into the unfathomable being of God
without manner.[1]

What Ruysbroeck is saying here is that the divine
Person is a distinctive reality existing only in self-
surrender. This is, in other words, a living paradox —
being is losing oneself. Continued existence as a Person
means continuously letting oneself go. Precisely where
all other beings are only able to continue by means of
self-preservation, the divine Person is above all distinguished by the fact that he has again and again to abandon himself. Being a Person, then, is not a simple reality,
something that is clearly delineated and can grow in its
own, well defined direction. It cannot be supplemented

by other elements, while at the same time being sufficient in itself. On the contrary, this Person is a complex reality, complexity itself, always oriented towards and intimately connected with what is different.

It is obvious that Ruysbroeck's conception of the Trinity cannot be meaningful to anyone who wants to hold "God" firmly within the mesh of an "objective" philosophy. Such a person can only envisage God as a conglomerate of four definitive "beings" — the three divine Persons plus the deity, the super-being. He cannot conceive of there being life in God. What, after all, should three Persons, who are in themselves clearly defined and complete, be able to do, other than either preserve themselves or be merged, in irrevocable self-annihilation, into the one, all-embracing being of God? Their transition towards the tranquil ground of God's being is, such a person would reason, one definite action which puts an end to all further life. Going outside themselves and giving themselves up would certainly mean dying.

Ruysbroeck, however, did not take a complete, objective datum as his point of departure. For him, God was the complex reality of the Person and therefore entirely and endlessly life. He made use of composite sentences and of a complementary or dialectical interplay of phrases such as "insofar as . . .", for, in his opinion, only such structures could point to the inexhaustible reality of God. Clearly, he could not work with the sort of language that set up boundaries and tried to enclose everything in separate compartments. "You may therefore observe," he wrote in "The Little Book of Enlightenment," "that God's nature is eternally active insofar as it is three Persons and it is eternal rest and undivided insofar as it is a single being."[2]

What the Persons give up is their personal nature,

their "distinctive nature" as Persons. This and similar terms such as "nature" and "the manner of Persons" are repeatedly and consistently used by Ruysbroeck in his writings.[3] It is moreover clear from his use of these expressions that he regarded the "Person" at all times as a dimensional reality, one single reality containing the two complementary aspects of being and distinctive nature. Being or "essence" points to the fact that what we have here is a concrete being. The other aspect of God, his "distinctive nature," self or "Person," also points to the same being or essence, but insofar as it is a reality which possesses itself, controls itself and experiences its being given in a unique and personal way. If God's being or essence is to be, then his being a Person is to be himself.

Both elements — the essential being and the personal being — must, of course, always exist together. In isolation, a being would be no more than a thing and a person would at the most be an idea. What the person, however, has to give up continuously is not the aspect of essential being, his very existence, but rather the aspect of being a person, in other words, his distinctive mode of existence, the way in which he fulfils what has been apportioned to him.

We would not be so very wide of the mark if we were to illustrate what we have said above by asking what is usually meant when it is said of a person that he is completely changed. What is *not* meant by this is that a certain individual who existed previously now no longer exists. (One being has not, in other words, disappeared from creation, nor has a new being suddenly appeared.) What *is*, on the contrary, meant is that this same person has begun to experience differently the being that has been given to him. (A new and different reality has, in other words, come about — the person is made new or renewed and made different or changed, although he has not become a new being.)

In this way, then, a man can take all that he is and has for a long time in one definite direction. He can be in pursuit of power, for example, he can be looking for security or he can love. In other words, he has a certain personality. But this personality can undergo a metamorphosis. (And this, as we all know, often comes about through the shock of meeting the other.) A person who has behaved stupidly with that precious being that has been given to him, acting like a dwarf within his being, can now, for instance, experience that same being like a giant, in a completely different and royal way. His old personality comes to an end, while his essential being remains. In other words, what we have is a person, because a genuine mutation is possible, without annihilation.

It is therefore important to understand a little more completely Ruysbroeck's view of God's being, that tranquil and obscure ground into which the Persons disappear. Is it a vague and unspecified being situated entirely outside the sphere of the personal, a completely abstract background, quite unconnected with life and personal relationships? It has often been suggested (in fashionable theological circles) that this was Ruysbroeck's idea of the divine being. It is, however, a view which he knew, but rejected. What is even more important is that he was able to provide his own positive description of God and of God's being, which is quite different.

The belief that God's being is a kind of background against which the divine Persons and all creatures are reflected and into which everything is bound ultimately to flow was unacceptable to Ruysbroeck. For him, this idea was simply a naive projection made by men whose experience of God himself was very limited. Those who describe the divine being in this way have, he claimed, really only experienced the deepest ground of their own being,[4] relying on their own efforts, talents or even techniques, in a "natural rest in emptiness"[5] which is peculiar to the creature. They have, Ruysbroeck insists, reached the point where they regard the divine being as a lifeless ground:

They have been raised up to the level of not-knowing and of vagueness. They are therefore united to this state and regard this vagueness as God himself. Although they do not love God, they have undivided rest and this is why they have the impression that, in eternity, all differences in life and reward and all distinction will pass away. They believe that nothing will remain but an eternal being which simply is, without personal distinction either in God or in creatures.[6]

How, then, does Ruysbroeck himself describe God's being or the unity within which the Persons as it were place a distance between themselves and their distinctive nature, in order to rediscover that nature and experience it in a more intense way? As our point of departure, we may take a rather long, but very synthetic passage from Ruysbroeck's "Spiritual Tabernacle":

In God there is also the distinctive phenomenon of being burnt. This is nothing but the unity of the divine nature which is called Father because it is an eternal activity. It is a fruitful activity, in the sense of being the origin of eternal activity. On the one hand, the entire activity of the Persons is aroused by this unity — the seeking and desiring of the Persons for unity has its origin in this unity. On the other hand, this unity includes all the seeking made by Love and, what is more, by surrendering itself — it devours and consumes in itself the different nature that it had once activated. This unity is therefore the ground and the point of rest of all Love — it draws everything that loves into itself and transforms it into its own form. In this being burnt, the Person continues to lose everything that is peculiar to itself. This being merged is as such undivided — there cannot be any difference in it. Yet the Persons continue to exist for ever in God with their own distinctive nature and their own specific activity.[7]

In this text, Ruysbroeck stresses one important aspect of his teaching, namely that the unity of the divine nature — that is, God's being regarded as activity — is the Father. In the "Kingdom of Lovers," he says very much the same thing: "The unity of the Persons is the Fatherhood."[8] In the "Spiritual Espousals," he speaks of the Father as being identical with the divine being and with the unity of the divine Persons: "The Father is the beginning of all Godhead, according to his Being and his Person."[9]

In asserting this, Ruysbroeck certainly takes us a long way from the idea of God's being as a vague, primordial ground or a kind of super-being existing a long way behind the three Persons of the Trinity. What he maintains is in fact almost exactly the opposite — that the divine being is the Father. In itself, however, this assertion does not tell us very much. We may be able to accept fairly easily — especially if we interpret the statement at a rather superficial psychological level — Ruysbroeck's calling the Father the unity of the Persons, but how can God's being be called Father without reducing the Son and the Spirit to the level of lesser Persons, a level at which they are no longer seen as the same God? Another passage from Ruysbroeck's work ("The Spiritual Espousals") can help us out of this difficulty:

And in the delectable inclination of his spirit he (man) conquers God, and becomes one spirit with him. And in this union in the

Spirit of God he comes to a delectable savor and possesses the divine Being.[10]

What Ruysbroeck is saying here is that God's being and the Persons of the Trinity are the same, but precisely in this sense — that the Father is the divine being possessed in a certain way and that the Son is the same divine being experienced in a special, son-like way. God's being is the one divine being, but only exists in three different and personal ways. This reveals the inexhaustible life of the Trinity and is a continuous and constantly repeated seeking for and finding God's being as it shines through and in the other Person.

What therefore must be clear by now is that the self-abandonment of the divine Persons is not in any sense a being absorbed forever in a vague, undefined being. It is not a situation in which the three Persons of the Trinity play a provisional game of love, as it were, involving Father, Son and Holy Spirit, each of whom then leaps individually and forever into the divine being, where they enjoy a definitive and inviolable state of blessedness. On the contrary, the personal level and the level of essential being are situated within each other, even though they are not, in themselves, identical. The Persons find the divine being only through and in the Other:

The divine Persons are merged into the unity of Persons; they hang naturally and delectably in the very being of God himself. This fathomless being is undivided light, the very being of the Godhead which shines through and in the unity of Persons.[11]

At a certain point, man abandons himself and falls into the fathomless abyss of pure blessedness, where the three divine Persons possess their own nature in an essential unity of Persons and in an interpenetration into each others' being.[12]

The process of merging into the divine being and of sinking into perfect blessedness cannot therefore be separated from the mutual encounter that takes place between the three Persons. This essential coincidence of the Persons is closely connected with the contest of love with the Person who is always different. It is through that Other that a Person is enticed out of his distinctive nature and becomes absorbed into the being. At the same time, however, it is also the Other, seeking his own blessedness, who again and again confirms a Person in his own distinctive nature:

Because there are. in the Godhead, the Persons who continue to fascinate each other, the happiness of the unity can always begin again and this enjoyment of unity, which is always open and never grows stale, makes the Persons seek each other with new enthusiasm. It makes them accept each other again as they did the first time. And all these different moments are found in the one instant — they are one, eternally now.[13]

This community of love which exists in the Trinity is therefore a continuous reception *from* the Other, which is possible in an unending abandonment of the distinctive nature of the Person. (Ruysbroeck's teaching here is remarkably close to that of Richard of Saint Victor, who defined the Person as ex-sistentia, "standing out of" or "from.") The Son, in other words, is only Son *from* the Father and he is all the more Son in that he abandons his distinctive nature as Son in a pure orientation towards the Father. It is moreover precisely his being from the Father and his orientation towards the Father that makes him not something (a being) or someone (an isolated personality), but rather Son, divine Person. If the Son were ever to look back in self-satisfaction at his being a Son or to try to exist simply from himself as Son, he would wither away, becoming no more than a pure individual. Life would cease.

For Ruysbroeck, however, God was characterized by an unceasing newness:

In their unity, the divine Persons embrace each other with an everlasting satisfaction and in an inexhaustible and ever seeking love. And this is constantly renewed in the living life of the Trinity. For there is always new discovery in new bringing forth and new giving in new embracing, with an ever new stream of eternal love.[14]

What happens in man's experience of unity with God is analogous, since the relationship is that between the creature and the Creator. The complexity of the life of the Trinity is experienced in the encounter between man and God, in which the created person, who possesses a finite existence, meets the Creator God, who lives in infinite being. In other words, man has, in one way or another, to transcend his limited, created existence. This, however, does not take place, according to Ruysbroeck, by man's being annihilated as a being. What has to be broken through in this case is simply man's distinctive nature, which is his created personality:

If we wish to be clothed with him (Christ), this must take place by means of his grace. This is able to make us love him so much that we shall be able to abandon ourselves and overcome our own created personality. In this way, we become one with his Person, the eternal Truth.[15]

The distinction between "being" and "distinctive nature" therefore continues to play a part in man's becoming one with God. The Other draws man out of his distinctive nature in order to lead us into the divine being:

If we are open to what happens outside the sphere of ourselves, then we become aware that the Spirit of God is drawing us out of our selves and making us merge into and be lost in his Self. He then leads us into the super-essential being of Love, that Love which enables us to reach the being of the Other.[16]

In this situation, a reciprocal giving and receiving takes place between God and man:

For the Spirit of God demands of our spirit that we at once surrender ourselves out of ourselves into God and that we at once receive God into ourselves and comprehend him.[17]

Whenever man receives God, moreover, this takes place not in the limited sphere of his own distinctive nature, but in his essential being, where he is completely open:

He (Christ) has given us his Godhead above all created being and his highest being, which we possess in everlasting blessedness above ourselves in our being.[18]

What takes place in this state is rather that man is enabled to enjoy God above any consciousness that he may have of being created, of his own distinctive nature and of his difference from God:

For through delectable love he passes beyond his created nature and finds and savors the riches and the joy which are God himself.[19]

There is revealed the obscure silence which is rest, far transcending all definiteness. We have died in this — and yet we live, but above ourselves. This is now our enjoyment and our highest blessedness. There, in God's being, our super-essential being, is an eternal silence. There, in the unity of Persons, no word is spoken.[20]

It is, however, important to notice that the same man

continues to lead an independent existence and, what is more, he leads this simultaneously:

We live constantly in our own being through love and we also die constantly in God's being through enjoyment. And that is why this is called a dying life and a living death.[21]

This brings us to the very heart of the phenomenology of the experience of love, which we must now discuss in greater detail.

3. From Actively Becoming One to Resting in Unity

In his "ordinance" of the experience of love, Ruysbroeck proposed two essential aspects — "becoming one" and "unity." At the beginning of this part of the book, we quoted a passage from Ruysbroeck's treatise on "The Perfection of the Sons of God," in which he described this process of becoming one as our "leaving ourselves and all that we do, so that we can, dying in love, enter the essential riches of God." In the same passage, unity is described in this sentence: "There we shall finally possess God, losing ourselves eternally in him." At the beginning of Part II we also discussed the organic relationship between the various aspects of this unity with God and later, referring to certain passages in Ruysbroeck's work on the Trinity, we showed how he regarded the Person as both "essential being" and "distinctive nature" ("self" or "personality"). We are now sufficiently well prepared to be able to examine a number of texts in which Ruysbroeck deals explicitly, in the phenomenological sense, with this process of becoming one and this unity.

The best way of obtaining some idea of the precise meaning of becoming one and of unity here and of the difference between them is to consider the state of the "self" in these aspects. In the process of becoming one,

this self remains the touchstone of every other reality.
The reality of the other — his offer — must fit within a
given framework of its own. The riches of the other and
his different being must endure the measure and the
form of the self in order to be accepted as reality. All
that can be "understood" here is a translation into structures of its own, in other words, an empoverishment of
the reality. What I cannot grasp, that is, as I am now,
must remain outside — the other as such is bound to be
alien to me. All love and unity existing at this level must
remain imprisoned within the capacity and the activity
of that self. There is certainly an authentic form of love
and unity at this level — Ruysbroeck never condemns
the experience of "friends" who are not able to transcend this stage of becoming one, but he regards it as an
experience which goes no further than a process of "becoming like."

This being or becoming like is a very important element in Ruysbroeck's phenomenology. The term occurs
again and again in his writings, usually in conjunction
with "one." At the same time, Ruysbroeck succeeded
better than almost anyone else in situating this aspect
of the experience of unity in a very convincing way.
Most spiritual writers have emphasized the compelling
need — for those who want to become one with God —
to shake off the burden of being unlike the Other and, by
the practice of the virtues, to become as far as possible
like him.

What Ruysbroeck says in this context is completely traditional, in that he insists on this likeness as a condition
for all unity, no matter at what stage of the spiritual life
man may be. In his "Kingdom of Lovers," for instance,
he writes: "No one can enjoy God if he is not like
Christ and his holy Church. Through likeness he can

become one with God" and later in the same book: "Without this being like, no one can become one with God, either now or in eternity."[1] As we shall see later, Ruysbroeck goes even further and claims that this like- .ness continues not only to exist but also to grow, how- ever deeply and entirely man's unity with God and his sinking into the Other may be.

Where Ruysbroeck shows real originality and depth, however, is in pointing out that this likeness is at the same time both absolutely necessary and insurmountably secondary. He demonstrates why being like God is a very important condition for unity, but can never be the cause of that unity. It is, in his view, indissolubly linked with being one with God, but the two are never the same — they are complementary aspects of the one living phe- nomenon. The passage containing the most detailed ac- count of this likeness can be found in Ruysbroeck's "Kingdom of Lovers," just at the point where he is com- pleting his description of the life of longing for God to that of seeing God. Let us look at part of that passage:

As far as this aspect of the experience of unity is concerned, the saints — whether they are in a state of grace or already in the state of glory — are always a likeness of God. Grace or glory can never be so great that they go beyond all measure. At the same time, no one can possess unity unless he possesses it in measureless love — that is why likeness can never reach unity and yet remain likeness. And we can never lose this manner of likeness in eter- nity, because, in eternal life, glory continues to exist and can never pass away. And in this aspect of unity, man sees whether it is now in a state of grace or in the state of glory, according to the created mode of existence that is peculiar to him.[2]

This likeness can only be acquired through authentic divine gifts — graces, virtues and good works — and, what is more, it also continues to grow in eternity.

Why, then, does this process of becoming one never become, automatically as it were, a state of being one with God? Why can it not be taken so far and made so perfect that there is no difference between the partners, in other words that God and man ultimately come together in perfect unity? The cause — the one cause — of this inevitable division between being like and being one can be situated and demonstrated at two levels. The first of these levels is that of objective being. At this level, it is man's created nature which preserves the difference between these two aspects, a distinction which moreover persists forever. It is true, of course, that this created nature is transcended at the summit of the experience of unity — we saw, towards the end of the previous chapter, how we must "overcome our own created personality" and how man, because he is a person, is able to "abandon" his own finite and limited mode of being and "in this way, become one with his (Christ's) Person, the eternal Truth."

This created being, however, never disappears. Man's finite being continues to exist and unity with God continues to be rooted in a basic structure — that of man's relationship as a creature with God. Because of this, the experience of unity is always

An eternal hunger that shall never be appeased. This is an inward longing and striving of the capacity for love and of the created spirit for a good that is uncreated. . . . Behold, here begins an everlasting longing and striving towards an end that is never attained. . . . For there is no vessel ever made that can encompass the riches that are uncreated.[3]

The last sentence in this quotation from the third book of "The Spiritual Espousals" clearly echoes the classical adage of "objective" philosophy, according to which all things have their place in an ordered structure: *quidquid recipitur, recipitur ad modum recipientis* ("everything that is received takes place according to the measure of the receiver") . It is evident, then, that Ruysbroeck knew and acknowledged this rule and that he gave it an important place in his teaching. On the other hand, by showing precisely why it refers to only one aspect of the experience of unity with God, namely that of becoming like God or one with him, he prevented the state of being one as such from being undermined. According to Ruysbroeck's phenomenological teaching, then, this being one with God is in no way obstructed by man's permanent limitations as a creature — these constitute only one element among others of the experience of unity between persons.

What is the main characteristic of this likeness to God experienced at the level of the mystical life? It extends in fact as far as man's possibilities and his power themselves reach: "By becoming like God, the soul ascends as high as it can in unity with him. This is the highest point of resemblance."[4] However far this reaching towards God may go, however, it never becomes unity: "The more graces man receives and the more virtues he practices, the higher he rises and the more like God he becomes; but, as far as this aspect is concerned, he still only resembles God and is never one with him."[5]

This is so because becoming like God always takes place according to the special manner of the one who is becoming one. I may perhaps imitate God in a perfect manner. I may become his image and likeness as fully as I can. This can, however, never be a state of being one, because *I* am the one who acts and who make mine what belongs to the other. *I* am always the principle of my own life and however much I may become like

God, my own special nature remains unaffected. Although I am moving in the right direction, my special nature is even given a firmer foundation. The distinction between man and God continues, in other words, and even in becoming like the Other he can never succeed in breaking through his isolation. Ruysbroeck therefore insists that man must become like God "without manner,"[6] that is, *not* according to his special manner. As long as I am there in my special manner and the Other has to be appropriated by me according to my special manner of becoming one, passing through that manner, as it were, there can be no true unity. I may become more and more like him, but he can only be experienced in himself as the Other. Let us turn now once more to the way in which Ruysbroeck examines the relationship between this likeness to and oneness with God in activities of various kinds.

In becoming one with God's Spirit, we are testifying to our own activity and to the efficacy of God. In our activity we are always at the level of becoming like God, for we feel that our contemplation and our seeking are directed towards Someone who is different from ourselves. In this way we can become like God. When God is active, however, we are formed by his Spirit and "overformed" by his clarity and his love. In this way, we transcend likeness and become sons of God in grace.[7]

The movement of becoming one with God is characterized above all, as we have seen, by man's self, his special nature as a creature. In unity with God, on the other hand, this self is overcome by the riches and the otherness of God. The oppressive, restrictive framework is broken and the person is set free to enter the world of the Other. Ruysbroeck expresses this experience in the following passage:

The greatest heat is present where our spirit is burning and, of its own accord, longing for God. Here it experiences the love of God, but still in itself, a divine impulse, experienced and measured according to its own measure. It is more than hot where the spirit is burnt up, is freed from itself and "overformed" by God. When the spirit has been burnt up and absorbed by the Other and when it has become one spirit with him, it is pure love in being.[8]

In a second passage in another treatise, Ruysbroeck confines himself to the difference between "burning" and "being burnt up," which is parallel to "becoming one" and "unity." Ruysbroeck uses the term "being burnt up" to describe man's total loss of his own special nature.

In standing in the presence of God, man feels in his spirit an eternal burning in love. This movement never ceases and its beginning lies outside itself. He feels at one with this burning in love in search of the Other. He also always feels that the spirit burning in him with a love that is eternal makes him leave himself and enter the Other. He always feels himself being burnt up in love, for he is "overformed" in unity with God. Insofar as his spirit burns in love and makes him long all the more, he can look back at himself and observe the difference and distinction between himself and God. In being burnt up, however, in love for God, he is simple and is therefore in no way different from the Other, feeling nothing but unity.[9]

This phenomenology of becoming one and being one with God is suggested by Ruysbroeck in many other images and combinations of words: "sinking in love and sinking away from ourselves," "raising ourselves up and transcending ourselves," "banishing and driving out of ourselves," "melting and melting away, being drawn into the whirlpool and perishing in it."[10]

The most striking example of the two aspects of becoming one and unity, however, is another passage from

"The Perfection of the Sons of God"[11] in which Ruys-broeck describes the "friends" on the one hand and the "sons" on the other, identifying becoming one as the former and being one as the latter. It is, however, important to bear in mind two questions in considering these figures of the friends and the sons of God. The first is the question of how to situate these two groups of Christians in relation to each other.

God's friends are genuine believers who experience a perfectly authentic and meaningful form of unity with God: "They are always ascending to God with sincere faith; with real hope they expect God and their own blessedness and with mature love they adhere to God and are rooted in him. All this means that they have received good gifts — they please God and God pleases them. . . . God has chosen them from all eternity and from all eternity their names and their works are written in the living book of God's providence."[12]

As for the sons of God, Ruysbroeck stresses that "all good, believing men are sons of God" and that the,difference between "ordinary" and mystical believers — between faithful servants, friends and sons — is to be found in the degree of consciousness of the same fundamental — sanctifying — grace. For Ruysbroeck, there were not any separate levels of different kinds of grace. There was, however, a difference in the experience of God. Not everyone is conscious, Ruysbroeck insisted, of what God is for him in precisely the same way: "All good, believing men are born of the Spirit of God and God's Spirit lives in them and moves them and impels them — each one in his own manner and according to the measure of his suitability — towards the virtues and good works by which they will please God. Some men, however, I call faithful servants and others trusted friends or secret sons, because of the different manner in which they turn to God and are spiritually active. And yet they are all servants, friends and sons, for all serve and love and seek the same God and all live and work from the free Spirit of God."[13] This is, of course, an extension of the fundamental and concisely expressed teaching about the mystical union with God "without means" provided in "The Spiritual Espousals." There, as we saw quite early in this book, Ruysbroeck said: "This is common to all good men. But how that may come about remains hidden from them all their lives if it be that they are not inward and untrammelled by any creature."[14]

Let us now turn to the second point that should be borne in mind regarding the figures of God's friends and his sons. For Ruysbroeck, the mystical son of God was above all the figure representing the richest spiritual experience. This does not mean, however, that the son is the ultimate and highest step on the ladder of perfection, the Christian who has climbed forever above the lower steps. The son is certainly not a servant or friend who has been promoted to a higher rank — he is rather a servant or friend who experiences what it is to be a son. As a son, he continues to do what he did as a servant or friend — no difference would appear on a photograph — but he does it in the light of a different experience. The same virtues and the same activities are translucent to the "son," whereas, when he was a friend, they were opaque, a screen or a "means." Now, as a son, he experiences "without means" why and for Whom everything occurs — God himself has become the principle of all his activities. That is why Ruysbroeck is able to affirm that "the trusted friends of our Lord are always faithful servants wherever that is necessary."[15] This is no more than an application of that aspect of the mystical experience of unity with God which we have already discussed and will elaborate further on, namely that being one with God is a way of life which forms an organic whole containing an interaction of complementary elements.

Let us briefly consider at this point the teaching which expresses Ruysbroeck's ideal of the mystical life — the "common life" of action and contemplation:

God's friends are in possession of their spirit and their actions are of their own special nature. They choose to cling to God in love. They are able and wish to live for God . . . and that is why they remain full both of themselves and their activities are a veil. . . . And even though they feel that they are becoming one with God in clinging to him in love, they are always conscious of the difference and distinction between them and God in that process of becoming one.

Ruysbroeck continues in the same vein:

They feel themselves to be raised up to God. They burn with love, but preserving their own distinctive nature, are not burnt up and consumed in the unity of love. God's friends experience in themselves nothing but a living ascent in love in various ways according to their own special manner. The sons of God, on the other hand, experience without manner one single all-embracing movement of dying into the Other.[16]

Later in the same treatise on "The Perfection of the Sons of God" there is a passage describing in pure phenomenological terms the movement towards the total loss of this distinctive and special nature:

This sinking away from ourselves is far above all virtues and all exercise of love. It is nothing but an eternal going out of ourselves, which takes place in the total attention that we have for the Other. We leave ourselves and go into him, as into blessedness. For we feel an eternal movement out of ourselves into the Other. This is the most inward and most hidden difference that we can feel between ourselves and God, for beyond this there is no more difference.[17]

The same aspect of "sinking away from ourselves" and going into the Other is also expressed in explicitly Christian terms in another passage, this time in "The Twelve Beguines," in which Ruysbroeck is concerned especially with the difference between man's and God's spiritual activity:

For it is where our spirit and all our powers fail in their activity that the Spirit of our Lord is active above our powers and our activity. It is there that we are formed by the Spirit of our Lord and that we suffer his activity, which includes all of ours. It is in passivity that we grasp him. In our activity we always fall short and cannot grasp him. And above our activity he is active and we are passive; we grasp him in suffering above all our activity. And this is possessing God without grasping him, that is, in suffering and not grasping.[18]

Finally, let us quote another, similar passage from Ruysbroeck's treatise on "Seven Steps in the Scale of Spiritual Love," which will at the same time serve to introduce the next chapter:

Our activity is to love God and our enjoyment consists in letting ourselves be embraced passively in God's love. The difference between love and enjoyment is the difference between God and his grace. It is where we adhere to God in love that we are spirit. Where he deprives us of our spirit, however, and "overforms" us with his Spirit, we are enjoyment.[19]

4. "Enjoyment" or Being Entirely in God

One of the most important questions that has to be considered in any discussion of the unity between God and man is that of "being in God" (the traditional term is "immanence"). Is there any moment at which God gives himself totally as God? Is there a time when man has nothing more to long for? This question arises in Ruysbroeck's phenomenological teaching mainly within the context of the theme of "enjoyment." Perhaps this would be better expressed if we were to say that he makes this undeniable reality tangible in that aspect of the experience of unity with God which he calls "enjoyment." In this chapter, we shall first try to ascertain the precise nature and meaning of this aspect of unity. We shall then deal with two points in greater detail, by analyzing the concept of "enjoyment" and finally by determining the particular part that it plays within the whole experience of unity. In "A Mirror of Eternal Blessedness," we read:

There follows the third point of the living being — we are one with God above all the exercise of love in an eternal enjoyment, that is, above all activity or passivity in a blessedness which consists of being emptied of our special nature and above the process of becoming one with God in total unity with him, in which no one but he can be active. For he himself is his activity and that is also his nature. In this activity we are emptied of ourselves and "overformed" and one with him in his love. But we are not one in his nature, for, if we were, we would be God and would no longer exist ourselves. This ould be impossible. In unity, however, we are above reason and without reason and in clear knowledge. We are no longer conscious of any difference between ourselves and God because we are above ourselves and stripped of our spirit above all order in his love.[1]

This state of "being in God" is usually expressed in Ruysbroeck's writing by the standard term "enjoyment," although he also uses other expressions such as "rest," "satisfaction" and "blessedness." Again and again he points out that this enjoyment, in all its different forms, is always "above" the sphere of activity or, seen from the point of view of man's activity, that human striving must always remain "below" enjoyment. Why, then, does Ruysbroeck lay such stress on this lasting difference between the two levels? He does this, it would seem, because it was for him the only way of guaranteeing the real state of being in God. If there were anything more to be gained from the experience of enjoyment as such and if there were still even the slightest need of further activity, then it is clear that total unity with God could not have been reached. In that case, there would still be a distance between man and God and if unity had been achieved, it would only have been temporary and therefore not genuine unity at all. In "The Seven Bolts," Ruysbroeck writes:

And then comes the seventh bolt, which is raised above all the others. By this I mean that there is above all activity a quiet rest, empty of all activity. Above all holiness and the practice of virtues there is a simple blessedness. Above all hunger and thirst for God and above all love and seeking for him there is an eternal satisfaction.[2]

In his treatise on "Seven Steps in the Scale of Spiritual Love," Ruysbroeck also says that

Enjoyment is above all our activity and we cannot grasp it. And our activity is always below enjoyment. We also cannot include it in enjoyment. We always fall short in activity and can never love God enough. But we have enough in enjoyment — we are everything that we want.[3]

In a passage from "The Spiritual Espousals" too, we find an extremely striking reason why this enjoyment of God is so exalted — it is, in Ruysbroeck's words, a state of rest which has become a perpetual unrest:

And in this light the spirit sinks away from itself into a delectable rest, for the rest is without manner and is unfathomable. And man cannot recognize it for what it is except with himself, that is, with his rest; for since all manner of recognition and comprehension consists in manner and in measure, it cannot satisfy us, but rest becomes a perpetual unrest.[4]

A vital part is also played, in this aspect of unity with God, in which enjoyment is far more important than man's activity, the acquisition of virtues or any reduction to the level of human taste or ability, by the simple yet profound theme of "love that is concerned with itself and satisfied with itself in all its desires."[5] In the same treatise, we read:

Wherever we experience this unity, we are one being, one life and one blessedness with God. There everything is consummated and everything is made new. For where we are overwhelmed in the wide embrace of God's love, every man's joy is so great and so much part of himself that he cannot think of or distinguish anyone else's joy. For in this state, this man has become delectable love, which is everything in itself and which can do nothing of itself and has no need to look for anything outside itself.[6]

Ruysbroeck gives us one of his finest descriptions of this state of enjoyment in a passage on "satisfied love" in "The Twelve Beguines":

Satisfied love is exalted above everything. It is concerned only with itself and with nothing else. It is the perfect fulfilment of all striving after virtue. It is above all burning heat and is like a fire of burning coals which consumes all matter and everything that is alien to it by taking it into itself. And it is itself the most sublime degree of love. In it there is neither coming nor going and the passionate seeking for love and virtue no longer exists in it. It is like burning oil which has burnt up and consumed everything that is alien to it and is now satisfied and at the stage of pure fire. Satisfied love lives in God and God lives in it. There is no place in it for what is different.[7]

Although he is normally so balanced and sober, Ruysbroeck at times becomes enthusiastic, especially in his descriptions of the state of blessedness of the man who is entirely in God. At the same time, the Christian who is at all familiar with the traditional sensitivity of the Church with regard to any teaching that savors of pantheism and seems to undermine the integrity of God as God is bound to be astonished by Ruysbroeck's audacious language when he speaks of man's blessed state of being in God. It is obvious that it is hardly possible to go further than he in affirming man's complete unity with God in mystical experience. There is no hint, when he writes about this state, of caution or reticence. In the "Seven Steps," he describes this "blessedness without any difference" in unrestrained language:

There follows the seventh step, the most noble that can be experienced either in time or in eternity. This occurs when, above all our recognition and knowledge, we experience within us an unfathomable not-knowing, when, above all the names that we give to God or to creatures, we die and pass over into an eternally nameless one in whom we lose ourselves. And it happens when, above all exercise of virtues, we look into ourselves and discover eternal emptiness in which no one can be active and, above all blessed spirits, we experience an unfathomable blessedness in which we are all one and we are the same One who is blessedness itself in itself. And it takes place when we see all the blessed spirits sinking away from themselves in their being and passing into the Supreme Being, in an unknown and unknowable darkness without manner.[8]

A passage of similar enthusiasm occurs in "The Little Book of Enlightenment":

Although the creature remains a creature, all loving spirits are one enjoyment and one blessedness with God, without any difference. For the blessed being that is enjoyment of God and all of his loved ones is so uniquely simple that there are neither Father, Son and Holy Spirit with distinction between Persons nor creatures. But all these enlightened spirits are elevated far above themselves in an enjoyment without manner which is a superabundance above all the fullness that any creature has ever received or could ever receive. There all exalted spirits are, in their Supreme Being, one enjoyment and one blessedness with God without any difference. And this blessedness is so simple that no distinction can ever arise in it.[9]

Is there any other mystical writer, following any tradition at all, who has described the experience of being entirely in God with more conviction and power than this? One has the impression that Ruysbroeck had no inkling of the theological pitfalls that lie concealed in such expressions as "one blessedness with God without any difference" — he is so artless in his testimony to this state of being completely one with God. He is quite unrestrained and self-assured and this is without any doubt because he is above all a phenomenologist. He does not try, as so many theologians have, to solve the problem of the relationship between personal perfection and un-

limited blessedness. He does not discuss the objective
question as to whether the saints in heaven are able to
enjoy perfect happiness when they observe that everyone has his special place in the heavenly hierarchy and
that one blessed soul is therefore greater than another.
From his own experience — not as the result of rational
thought — Ruysbroeck knows that different elements
can co-exist in human experience. Blessedness as such —
the absolutely unadulterated spiritual quality of unbroken unity — and personal blessedness are not mutually exclusive. The one aspect of man's complete merging
into the One who is nameless without ever going back
to himself and the other aspect of his possessing his own
particular happiness do not exclude each other, but in-
teract at the deepest level. Both aspects are included
within the same reality of unity with the Other. Ruysbroeck is therefore able to affirm with complete self-
confidence and without fear of contradiction that every
blessed soul has its own particular state of blessedness.
Order, merit and precedence — these continue to exist:

We shall remain eternally in ourselves and be blessed and in the
place allotted to us in the glorious hierarchy of heaven, each one
according to the measure of his virtue and his love. But we shall
also enjoy God above ourselves (that is, "above every distinction
and order of merit") in the unfathomable love that is God himself.[10]

It is clear, then, that Ruysbroeck regards the blessedness of each believer who is accorded a special place
according to his merits as only one aspect of a much
richer and more complex whole. That is why he is able
to teach that this aspect of individual blessedness can
never exclude or overshadow the state of blessedness as

such. He stresses this in several treatises. Here is one example:

The luxury that God gives is the same for everyone but not everyone is capable of receiving the same. In any case, there is for everyone who is involved in the process of becoming one the superabundant possibility of more enjoyment. But when a man is lost in the darkness of the desert there can be no more enjoyment because there is neither giving nor taking there, but only one simple being — God, with all those who have become one with him, is there, sunken away and lost. They can never find themselves again in this undivided being, for it is pure, unique simplicity. This is the highest blessedness that exists in the kingdom of God.[11]

In addition to such words as "enjoyment," "rest," "satisfaction" and "blessedness," Ruysbroeck also uses another term to express the authentic experience of God's immanence. This is the mutual "possession" of God by man and man by God. At a given moment in the mystical experience of unity, nothing more of God remains hidden from man. There is nothing more still to be attained by him. Nothing is inaccessible to him. Perhaps the most remarkable aspect of these texts dealing with man's possession of and being possessed by God is something that is not fully expressed in the passages about his enjoyment of God, namely that this total possession is above all reciprocal. In other words, God is really possessed by man and man is genuinely at the same time his property, God making his home in him. We may therefore say that God becomes the very principle of our life, because we live entirely in him and our activity is fully incorporated into his. This is the definitive fulfilment of the process of "being formed" described in other texts that we have examined:

We possess God in sinking away from ourselves in love and in losing ourselves. Then God is our property and we are his. And we continue to sink away eternally, without returning, from ourselves and into our property, which is God.[12]

The image of the throne, which Ruysbroeck also uses in other texts, expresses the same idea of mutual possession in enjoyment:

Thrones are those who possess God in a delectable adherence to the Supreme Being and are themselves possessed by God as his throne and rest. They are one without distinction in the simple enjoyment of being.[13]

We must now return to the central concept of "enjoyment" and see how, in two passages especially, Ruysbroeck defines it more precisely. In the first of these texts, in "The Perfection of the Sons of God," he distinguishes three aspects of enjoyment — "rest," "passing away" and "dead-lost" — in an analysis which is particularly subtle and at the same time not difficult to grasp. Although Ruysbroeck describes various stages in this process, we should not forget that what he is attempting to define throughout is always the same — unity with God. The process analyzed is simply that of the gradual unfolding of man's authentic possession of and being possessed by God and it would be a distortion of this structure to see it — perhaps unconsciously — simply from the point of view of a growth towards and an ascent to God.

The culminating experience of enjoyment has three aspects. The first of these is rest, when the self has reached the one he loves and is at home there. He is possessed by the loved one in pure and essential love. The spirit is overcome by the love of the loved one. He is in possession of him and at rest. The second aspect is a passing away into God. The spirit sinks away from himself, without knowing who he is, where he is or how this is happening. This is followed by the third aspect, the last one of which the spirit can be conscious. Here he perceives a darkness which he cannot enter with reason. In this, he feels himself to be dead and lost and completely one with God without any difference.[14]

In a second passage, this time in "The Spiritual Tabernacle," Ruysbroeck analyses man's enjoyment of God and situates it within the whole experience of unity. It is true that man cannot hope to come to a full enjoyment of God by his own activity. It is also true that this state of blessedness transcends all the stages that precede it and all forms of appropriation — it can never be the result of purely human effort. Nonetheless, this most profound state of unity with God is never a phenomenon that is totally isolated from all man's attempts, however transitory they may be, to become one with him. Our striving towards and our ascent to God cannot touch this quiet enjoyment, but possession by God can, on the other hand, have an effect on the mystic's active seeking. Spiritual experience as a whole can be seen as functioning in an ascending order. It is therefore clear that Ruysbroeck's definition of "enjoyment" works in the opposite direction — in descending order — since he is obviously pointing to the effect that the climax of that experience (enjoyment of God) has on the lower stages.

It hardly needs to be said, of course, that Ruysbroeck is here looking at the whole question pre-eminently from the perspective of the mystic who is in full possession of God. We may also say in this context that this is his constant standpoint and that he describes almost every level of spiritual experience from the culminating or terminal point of that experience, the creative enjoyment of God. We need only to recall here that, in his view, even the simplest virtues are rooted in the highest Love and unity and that he believed, as we have already seen,[15] that God's mystical "touching" of man's innermost being occurs before God's effects flow out into the different powers. All these characteristics reflect a fundamental Christian teaching — that the Kingdom of God is there before man is converted to it.

In this delectable love there are three aspects. The first is that God shows himself to the spirit that is empty of all activity as the one with whom enjoyment is to be found. In the second aspect, the loving spirit escapes from himself and melts away into an essential enjoyment. This melting away in love is without manner and always without returning and its nature is enjoyable. For the spirit dies to itself in God, that is, in an experience of undivided simplicity and blessedness. We should understand this melting away as the expression of perfect, delectable love which always enters the Other and not as an active love that seeks, which goes towards the Other, but is always returning to itself. For enjoyment is a definitive resting which can no longer move or be moved. . . . The third aspect is that this possession of the Other in enjoyment is always satisfied and unmoved, so that there is no need to go on seeking, but the burning and melting away is always being renewed, before the face of that enjoyment. And so this love forms part of a greater whole, in which the ascent to God continues and the spirit tries to grasp what it has already come to possess in delectable rest.[16]

This analysis of the state of enjoyment leads us to another central theme in Ruysbroeck's phenomenology— his conception of unity as a living reality in which no single aspect of the experience is isolated from any other aspect. We must now examine this theme a little more closely, since an understanding of it will help us to see Ruysbroeck's two teachings — man's being entirely in God and the lasting difference of God — more clearly in relation to each other.

5. Unity and the Lasting Difference of God

In the texts that we took as examples of Ruysbroeck's treatment of the theme of "enjoyment," we considered, among other aspects, the stress that he laid on the authenticity of man's experience of unity with God. There is, in Ruysbroeck's view, no distinction in this unity between the two persons — man is "burnt up," "consumed" and "sunken away" in God. But, in dwelling on God's immanence in this way, did Ruysbroeck at the same time also stress God's lasting difference? He described in unequivocal language man's being entirely in God in total unity, but did he also place equal emphasis on God as the one who is always greater than man, on God as "inaccessible light," to use Paul's term, on the God of the Judaeo-Christian tradition who is always different and, in the scholastic terminology, transcendent? This paradox of the inexhaustible nature of God in his unity with man is at the same time a question of central phenomenological importance. It is therefore at this level of the structure of human experience that we must now consider in greater detail the lasting difference of God by examining a number of texts in which Ruysbroeck deals with this question.

If we are to analyze this important matter correctly, we should distinguish two different aspects and con-

sider them in conjunction with one another. The first
aspect can best be expressed in the form of a series of
questions. In unity, does man become one with God to
such an extent that this unity is ultimately no more than
a lifeless identification? Is the state of being lost, described by the mystics who have experienced this unity,
a situation in which nothing remains of man as a creature
and in which he is simply absorbed into some vague,
undefined being? Is the highest state of blessedness nothing but an abscence or a disappearance, having no deep
effect on man as such? If the mystic does in fact emerge
from the depths of this experience and appear again, is
this return a significant event which would embarrass
those who are in favor of a completely abstract concept
of "nirvana." If, moreover, he also declares that he cannot give us any information about his experience, are
we to take this as meaning that he has brought nothing
back with him, that he knows no more and that he is in
no way changed by the experience? Ruysbroeck deals
with this first aspect of the difference of God under two
headings, both of which we shall consider in this chapter — first, that the tension continues to éxist in the
relationship between the persons and secondly that unity
is a living, organic whole.

The second aspect of the lasting transcendence of God
can also be formulated in a series of questions. What is
the quality of this supreme unity? Quite apart from its
effect on the mystic himself, how does the world in
which he is lost look? In the long run, cannot everything
be reduced to a rather dull experience, since unity with
God and mutual possession clearly amount to something
unoriginal, an illusion that on closer inspection has
nothing to offer but the patient cultivation of ground
already well known. Is it not true to say that God him-

self may be no more than a beautiful book which, we
suddenly discover, we have already read? We shall see
what Ruysbroeck has to say about this aspect of the
reality of God in the last chapter of this book.

1. The Tension Continues to Exist in the Relationship between the Persons

Before examining the passages that we have chosen
to illustrate Ruysbroeck's phenomenological teaching
about the lasting difference of God, it is important to
note that he speaks again and again, usually in com-
pressed philosophical or theological statements, about
the folly of those Christians who regard unity with
God as a complete merging together of two beings. He
uses the word "beings" in the sense of precisely defined
matters. It is true, of course, that he makes such statements as "and then we become one being with God,"
using a manner of speaking which, from the fourteenth
century onwards, sent shivers down the spines of ortho-
dox and philosophically trained readers, because they
suspected that Ruysbroeck was teaching the same kind
of pantheistic heresy which he accused others of teaching.

Only a fundamental semantic study, such as J. Alaerts',
of the way in which the Ruysbroeck uses such terms as
"being," "essence," "essential" and "superessential" can
help us to understand this problem and overcome the
objections that it raises.[1] In the meantime, however, we
may say that his "essential" terminology is in no sense a
medieval echo of Aristotelian teachings. In his writings,
"being" or "essence" has a special and rich meaning
which cannot be reduced to that of the earlier *essentia*.
In his teaching, the word evokes realities which lie outside the framework envisaged by Aristotle and his fol-

lowers. When Ruysbroeck speaks of "becoming one being with God," he does not in any sense mean that the divine being and man's being are merged together. What he is suggesting in this use of the word is a mode of being in which God and man are one. It is not difficult for us now to sense the existential verbal tonality of Ruysbroeck's use of the term "being."

In addition to making a number of doctrinal statements of this kind affirming God's different being, Ruysbroeck also writes in a way in which the healthy realism of the Low Countries is combined with deep phenomenological insight. An example of this can be found in a passage in his treatise on "The Perfection of the Sons of God" in which he points out that blessedness, if it is really to be blessedness at all, must have a concrete effect on man. What would happiness in unity with God mean if it were to be situated simply in the hereafter and have no reference to man here and now?

In the passage that follows, Ruysbroeck discusses our "knowledge," which does not enable us to "know" how blessed we are, although we can know that we *are* blessed. We are always failing in our attempts to measure our progress and fit it into a frame, but that does not mean that we do not know that there is an endless need to measure and that there is something that has to be enclosed in a framework.

The unfathomable clarity of God surrounds us in unity and "overforms" us with itself. In this way, we are as it were annihilated by God and created anew by him. We sink away into love to the point where we possess blessedness and are one with God. But while we are becoming one with him there is still a living knowledge and an active love in us. . . . If it were possible for us to be blessed without knowing, then a stone could also be blessed, for it knows nothing. If I were the lord of the whole world and did

not know, hat would I care? And that is the reason why we shall
always know that we taste and that we possess.[2]

How, then, does Ruysbroeck express this characteristic of God as the one who is always different? He does
so by stressing the continued existence of the polarity
between God and man within the state of perfect unity.
What is particularly masterly in his account, moreover,
is that he never allows this tension, which never ceases
to exist, to become reduced to the level of a hidden
disruption of man's state of being entirely in God. Speaking from personal experience and as a phenomenologist,
he claims with confidence that the man who is one with
God can only confirm that unity consists of both the one
and the other. Precisely as a person, a man can experience both the one and the other, that is, the different
aspects of the one "psychological" reality. "One" and
"different" are not various things experienced in sequence, but rather complementary aspects of the one
spiritual state of unity between the divine and the human persons:

And so we live entirely in God, where we possess blessedness, and
we live entirely in ourselves, where w raise ourselves up to God
in love. And even though we live entirely in God and entirely in
ourselves, we live only one life. But it has two opposite aspects.[3]

In another passage in the "Twelve Beguines," Ruysbroeck says very much the same:

And although we feel ourselves to be raised above ourselves and
one with God in love, we still remain eternally different from him
in our spirit and in our thoughts. And between the unity with God
and the difference from him that we are there is a constant tension, so that we have always to try in love to leave ourselves and
overcome this distance. Our blessedness consists of this.[4]

In "The Seven Bolts," Ruysbroeck makes use of a comparison to illustrate the relationship between this unity and difference:

In unity we move as it were towards a point from which all lines extend and at which they all converge. In the point itself the lines lose their own name and can no longer be distinguished from each other and from the point. There, they are the unity which is characteristic of the point itself. But the lines still remain what they are — converging lines. In the same way we too will always preserve our own created mode of being and yet at the same time, in a constant losing of ourselves, eternally enter the Other's being.[5]

Ruysbroeck describes this experience quite often in various texts, sometimes with an interesting addition outlining what the person really is. He does not, of course, use "anthropological" arguments to prove that his description of unity with God is meaningful or plausible. All that he does is to say that man comes to know himself in this unity as a being capable of growth and extension. A table is simply a table, but man is essentially, in his very being, a power capable of concord between himself and the other, a being of known possession and new conquest. Man's spiritual being is not broken when it is broken through; it is as such unbroken growth. And it is spiritual only insofar as it becomes continuously wider. In the experience of unity, it is completely overwhelmed, abandoned and "annihilated" and it is then that it really *is*.

There are two aspects of love — unity and difference. Unity in love cannot become difference and difference cannot become unity. In love there is one spirit which is divided between these two aspects. The difference makes man blessed by enabling him to stand before God and contemplate him with eternal admiration. Unity in love is supreme blessedness, rest and enjoyment with God in eternity.[6]

The following quotation from "The Spiritual Espousals" can be compared with the above text from "The Twelve Beguines":

The inward man possesses his life in these two manners, that is, in rest and action. And in either he is whole and undivided, for he is wholly in God, where in enjoyment he rests, and he is wholly in himself, where actively he loves.[7]

Unity with God does not mean therefore that man as a person simply disappears. But we may go further than this and say, with Ruysbroeck, that man not only continues to exist as a person in the state of unity with God, but also becomes even more a person. We have already seen how "unity" calls for a continuously growing "likeness." Towards the end of his "Spiritual Espousals," Ruysbroeck also observes that "the most excellent and the most profitable contemplation to which a man can attain in this life" is not a situation in which an ethereal contemplative is likely to find himself, but rather the state in which "man remains free and master of himself, increasing in every form of meritorious living. . . . in inwardness and virtue."[8]

Ruysbroeck is clearly convinced, then, from his own experience, that man becomes even more human and a richer personality by becoming more like God, but at the same time he also stresses — and in so doing reveals a fundamental change in perspective — that this is something that is not the result of an attempt to achieve unity, but something that occurs because unity has already been achieved. The man who is actively seeking God tries, by the practice of virtues to become like God and, at the same time, wants so to speak to attract God's attention. What happens to him in this ascent to God is that his seeking does not cease to exist, but rather loses its aspect of acquisition and seizing. He continues to seek and indeed seeks more than ever, but he does so now rather as a consequence or reflection of being one with the Other. He no longer seeks in an attempt to reach God. Sunken away from himself and living the Other's being, the mystic is now able to see from the point of view of unity with God what he must be for the Other. He possesses God, but he has been given such superabundant riches that new energies are constantly being released and new efforts are constantly being made to ensure that the Other has a suitable home:

The process of becoming one between us and God is a consuming fire. And that is why, when we turn to this fire, it makes us new again and again and sets us alight in new love, so that we must always go on seeking.[9]

There is, in this state, no longer any question of man's having to continue to be active in order to reach the Other or of his being able to appropriate some sphere or territory that God wants to keep to himself. At this stage, the mystic is no longer dwelling in himself as he was at that first, rather naive stage when he believed that he might, as the result of exercising the virtues, take the whole ocean into himself and his own familiar experience. On the contrary, at this point of development, we are concerned with the Christian who is one with God and at the same time conscious that God is always immeasurably greater than he is and different. This God, however, never ceases to set man alight in the unity that exists between them:

Love without measure, which is God himself, reigns in the purity of our spirit like the heat of burning coals, making both God and man one. It spits out glowing, burning sparks which touch and

set the fiery love alight again. Heart and senses, will and desire
and all the strength of our soul, in storm and fury, in storm and
fury and in pure love without manner — these are the weapons
which we use in our struggle against this terrible and mighty love
of God which burns up and swallows all loving spirits. It arms us
with its gifts, enlightens our reason and offers, advises and teaches
us, so that we can resist and fight to maintain our right in love
against it for as long as we can.[10]

2. Unity as a Living, Organic Whole

Having outlined the way in which Ruysbroeck deals
with the first element in the essential and lasting difference of God as a continuing tension between the persons involved in the state of unity, we can now turn to
the second phenomenological element mentioned above.
In considering this, we must see how Ruysbroeck describes the interplay in this unity between man's state
of being entirely in God and God's lasting characteristic
of being greater than man. In the preceding section, the
first element was expressed in terms of a polarity between persons who are constantly involved with each
other. In this section, we shall see how the second element is described in different terms, namely as stages in
the process of becoming one with God. In the first
theme, we saw how the ideas of "unity" and "person"
were stretched almost to breaking point, the conceptual
language of an earlier period being scarcely able to express the real quality of the unity between God and man,
which is, as we have seen, is both "the one and the
other."

Ruysbroeck always takes as his point of departure the
facts of his own experience. In this case, as in others,
he does not make use of speculative thought to solve the
problems confronting him. He does not try to make the
phenomenon of man's unity with God intelligible by

constructing rational links between the two partners. All that he attempts to do is to take into account and recognize as valid the special dimension both of the persons involved and of the state of unity itself.

In the passages quoted in this second section on the unity between God and man, we shall see how Ruysbroeck consciously reveals the successive stages that can be distinguished in the process of man's ascent to unity with God. The whole process is made translucent by the author who, because of his own experience and his profound reflection about it, delineates the entire framework of his "ordinance," with its clearly defined surfaces of becoming one and final unity with God, so that it appears ultimately as one single living and organic whole. What is more, since Ruysbroeck is such a great writer and a master of the paradoxical style, it is possible for him to make an otherwise purely mechanical and chronological process live for us.

Let us first look at two texts written from the vantage point of becoming one with God. In both, the mystic seems suddenly to be genuinely surprised by his discovery that the one who is seeking has really already found and that the experience of becoming one is already an experience of authentic unity itself.

We recognize by this that, in the course of our becoming one with God, there is already present a loving embrace shared by God and us and our striving to love and all our activities are already fulfilled and crowned.[1]

The different aspects of becoming one and ultimate unity are therefore mutually complementary and cannot be separated. They are not, however, interchangeable, nor is the one ever reducible to the other — the embrace of which Ruysbroeck speaks is not the direct cause of the activities, nor is it the result of a successful process of becoming one. In this second passage too, Ruysbroeck still has this process in mind, but once again he shows it to be a becoming one which is already a state of unity:

Purity of the spirit is to be united with God's Spirit. There are two inseparable aspects of becoming one. We feel within us how we become united with God and how we achieve unity with him, his Spirit having an effect on us and our spirit being lost in him.[2]

Just as the aspect of becoming one contains within it that rest which is a feature of the following phase of unity, so too does that later stage contain something more, namely the previous stage of becoming one, which is not yet completed:

In the state of unity with God, the spirit perceives that he has, through love, sunk away from himself into the depths and that he has raised to the heights and has become lost in the distance. And he feels that he has gone astray in the wide spaces. He feels too that he is living in an unknown place that he knows well. He feels as though he has fled away from himself into unity with God, but only in and through the unceasing process of becoming one. He knows that, through dying, he has entered the living reality of God. And there he experiences one life with God.[3]

A particularly striking description of this situation can also be found in Ruysbroeck's "Spiritual Espousals." In this long passage, the author first outlines the phenomenon using the terms that we have already encountered — "likeness" and "unity." To begin with, he seems hardly to be concerned with the mysterious intertwining of the two aspects and stresses above all the transition from "likeness" to "unity." Later, however, he goes back, penetrates to a somewhat deeper level and explains, with the help of the terms "activity" and "rest," the real nature of loving God. This text shows us above all that the different aspects are really the same living reality:

And each hour our likeness to God is submerged, and dies in God and is made one with God and remains one; for charity makes us to be made one with God and to remain and dwell one with him. And yet we preserve an everlasting likeness in the light of grace or of glory, where we actively possess ourselves in charity and in virtue. And we preserve a unity with God above our works in a nakedness of our spirit in the divine light, where in rest we possess God above all virtue. For charity must evermore be active in our likeness to God and unity with God shall rest eternally in a delectable love. And this is our commerce in love.

For in the same instant and the same hour, love is active and rests in her Beloved. And the one is strengthened by the other. For the higher the love, the greater the rest; and the greater the rest, the more fervent the love. For the one lives within the other and whoever does not love does not rest and who does not rest does not love. Yet it seems to such a good man that he neither loves nor rests in God and this same seeming comes from love; so that he may yearn to love more than he is able, it seems to him that he falls short. And in this work he savors both love and rest, for no one can understand how one loves actively and rests delectably, except for the man who has forsaken himself and is free of himself and is enlightened.[4]

This presentation of different but complementary aspects of man's unity with God is also to be found, in a terse form in "The Perfection of the Sons of God," in a section in which Ruysbroeck describes the "spiritual life." New energy, he says, always comes freely "out of" — which is not the same as "through" — already possessing and, although this possessing is never disrupted and the act of acquisition never has to be repeated — on the contrary, man continues without interruption to possess — it is renewed again and again, thanks to the new activity:

> Out of this becoming one man's desire is always stimulated and roused anew to new inward activity. And while it is active the spirit is rising to become one anew. In this way, both man's activity and his movement to become one are constantly renewed.[5]

As Ruysbroeck suggests in this passage, the same experience of unity as a living reality can also be defined, as it is in "The Spiritual Tabernacle," as continuing to exist while active love goes on seeking.[6] There is certainly a close link between the various steps in the experience of mystical love, but this does not mean that there is an accumulation of systematic acts of acquisition. There is a sequence of events, but this is not chronological. Ruysbroeck makes this clear in a passage in his "Seven Steps":

> Stripped of ourselves and of our own activity, we should therefore go into an enjoyment of God and at the same time go out of ourselves in good works, while remaining always united to the Spirit of God. This is what I mean. It is similar to when we open our eyes, look and then close them again, so quickly that we are not conscious of it. In the same way, we die in God and live out of God, yet always remain one with him. So too shall we go out of ourselves and go in with love, all the time clinging to God and remaining united to him without any movement.[7]

Whereas in a pheneomenological context Ruysbroeck uses such terms as "becoming one" and "unity" with God, in psychological passages he prefers to express these ideas by speaking of love which is "active" or "essential." As long as man remains enclosed within his own self, his activity in love will always be prevented from breaking out of the restrictive framework of that self and therefore an activity that is confined to seeking and acquiring. As soon as he has left the confines of his own self, however, he becomes capable of a different kind of loving activity. This love transcends the limitations of the human self, is not restricted and therefore no longer seeks what is within its power to grasp. In the last passage that we have chosen to include in this chapter, Ruysbroeck takes as his point of departure not the difference between these two kinds of love, the "active" love of becoming one and the "essential" love of unity, but the nature of love as such, in its paradoxical fullness:

All our activities are contained in our response to God's love and all his activities and his gifts are found in that love. In all our free reactions to God we shall therefore live with continuous love. For we must live in this way — by experiencing how, in every one of our free reactions to God's love, our loving heart is burnt up and melts away and by feeling ourselves sink away into God in praise of the highest good.[8]

In conclusion, then, we may say that Ruysbroeck wants us to "find love with love," as he expresses it in "The Little Book of Enlightenment,"[9] and this means that we should expect to experience unity with God in becoming one with him.

6. The Inexhaustible Experience of Being in God

1. A Lasting Superabundance

In the previous chapter, we discussed the question of God's lasting difference or transcendence and concluded that man experienced this difference above all when he was united with God, this unity being in no sense an identification with God, but rather a developing and dynamic life with him. We saw that unity with God was, in Ruysbroeck's view, "being" or "essence," in the existential, verbal sense of the word, a mode of being in which tension between the two personal poles, God and man, always continued to exist. We also recognized that Ruysbroeck conceived this unity as one single reality containing different facets reflecting each other and being reflected in each other.

In that chapter, then, we made an initial and partial analysis of the phenomenon of God's transcendence and found that, according to Ruysbroeck, his lasting difference was situated in the fact that man never ceases to exist independently in the state of unity with God. The relationship is never discontinued. We also saw, especially when we were considering Ruysbroeck's descriptions of man's experience of being in God in the preceding chapter, that this relationship included an aspect of being absolutely "one without any difference." At the same time, however, a distance and an unending seeking continued to exist.

The question that we have to consider now is where this constant difference comes from? What Ruysbroeck does here is in fact to integrate two perspectives or rather to give new meaning to a well known Christian teaching (the result of speculative thought) without refuting that teaching. He does this by approaching it from the vantage point of the mystical experience of being in God rather than from that of rational thought. This teaching, which is based on an "objective" structure, is that the Creator and the creature are separated from each other by an unbridgeable gulf. Man can never become God — this is, as we have already seen, a constantly recurring refrain in Ruysbroeck's writing. A quotation from "The Little Book of Enlightenment" gives a very good example of his attitude:

But the creature never becomes God. For he becomes one only through grace and through love and these flow back into God. And so the creature feels in his inward contemplation distinct from God and different. . . . God gives himself into the being of the soul, where the powers are gathered and where they are combined in unity and are "overformed" by God. There everything is in superabundance. For there the spirit feels one truth and one riches and one unity with God. And yet there is still a movement forward — an essential difference between the soul's being and God's being.[1]

This is obviously a case where Ruysbroeck feels impelled to stress the lasting transcendence of God of a very special and, for the mystic, provisional kind. This is the difference between God and man which must be accepted as for ever insuperable in the context of the polarity between the two beings — God's Being and man's being — and which reveals that there can be no hope of genuine immanence, since God is in himself transcendent and therefore unattainable. Ruysbroeck's "movement forward" is ultimately no more than an expression of the unbridgeable gulf that always exists between God and man. In the light of this very limited view, another passage from Ruysbroeck's writing can only be understood as an invitation to go on seeking endlessly and hopelessly. Even "above all virtues and all exercise of love," man is apparently never able to rest and is always prevented from really possessing. This is what Ruysbroeck says in a passage that we have already quoted in a different context:

This sinking away from ourselves is far above all virtues and all exercise of love. It is nothing but an eternal going out of ourselves, which takes place in the total attention that we have for the Other. We leave ourselves and go into him, as into blessedness. For we feel an eternal movement out of ourselves into the Other.[2]

How, then, was it possible for Ruysbroeck, who was one of the most convincing and reliable witnesses to the state of unity between man and God and to man's condition of perfect happiness, to insist so firmly on the inseparable distance between the utterly transcendent God and his creature? He was undoubtedly able to do this because he drew not only on the "objective" structure, but also on his own presonal experience. Even though he fully recognized his position as a creature, he had himself experienced something more. The framework or structure continued to exist and within it, he knew, everything had its place, its definition and its limits, but this did not mean, Ruysbroeck believed, that nothing could take place within that structure. On the contrary, something could and did take place and this was of a different quality.

This event is the encounter between persons, the community of love, the life that calls for an objective structure, but is never identical with it. It is this which provided the mystic of Groenendael with his definitive and all-embracing perspective based on his experience of being one with God. This is the experience of "some men who, above all exercise of virtues, discover and feel in them a living experience in which are joined together the created and the uncreated, God and the creature."[3]

What happens, then, in this mystical perspective, to the insuperable distance between the creature and the Creator? Is it simply forgotten or placed in parenthesis by someone who disguises the grey fabric of reality with the bright colors of emotion? How is the lasting difference of God, his hopeless transcendence, integrated?

Ruysbroeck provides an answer to these difficult questions by insisting that the mystic experiences an aspect of being entirely in God.[4] We have already quoted a passage from "The Little Book of Enlightenment" in our chapter on "Being Entirely in God" in which Ruysbroeck speaks of "one enjoyment and one blessedness with God without any difference" as the, state of unity with God and says that "this blessedness is so simple that no distinction can ever arise in it." This state of, in other words, clearly one of being entirely in God.

Now this brings us to the most important and original contribution that mystical experience can make to a better understanding of the lasting difference of God. It is that this state of being in God, this divine immanence is a "superabundance." It is "an enjoyment without manner, which is a superabundance above all the fullness that any creature has ever received or could ever receive."⁵ Possession of and being possessed by God is always inexhaustible. Being in God is entire and authentic and leaves nothing to be desired. It is also a lasting superabundance.

The phrase "an enjoyable inclination towards God" occurs in the same passage from "The Little Book of Enlightenment." It means a movement which is already an enjoyment of God⁶ and it serves to characterize the transition to "being one without any difference" and falling into "superabundance." The same phrase, an "enjoyable inclination," is one that we have already encountered in our previous chapter on "Enjoyment or Being Enirely in God," when we quoted from Ruysbroeck's "The Kingdom of Lovers." The third aspect of the "ordinance" of man's encounter with God, Ruysbroeck claims, is

an enjoyable inclination towards and a clinging to God, which causes man and all his powers to flow away. He is surrounded on all sides and filled both within and without by a superabundance of riches much greater than he would ever have been able to desire for himself.⁷

In being entirely in God, then, the mystic is in this "superabundance." But the question remains — is this experience of superabundance in the long run not simply a rather enthusiastic way of saying that man, as a creature, is insuperably limited. Does it not mean that God in fact never gives himself entirely and that what is here claimed to be an inexhaustible experience of being in God is really no more than a threatening surplus or a hopeless journey from partial and provisional possession to an illusion of blessedness?

Light is thrown on this whole problem by another text — one which we have already quoted at the be-

ginning of our chapter on "The Life of the Trinity" —
in Ruysbroeck's "The Kingdom of Lovers."[8] In this
passage, the author shows how both the divine Persons
and man himself in God's being in "an experience of an
enjoyable inclination into the unfathomable being of
God" and the passage continues: "here God and all
those who are united with him suffer the 'overforming'
of this simple light." Then, in a striking sentence, Ruysbroeck returns to the theme of superabundance: "In this
suffering, the soul becomes conscious of the coming of
the one whom he loves, because it receives more than it
can desire in this enjoyable unity."

This "enjoyable inclination" is not the exclusive preserve of man, the limited creature. It is also something
which the divine Persons experience, even though they
enjoy a superabundant blessedness. What we have here
is pure transcendence, not only with regard to the capacity of man and all creatures, but also a transcendence in itself with regard to every definition and every
form of status quo. The ultimate divine reality itself is
thus in no sense a block of granite or a massive pedestal,
nor is it an end, but above all a "living Ground," an
ever new Beginning. Continuously included by the divine
Persons and the "blessed spirits," it is itself never exhausted. This eternal Life is described most vividly by
Ruysbroeck in the final pages of his "Spiritual Espousals."

It is in fact from this sublime experience of unity
with God, this inexhaustible state of being entirely in
God, that Ruysbroeck views the distance between God
and man. The lasting difference between them is seen
as an integral part of the state of blessedness and as the
other side of the coin of their indissoluble togetherness.
Movement is seen as the result of rest and seeking as

the reaction experienced by the one who has found a superabundance. Who was the mystic who said that the bee still buzzed and moved its wings while it was sucking honey? An expression like "a continuous enjoyable inclination into the Other" can be seen in this light, not as a confession of tragic impotence, but as a statement of infinite happiness. The difference between the Creator and the creature, man, becomes simply a reflection, on the surface of the objective structure, of the inexhaustible character of God himself. The gulf between God and man is bridged by mystical experience and the two are integrated in mystical unity. Ruysbroeck, as we shall see later, never thought of man as a closed reality, something made to measure. He saw him as infinitely open, but at the same time as incapable of grasping the living Ground of God, however wide his power as a creature might stretch. Nonetheless, this very failure was, for Ruysbroeck, a "blessedness" for man. There was no question of obliterating the distance between God and man or of denying the existence of the objective structure. What he attempted to do was rather to throw an entirely new light on the whole question by integrating it into the unpredictable experience of mystical unity between God and man.

In order to have any idea at all of the real meaning of God's transcendence for Ruysbroeck, it is necessary to rid one's mind for a moment of all a priori ideas and clearly defined concepts and to allow a completely original reality the opportunity to express itself. Or, put in a rather different way, we should place ourselves in a position where we accept that God's being is a superabundance and that the only way of being entirely in him is to allow ourselves to be overwhelmed by him. Clinging to any idea that reduces this state of being in God to an identification and God's lasting difference to what is simply unattainable is to prevent oneself from having any access at all to the reality that Ruysbroeck is describing from his own experience.

Let us now conclude this section with a number of short texts in which Ruysbroeck attempts to lead his reader into an experience of what he himself experienced — definitive unity with God which, for all its certainty, was always an infinite adventure, a state of complete satisfaction, yet without the slightest trace of boredom:

> Then one comes to rest. Then one will possess and grasp the Other. And in grasping one is at once open to receive more. And this is eternal Life.[9]

> This fruit is so fathomlessly sweet in our throat that we cannot consume it and transform it into ourselves. On the contrary, it consumes us and transforms us into itself.[10]

> God's clarity has completely embraced us, grasped us and penetrated us. And it has opened our simple gaze so wide that our eyes must remain open forever — we cannot close them.[11]

Finally, a passage that we have already quoted in the chapter on "Enjoyment or Being Entirely in God" is extremely relevant in this context:

> In the state of unity with God, the spirit perceives that he has, through love, sunk away from himself into the depths and that he has been raised to the heights and has become lost in the distance. And he feels that he has gone astray in the wide spaces. He feels too that he is living in an unknown place that he knows well. He feels as though he has fled away from himself into unity with God, but only through the unceasing process of becoming one . . .[12]

2.   "Without Manner and Without Fashion"

Ruysbroeck described his experience of the lasting

difference of God most brilliantly and completely in those passages in which he was writing about God's being "in which the Persons and all blessed spirits are one," as well as in texts dealing with a question which was fashionable at the period — the nature of love.

In his treatise "The Seven Bolts," for example, the Master of Groenendael, without in any way writing in a frantic or confused language, takes lyrical flight in an attempt to express his own profound experience and is driven from one paradoxical statement to another. Following what may appear to be a somewhat scholastic process of analysis, the flood of words in this particular text can be divided into two currents. This will in no sense destroy the fundamentally paradoxical nature of the passage — on the contrary, it should bring that paradox more sharply into focus. These two currents are those of God's transcendence or lasting difference and of his immanence or being in us. Under the first heading, transcendence, we can list the following concepts: immeasurable; above all manner, above all activity and the practice of virtues; unfathomable flood; without manner; wild and turbulent; losing one's way; no manner, no road, no path, no foundation, no measure, no end and no beginning. Under the second heading, God's immanence, can be grouped such terms as burnt up; quiet, untroubled; quiet essential love; enjoyment; flowing away; the blessed state of unity. In this text, then, the author blends together the ideas of transcendence and immanence:

God's being can be imagined in this way: as if you were to see the heat of an immeasurably great fire in which everything is burnt up in a satisfied, glowing, untroubled fire. That satisfied essential love which is enjoyment of God and all the saints should also be seen in this light, above all manner and above all activity and the practice of virtues. It is a satisfied yet unfathomable flood of riches and wisdom and all the saints have flowed away in it with God in an enjoyment without manner. And this enjoyment is wild and turbulent. It is losing one's way in a world where there is no manner, no road, no path, no foundation, no measure, no end and no beginning. There is nothing at all that can be perceived or distinguished. And this is the blessed state of unity that we shall all experience.[1]

Ruysbroeck says very much the same in another passage, this time in "The Spiritual Tabernacle":

At the fourth stage, God dwells in the simplicity of our spirit with his being. Here, then, we may leave ourselves, because of the clarity and riches of God and our becoming one with God, and overcome all things and leave all distinction and multiplicity behind us. If we do this, we shall enter the simple openness of our being and then we shall experience the infinite breadth and the abysmal depth of God's being. And this, to our simple way of seeing, is a turbulent emptiness into which no corporal or spiritual image can penetrate. If we contemplate and possess this turbulent emptiness in the openness of our being, we shall be at the fourth phase.[2]

In many of the passages in which Ruysbroeck attempts to describe this experience, he uses the word "undefined," because God's being and unity with that being was for him a reality which could not be defined. This does not mean, of course, that it is not a definite reality or that he regarded it as a vague, shadowy and empty husk, something fantastic or sentimental in origin. Nor is it the vague, undefined quality, the "neither this nor that" of the speculative thinker who refuses to make any positive affirmation about the nature of the ultimate reality.

There is, on the contrary, no doubt at all that Ruysbroeck was concerned here with a definite reality, but that this was a reality which resisted all attempts to embody it in any definition. We may say that this reality cannot be described or specified either as a whole or in its parts. It can be said that it is this or that or that something else belongs to it and this would be true of it, yet at the same time untrue, because there is something hidden in this reality that is of an entirely different order, something that cannot be defined, formulated or finally grasped. Any attempt to seize hold of it is real, but at the same time always too weak or rather unsound and unqualified. If we try to grasp this reality all that we learn is that it always eludes our grasp.

What, then, has Ruysbroeck to tell us about his experience of this reality- It is that he had a positive experience of what was undefined, an experience of "nothing." He was clearly not anxious to repel every creature in the hope that he would clear the way for an encounter with the transcendental God, nor did he claim — like so many authors, who give the initial impression of being more profound and more "absolute" — that he had nothing at all to say about the ultimate experience. What he was aiming to do was to provide some living understanding of that unity with God which, he knew, was endless Life. And he did this in a language which, projected into our world, was purely negative. After all, does not "undefined" mean the same, in our world, as non-being? But in God and in the experience of unity with him, "undefined" is the only possible definition and one of the few words that is able to point to the irrecoverable Life that exists there.

Another image that Ruysbroeck uses frequently in this context is that of the "abyss," "abysmal depth," "unfathomable deeps" and other words and phrases with the same basic meaning. We have already encountered the expression "the abysmal depth of God's being" in the quotation from "The Spiritual Tabernacle." In another passage in "The Kingdom of Lovers," the author speaks again of God's being, the ultimate state of blessedness, as an unfathomable abyss:

In the simple enjoyment of being they are one without any difference. In this simple unity of God's being there is no knowing, no desire, no activity. For it is an immeasurable abyss which cannot be actively fathomed.[3]

These negative words and phrases are not used speculatively. They are only employed in an attempt to express the author's experience of a positive and indeed overwhelming reality. This becomes even clearer in passages in which Ruysbroeck discusses two abysses or "deeps," as in the following text:

Delectable love is unfathomable. And the unfathomable deeps of God call out to other deeps; that is to all those who are united with the Spirit in delectable love. This inward calling is the overflowing of an essential clarity. And this essential clarity, set and embraced in an unfathomable love, causes us to lose ourselves and flow away from ourselves into the unknown darkness of the divinity.[4]

What does Ruysbroeck mean by the sentence: "This inward calling is the overflowing of an essential clarity"? Light is what the mystic is pointing to — a unity with God in clarity. But the only way of indicating the special nature of this unity, without violating the transcendence of God within that unity, is to speak of a struggle between two abysses. In this wonderful combat, the one abyss swallows the other only because it surrenders too much to the other and this results in an "overflowing of an essential clarity."

The way in which unity with God is a life of blessedness is expressed very beautifully in a passage in "The
Kingdom of Lovers" by Ruysbroeck's use of the image
of abysses becoming deeper and deeper in an endless
interchange:

Since the light by which we contemplate is immeasurable and
what we contemplate is an abyss, the one can never exhaust the
other. But in our most enjoyable beholding of the supreme majesty
of God, we gaze and contemplate eternally, though not according
to our special manner as men. It is in this way too that the Father
also gazes at the abyss of his being by means of this eternal
wisdom.[5]

In another passage in the same treatise, Ruysbroeck
echoes what is said in the above text and at the same
time lets the theme of the "nature of love" be heard
quite clearly:

For, through enjoyment, they have fled away from themselves and
have lost themselves and have come to possess God as a luxury
without manner that cannot be grasped. And they are also possessed by God, similarly without manner. This being without
manner in unity can never be exhausted and can at the same
time never be found by active love, either God's or any creature's.[6]

We have already pointed to the difference between
"active" and "essential" love in Ruysbroeck's writing
and to the way in which he regards them as closely intertwined.[7] In addition to these two kinds of love, or
rather two aspects of the same love, Ruysbroeck also
speaks of a third, and this is the definitive aspect of the
one love — "love without manner."

From whatever standpoint he approaches this ultimate — and first — reality and whether he regards it
as God's being, as blessedness or as love, Ruysbroeck is

clearly fascinated by its special quality, namely that it cannot be defined. What applies to things also applies, in a special way, to this activity of love. Every thing is that thing because of its definition — it *is* by virtue of the fact that it is distinguished from the rest. Precisely because it is defined, however, it is also limited and enclosed. This is why no thing — and no god with the same basic characteristic — can ever sanctify us or make us blessed. Its limitations are always visible.

If, then, love were in some way capable of being defined and had its own special way of functioning, then it would inevitably fall in one way or another into repetitions. It might continue to exist and even grow, but it would always develop in the same direction and become a fixed and regular exercise. What Ruysbroeck means, then, when he applies the words "without manner" to the activity of love is that love breaks through all "manners" or modes. (In passing, we may note that here he touches once again on the theme of the lasting difference of God and on that of unity.) Love can again and again be grasped by man and it is expressed repeatedly in definite "manners," but at once transcends them. In this way, it remains, for the one who is entirely one with it, always new. Love is, in other words, nothing but life. In its deepest essence, it is pure Life; not "this or that," but Life itself.

It is clear from this that the expression "love without manner" as used in this way by Ruysbroeck can refer to two different stages in the experience of love. Usually it applies to the aspect of love that forms a transition between "active" and "essential" love. This is the moment at which love itself with its "manners," which define it and are defined by it, is broken through. In this case, "love without manner" is the same as "falling short in love"⁸ and "going out of ourselves in love."⁹ It is the activity which is peculiar to the spirit that escapes from itself — this is expressed very strikingly by Ruysbroeck in his description of the "friends" and the "sons" of God.¹⁰ This aspect of love, then, is what unites man with God:

For the inward love of our spirit, that is, love without manner, is unceasingly active in going out of itself and making the spirit without love, that is, making it new in love. For, in its activity in going out of itself, the spirit transcends itself and becomes love itself, that is, essential love, in the ground of its unity.¹¹

In this context too, it is helpful to consider a passage from "The Spiritual Espousals," since this text shows rather more clearly perhaps how this "love without manner" is the result not of man's own efforts, but of God's superabundant gift. In addition, this text is important in that it draws attention to a characteristic feature of Ruysbroeck's mystical teaching, namely that the same phenomenon or experience is always recurring at different levels in the mystical life. This brings us to the aspect of divine influence on man's highest powers:

From such men God demands more than they can achieve. For he manifests himself to them so rich and so merciful and so immeasurably good, and in this manifestation he demands of them love and honor according to his worth. For God wishes to be loved by us in accordance with his excellence and in this work all spirits fail; and so love is without manner and without fashion. For our spirits do not know how to add yet more to the love that they already bear, for each spirit's capacity for love is finite. And therefore the work of love is constantly begun afresh.¹²

In another passage, Ruysbroeck uses the same words "without manner" in the context of a description of man's definitive state of unity with God, in which he has already sunk away into the Other. In this case, the author's aim is to point to the inexhaustible nature of possessing and being possessed by God and to God's lasting difference within the state of unity:

And this state of being sunken away in love into the Other is always a clinging to and a following of an active exercise of love without manner, for love cannot be still. It has to know and taste the unfathomable riches which are its very foundation.[13]

What was manifested at the aspect of becoming one with God as an activity that breaks through our own "manners" also exists now at the level of unity with God — we are conscious of the fact that this is a force which not only breaks through our own definitions, but also is in itself impossible to define or to limit.

We can conclude this section by quoting a short text, which is almost a formula, taken from "The Twelve Beguines." This sums up much of what has been said in this section. The "giving and taking" that is peculiar to love means that it is always setting itself free in order to attain the Other, but is not defined or delimited in any way by this constant progress towards fulfillment:

It is the nature of love always to give and to take. But love itself is not a still being. Giving and taking — a distinction in the experience of love — will always remain.[14]

3.   An Encounter That is Always New

The reason why God's being is both superabundant and incapable of definition is that it is ultimately a being that is always possessed by a Person. In other words, it is only in and through the Other that access can be gained to this being. It should have been made clear in our examination in the second chapter of this book of some of Ruysbroeck's texts on the life of the Trinity that this ultimate reality is not a vague background behind the Persons, but rather a relationship between the Father, the Son and the Holy Spirit. Ruysbroeck makes a distinction in his reflection about the mystery of the Trinity between the divine being and the divine Persons, seeing them as different aspects of the same reality. The same mystery, however, seen as a reality revealed in Jesus Christ, is always Father, Son and Holy Spirit, one God in three Persons, and never a being either before or after the divine Persons. What is more, as we also saw in the same chapter, Ruysbroeck regarded this as the "model" par excellence of the mystic's relationship or community of love with God. In this perspective too, it is true to say that "the Father is the beginning of all Godhead, according to his Being and his Person."[1]

In what sense, however, is this "personal" character of God the cause of his lasting transcendence? What connection is there, according to Ruysbroeck, between the divine Person and God's being "without manner" and the lasting and inexhaustible character of that being? In "The Spiritual Espousals," we read:

For the Father gives all that he is and all that he has to the Son, except only his attribute of Fatherhood, which he himself remains. And therefore all that lives in the Father, concealed in unity, lives in the Son, flowing out and made manifest; and evermore the simple deepness of our everlasting image remains hidden in darkness and without manner.[2]

Everything that the Son has, then, comes from the Father. He is given in full the being of God — all unity and being in God without any reservation at all. Only the giving itself — the Father's "attribute of Father-

hood" — never becomes the possession of the Son and
never becomes the Son himself. That is why the "simple
deepness" always remains undefined for the Son, who
must always relinquish his own distinctive quality to the
Father whenever he enters the divine being or is in it.
(The Son is not a son because of what he possesses, but
because he is able to receive again and again; this applies
to all sons.)

The Son must, moreover, also become "without manner" — he has to undergo the transcendence or difference of God when he becomes one. For the Son, possession is as impossible as an extension of himself. He can
only possess, as it were, by losing himself in the Father
who is always different.

Just as, through the Father, the Son is one with an
inexhaustible being, so too is the Father overwhelmed
by the way in which the Son offers him being. With
enjoyment he contemplates this being, which is really
being in — but he always does this "without manner":

But in our most enjoyable beholding of the supreme majesty of
God, we gaze and contemplate eternally, though not according to
our special manner as men. It is in this way too that the Father
also gazes at the abyss of his being by means of this eternal
wisdom.[3]

In enjoying God's being in this way, the Persons
always surrender their distinctive character. In unity,
the state of being different continues to come to new
life. In accordance too with the model of what takes
place in God himself, the mystic experiences God as
the one who opens his entire being to him, but who at
the same time also never ceases to withdraw himself
from him. There is, then, an essential relationship with
a Person, in which man is in unity with the being of the

Other. This is above all the particular vision of the Master of Groenendael — a vision which was not shared by all mystical authors. Ruysbroeck has himself given us a description of the views of those who opposed his teaching in several passages in some of his treatises and a brief summary of his reactions to these deviations will give us a better insight into his own ideas.

In all the mistaken forms of spiritual teaching that he was in fact combating, Ruysbroeck was really opposed to only one fundamental heresy. This can be described as a false mystical passivity, quietism, premature rest or "false emptiness." Despite the variety of affirmations made by the different mystical writers criticized by Ruysbroeck, the one central error common to all their teaching about God and the state of blessedness arose from the fact that they spoke in the light of a false or at least of an incomplete mystical experience. This experience was of an imaginary process of becoming one with God. Their conversion was not to God, but to themselves.

Ruysbroeck himself says that they "sink themselves in natural rest," which is "nothing else but emptiness" and that they are "turned away from God and inclined towards themselves through natural love" and are "bowed down over themselves."[4] They therefore only discover themselves, not God, "losing their way in the inactive and blind simplicity of their own being."[5]

It is impossible for such people to see God, although they believe that they are simply contemplating the divine being in their own being. What, then, is the origin of this great error? These false mystics have undoubtedly discovered an aspect of God and are convinced of his reality. Ruysbroeck believes that their experience of God is only insofar as God is present in them as Creator: "They have become so simple and so united in an inactive way with the naked being of their own souls and God's being in them. . . ."[6] In this way, God can also be found in all other creatures: "And he gazes into the simple truth, which always shines in his being and in all beings."[7]

These false mystics fail in that they do not progress beyond this aspect of the divine reality. It is in his explanation why they do not advance further on the way towards unity that Ruysbroeck reveals how absolutely indispensable the personal relationship between God and man is in the mystical experience. These men do not reach unity with God, he insists, because they approach God by the wrong path. They are "without God's grace" and they are "not impelled forward by the Holy Spirit." They "want to know, but not believe; they want to have without hoping, to possess without loving."[8] In a word, they never become one with God because they will not lose themselves. "And therefore they cannot rise above themselves. What they experience is a natural inclination towards their origin, which is God."[9] Here Ruysbroeck uses an image which occurs both in "The Spiritual Tabernacle" and in "The Twelve Beguines": "However high the eagle flies, he does not fly above himself."[10]

We may conclude, then, that the "unity" with God experienced by such immature mystics was nothing more than an experience of an extension of their own being. They do not go out of themselves, Ruysbroeck teaches, to the Other who is always greater than they are, "for, above the rest that they find in their own being, they have no feeling for God or for the Other."[11]

In this context, it is valuable to quote a longer passage taken from Ruysbroeck's "Mirror of Eternal Bles-

sedness." Not only does it contain a number of well
formulated elements which provide a clear insight into
the author's anthropological teaching — it also and
above all reveals Ruysbroeck's own attitude towards
mature mystical experience.

And therefore we can become one with God, but cannot achieve
unity with him. This unity would mean that our being would
disappear and we would then neither know, nor love, nor be
blessed. But we should think of our created being as a wild and
savage desert, in which we must wander without mode or manner.
For we cannot go out of our being, nor can we enter the being of
the Other unless we do it with love.[12]

Here, as in other passages,[13] Ruysbroeck contrasts two
different worlds, but does not teach a false mysticism
by misunderstanding one or other of them. He presents
us on the one hand with the world of things or "beings"
in their mutual relationships of cause and effect and, on
the other, the world of persons in their own distinctive
relationship with one another, namely that of love. We
can put this in a different way by saying that he contrasts the material structure with life itself.

The experience of the false mystic may be very rich
and interesting from the psychological point of view, but
it takes place exclusively within the first of these worlds,
the material world of "beings." The false mystic certainly
discovers the divine being on the frontier of his own
being, which flows into a space that is so undefined that
it may at the same time also be the space where the
infinite God dwells. The false mystic meets God at the
boundary, but he never penetrates into the divine being
itself. Why is this?

Ruysbroeck gives two closely related reasons for this
ultimate failure on the part of false mysticism at the

end of the passage quoted above. The first is that the
man who is following the wrong path of mysticism cannot dare to "wander," because he has not become stripped of himself. This means that every mystical discovery
can only result in extending his own being, so that what
he achieves is always immediately cancelled out again.
The second reason is that the false mystic never gives
himself totally to God in a personal relationship. He has
not even the beginning of an understanding of what it
means to let himself be taken over by the Other and
thereby to experience his "greatest joy in what cannot
be embraced." Full, living and fruitful mystical experience, on the other hand, is found in true unity with God:

Unity is living and fruitful and it cannot be still and satisfied.
For it is continuously renewed in love because the lovers, who
dwell in each other and cannot be separated, visit each other
again and again. In that love there is attraction and following,
giving and taking, touching and being touched.[14]

The most important element of all perhaps in Ruysbroeck's mystical teaching is that our being in God is
an inexhaustible experience. This teaching, moreover,
was revealed to him within his experience of being one
with the Other in a relationship of love with the God
who is always new.

Let us conclude with one final quotation from the
Master of love, Jan van Ruysbroeck of Groenendael,
describing the coming of Christ the Bridegroom in the
life of mystical contemplation:

And the coming of the Bridegroom is so swift that he has always
come and is always dwelling within us with all his riches; and
ceaselessly and ever and again he is coming in his own person with
new clarity, just as if he had never come before. For to have come

consists in an eternal now, without time, which is constantly received in new joy and new delight. Behold how the gladness and the joy which this Bridegroom brings in his coming are unfathomable and immeasurable, for so is he himself. And therefore the yes of the spirit, with which it contemplates and gazes upon its Bridegroom, are opened so wide that they may never be closed again.[15]

Notes

GENERAL NOTE

All translations of passages from Ruysbroeck's treatises have been based on the texts prepared by the Ruusbroec-Genootschap. The four volumes of the Werken *(indicated by roman numerals in the notes) were revised and improved in the second edition, which was published in Tielt, 1944-1948. The original titles of Ruysbroeck's treatises and their usual English titles are:*

Het Rijcke der Ghelieven ....The Kingdom of Lovers
Die Gheestelike Brulocht ....The Spiritual Espousals
Van den Gheesteliken Tabernakel ....The Spiritual Tabernacle
Vanden Blinckenden Steen ....The Perfection of the Sons
of God
Vanden Vier Becoringhen ....The Four Temptations
Vanden Kerstenen Ghleove ....The Christian Faith
Vanden VII Sloten ....The Seven Bolts
Een Spieghel der Eewigher ....A Mirror of Eternal
Salicheit   Blessedness
Van VII Trappen in den Graed ....Seven Steps in the Scale
der Gheesteliker Minnen   of Spiritual Love
Dat Boecsken der Verclaringhe ....The Little Book of
Enlightenment
Vanden XII Beghinen ....The Twelve Beguines

PART I: INTRODUCTORY QUESTIONS

1. Saul Bellow, *Mr. Sammler's Planet,* (London: Weidenfeld & Nicolson, 1969), pp. 3–4.
2. Bellow, *op. cit.,* p. 280.
3. ·Bellow, *op. cit.,* p. 37.
4. R. D. Laing, *The Politics of Experience and The Bird of Paradise* (Harmondsworth: Penguin Books, 1967), pp. 22, 23. For the alienation of man from his inner world, see especially p. 50ff.
5. J. H. van den Berg, *Wat is Psychotherapie?* (Nijkerk: 1970), pp. 35-36.

For pathological illness in the context of the disappearance of spirituality, see p. 39.

6. "The Spiritual Tabernacle"; II, p. 330.

7. This choice is not made on the basis of personal preference or because I wish to exclude certain aspects of mysticism, but because my knowledge is limited. I have, for example, confined myself entirely to Christian mystical authors. R. C. Zaehner has covered a far wider field, including world mysticism, in his *Mysticism Sacred and Profane*. Among the important books that I have consulted in preparing this introductory chapter are:

Cuthbert Butler, *Westren Mysticism* (London, Constable, 3rd edn., 1967).

William James, *Varieties of Religious Experience* (London, 1902).

J. Maréchal, *Études sur la psychologie des mystiques* (Paris and Brussels, I, 1924, II, 1937).

A. Poulain, *Des Grâces d'oraison* (Paris, 1901).

Evelyn Underhill, *Mysticism* (London: Methuen, 1911)..

The most important work published on mysticism in the Netherlands is: St. Axters, OP, *Geschiedenis van de Vroomheid in de Nederlanden* (Antwerp, four volumes, 1950–1960). Ruysbroeck is discussed in Vol. II, *De Eeum van Ruusbroec*, pp. 213-291.

8. Walter Hilton, *The Scale of Perfection*, translated by G. Sitwell, London: Burns & Oates, 1953, pp. 153, 277, 278.

9. "The Spiritual Espousals," I, p. 206. All quotations in this book from "The Spiritual Espousals" are taken from Eric Colledge's translation of *Blessed Jan van Ruysbroek, The Spiritual Espousals* (London: Faber and Faber, 1952). This quotation will be found in Colledge, p. 147.

10. "The Spiritual Espousals"; I, p. 174; Colledge, p. 117.

11. Dag Hammerskjöld, *Markings* (London: Faber and Faber, 1964), pp. 90, 91.

12. *Vida*, chapter 18, § 15; *Obras completas* (Madrid, 1962), p. 73; *Cuentas de Conciencia*, 66a, § 10, *op. cit.*, p. 466. Both passages are substantially quoted by Evelyn Underhill in her *Mysticism, op. cit.*, p. 291, 2.

13. *Sermo super Cantica Canticorum*, 74, 5, *Sti-Bernardi Opera* (Rome, 1958), II, p. 242, 3. This translation is taken from *Bernard of Clairvaux: On Loving God and Selections from Sermons*, ed. Hugh Martin (London: SCM Press, 1959), pp. 122, 3.

14. Benedict of Canfield, an English Capuchin (1562–1610) active in France, is perhaps the most striking and influential figure at the beginning of the great movement in French mysticism. H. Bremond has written very well about him and about the circle around Madame Acarie in the *Histoire littéraire du sentiment religieux en France*, II, *L'Invasion mystique* (Paris, 1916), p. 152ff. He was directly and extremely influenced by mysticism n the Netherlands. His most important work was his "Rule of Perfection" (*Règle de perfection*, Paris, 1614), from which the quotation is taken (III, p. 293).

15. "The Spiritual Espousals"; I, p. 197; Colledge, p. 138.

16. *Ibid.*

17. "The Spiritual Espousals"; I, p. 143; Colledge, p. 87.

18. William of St. Thierry (1148) originated in Liège, but was active in France, first as a Benedictine and later as a Cistercian. He was a friend of Bernard of Clairvaux and his best known treatise is The Golden Epistle (Littera Aurea). Many of the mystics of the Netherlands, including Hadewijch and Ruysbroeck, took over several of the important themes that occur in this influential treatise, among them the theme of the "love that is knowledge." This quotation comes from the *Littera Aurea*, PL, 338, A–B.

19. "The Spiritual Espousals"; I, p. 146, 7; Colledge, p. 90, 1.

20. Dag Hammarskjöld, *op. cit.*, p. 169.

21. I, p. 197; Colledge, p. 139.

22. I., p. 200; Colledge, p. 141, 142.

23. Quoted by Poulain, *op. cit.*, p. 92.

24. *Règle*, III, pp. 320, 321; see also pp. 311, 312 and 332, 333.

25. Cuthbert Butler, *op. cit.*, p. 13; the Carmelite nun in question was Mother Isabel Daurelle of the Sacred Heart.

26. I, p. 168ff; Colledge, pp. 97, 101.

27. Colledge, *op. cit.*, p. 112.

28. Colledge, *op. cit.*, p. 112.

29. I, p. 170; Colledge, p. 113.

30. *Ibid.*

31. Augustine Baker (1575–1641) was an English Benedictine who was powerfully influenced by the mystics of the Netherlands and the Rhineland and also by the writings of Benedict of Canfield, although he was in many ways opposed to the latter's teachings and felt the need to modify them. His best known works are his *Sancta Sophia* (Douai, 1657) and his *Confessions* (London, 1952). For his description of the "great desolation," see the fifth chapter of his *Sancta Sophia,* III, 3. The quotations in this book are taken from the last edition of this work, *Holy Wisdom,* (London: Burns & Oates, 1950).

32. Baker, *Holy Wisdom,* p. 542.

33. Baker, *Holy Wisdom,* p. 540.

34. Baker, *Holy Wisdom,* p. 540, 541.

35. *Règle,* III, p. 376.

36. *Ibid.* p. 328.

37. P. Debongnie, *La Grande Dame du Pur Amour. Sainte Catherine de Gênes* (Bruges, 1960), pp. 35, 36.

38. *Broeder Gheraert, Prologhe,* ed. De Vreese, p. 8; quoted by J. Huyben, OSB, in *Jan van Ruusbroec, Leven Werken,* Mechelen and Amsterdam, 1931, p. 125.

39. Quoted by J. Huyben, *op. cit.,* p. 105.

40. The quotations here are taken from "The Spiritual Tabernacle"; II, pp. 321–33 and *passim.* This treatise contains a good deal of criticism of the contemporary situation, as does the treatise "The Seven Bolts"; III, pp. 98, 118.

41. "The Perfection of the Sons of God"; III, p. 26.

PART II: THE PHENOMENOLOGY OF THE COMMUNITY OF LOVE

1. The Different Aspects of Unity with the Other

1. III, p. 23.
2. *Ibid.*; III, p. 20.
3. *Ibid.*; III, pp. 19 and 20 *passim*.
4. *Ibid.*; III, p. 31.
5. *Ibid.*; III, p. 32.
6. Cf. "The Spiritual Espousals"; I, p. 248; Colledge, pp. 187, 188.
7. "Overforming" is a technical term used by the mystics of the Netherlands, similar to the term employed in other traditions, namely "transformation." Ruysbroeck's word "overformation" is better insofar as it suggests more clearly that the mystic is not simply absorbed into God or just disappears into him, but that he obtains a different principle of life.
8. I, p. 9.
9. "The Spiritual Espousals"; I, p. 221; Colledge, p. 160.
10. I, pp. 196–99; Colledge, pp. 139–40; cf. *ibid.*; I, p. 221; Colledge, p. 160 and "The Kingdom of Lovers"; I, p. 56.

2. The Life of the Trinity as the Model of the Unity of Persons

1. "The Kingdom of Lovers"; I, p. 71.
2. III, p. 289.
3. See, for example, "The Spiritual Espousals"; I, p. 243; Colledge, p. 179; "The Spiritual Tabernacle"; II, p. 34; "The Perfection of the Sons of God"; III, p. 19–21; "A Mirror of Eternal Blessedness"; III, p. 169; "Seven Steps"; III, p. 271.
4. See "The Four Temptations"; III, p. 52.
5. "The Spiritual Espousals", I; p. 228; Colledge, pp. 166–68; cf. "The Seven Bolts"; III, p. 105.
6. "The Seven Bolts"; III, p. 106; cf. "A Mirror of Eternal Blessedness"; III, pp. 191, 193.
7. II, p. 34.
8. I, p. 63; cf. "The Spiritual Espousals"; I, p. 248; Colledge, p. 185; "The Twelve Beguines"; IV, pp. 18-19.
9. I, p. 219; Colledge, p. 159.
10. *Ibid.*; I, p. 224; Colledge, p. 163.
11. "The Kingdom of Lovers"; I, p. 70.
12. "The Little Book of Enlightenment"; III, p. 294.
13. *Ibid.*; III, p. 290.
14. *Ibid.*; III, p. 289.
15. "A Mirror of Eternal Blessedness"; III, p. 169.
16. "The Perfection of the Sons of God"; III, p. 25.
17. "The Twelve Beguines"; IV, p. 31; Colledge, p. 28.
18. *Ibid.*; IV, p. 209.
19. "The Spiritual Espousals"; I, p. 247; Colledge, p. 188.
20. "The Four Temptations"; III, p. 56.

21. "A Mirror of Eternal Blessedness"; III p,. 217.

3. From Actively Becoming One to Resting in Unity

1. I, pp. 62 and 65.
2. *Ibid.,* p. 64.
3. "The Spiritual Espousals"; I, p. 199; *op. cit.,* p. 140.
4. "The Kingdom of Lovers"; I, p. 70.
5. *Ibid.,* I, p. 63.
6. *Ibid.;* I, pp. 94, 66.
7. "A Mirror of Eternal Blessedness"; III, pp. 207–8.
8. "The Twelve Beguines"; IV, p. 103.
9. "The Perfection of the Sons of God"; III, p. 8.
10. *Ibid.*
11. *Ibid.;* III, pp. 14–22, especially pp. 18–22.
12. *Ibid.;* p. 20.
13. *Ibid.;* III, p. 21.
14. I, p. 206; Colledge, p. 147.
15. See, for example, "The Perfection of the Sons of God"; III, p. 18; "A Mirror of Eternal Blessedness"; III, p. 148.
16. "The Perfection of the Sons of God"; III, pp. 18–20, *passim.*
17. *Ibid.;* III, p. 27.
18. IV, pp. 21–2; cf. *ibid.;* IV, pp. 25, 26; "A Mirror of Eternal Blessedness"; III, pp. 206, 207–8.
19. III, pp. 268–69.

4. "Enjoyment" or Being Entirely In God

1. III, p. 215.
2. III, p. 108.
3. III, p. 260–1.
4. I, p. 223; Colledge, p. 162.
5. "The Perfection of the Sons of God"; III, p. 23; cf. "The Seven Bolts"; III, p. 105.
6. "The Perfection of the Sons of God"; III, p. 39.
7. IV, p. 58.
8. III, pp. 265–66.
9. III, p. 294.
10. "A Mirror of Eternal Blessedness"; III, p. 184.
11. "The Kingdom of Lovers"; I, pp. 86, 87; cf. "The Seven Bolts"; III, p. 117; "A Mirror of Eternal Blessedness"; III, pp. 216–17.
12. "The Perfection of the Sons of God"; III, p. 27.
13. "The Kingdom of Lovers"; I, p. 73; cf. ibid.; I, p. 77–82; "The Spiritual Tabernacle"; II, p. 82.
14. III, p. 40.
15. See Chapter I of this volume ("The Different Aspects of Unity") and "The Spiritual Espousals"; I, p. 221; Colledge, p. 160.
16. II, pp. 361–2.

5. Unity and the Lasting Difference of God

1. The Tension continues to exist in the Relationship between the Persons

1. See J. Alaerts, *La Terminologie "essentielle" dans l'Oeuvre de Jan van Ruusbroec (1293–1381)*, doctoral thesis, Strasbourg, 1972.
2. III, p. 28.
3. III, p. 26.
4. IV, p. 59.
5. III, p. 116.
6. IV, p. 198.
7. I, p. 226; Colledge, p. 165.
8. I, pp. 246–7; Colledge, p. 188.
9. "The Spiritual Tabernacle"; II, pp. 99, 100.
10. "A Mirror of Eternal Blessedness"; III, p. 203.

2. Unity is a Living, Organic Whole

1. "The Spiritual Tabernacle," II, p. 355.
2. "A Mirror of Eternal Blessedness," III, p. 206.
3. "The Perfection of the Sons of God", III, pp. 6, 7.
4. I, pp. 216–7; Colledge, p. 156.
5. III, p. 6.
6. II, p. 354.
7. III, p. 269.
8. "The Spiritual Tabernacle"; II, pp. 88, 89.
9. III, p. 286.

6. The inexhaustible Experience of Being In God

1. A Lasting Superabundance

1. III, p. 293.
2. "The Perfection of the Sons of God"; III, p. 27.
3. "A Mirror of Eternal Blessedness"; III, p. 198.
4. See this book, Chapter 4 ("Enjoyment, or Being Entirely in God").
5. "The Little Book of Enlightenment"; III, p. 294; already quoted in Chapter 4 ("Enjoyment, or Being Entirely in God").
6. III, p. 293, line 33; see also "The Kingdom of Lovers"; p. 9.
7. "The Kingdom of Lovers"; I, p. 9; already quoted in Chapter 1 ("The Different Aspects of Unity')).
8. See also Chapter 2 ("The Life of the Trinity").
9. "The Spiritual Tabernacle"; II, pp. 2, 3, 365.
10. "The Perfection of the Sons of God"; III, p. 35.
11. "A Mirror of Eternal Blessedness"; III, p. 213.
12. "The Perfection of the Sons of God"; III, pp. 6–7; already quoted in Chapter 4 ("Enjoyment, or Being Entirely in God").

2. "Without Manner and Without Fashion"

1. III, p. 116.
2. II, p. 95.
3. I, p. 73.

4. "The Spiritual Espousals"; I, p. 223; Colledge, p. 162.
5. I, p. 78–79.
6. *Ibid.*; I, p. 72.
7. See Chapter 5 ("Unity and the Lasting Difference of God").
8. See, for example, "The Twelve Beguines"; IV ,p. 57.
9. *Ibid.*; IV, pp. 25, 59.
10. See also Chapter 3 ("From Actively Being One to Resting in God", especially the section on the "friends" and the "sons" of God").
11. "The Spiritual Tabernacle"; II, p. 65.
12. I, p. 185; Colledge, *op. cit.*, 116.
13. "The Perfection of the Sons of God"; III, p. 25.
14. IV, p. 96.

3. An Encounter That is Always New

1. "The Spiritual Espousals"; I, p. 219; Colledge, p. 159; already quoted in Chapter 2 ("The Life of the Trinity").
2. "The Spiritual Espousals"; I, p. 246; Colledge, p. 187.
3. "The Kingdom of Lovers"; I, pp. 78–9; already quoted in Chapter 6 ("Without Manner and Without Fashion").
4. "The Spiritual Espousals"; I, p. 229"; Colledge, 167–68.
5. "The Little Book of Enlightenment"; III, p. 279.
6. *Ibid.*; III, pp. 279, 298; "The Spiritual Tabernacle"; II, p. 336.
7. "The Spiritual Tabernacle"; III, p. 336.
8. *Ibid.*
9. "The Kingdom of Lovers"; I, p. 62.
10. "The Spiritual Tabernacle"; II, pp. 53, 336–37; "The Twelve Beguines"; IV, p. 42.
11. "The Little Book of Enlightenment"; III, p. 281.
12. III, p. 217.
13. See, for example, "The Little Book"; III, pp. 276–76; "The Twelve Beguines", IV; p. 30.
14. "A Mirror of Eternal Blessedness"; III, p. 213.
15. "The Spiritual Espousals"; I, p. 243; Colledge, p. 183.

CHARGED WITH THE SPIRIT

Mission Is for Everyone

Joseph G. Donders

ORBIS BOOKS

Maryknoll, New York 10545

The Catholic Foreign Mission Society of America (Maryknoll) recruits and trains people for overseas missionary service. Through Orbis Books, Maryknoll aims to foster the international dialogue that is essential to mission. The books published, however, reflect the opinions of their authors and are not the official position of the society.

Library of Congress Cataloging-in-Publication Data

Donders, Joseph G.
    Charged with the Spirit : mission is for everyone / Joseph G.
Donders.
        p.   cm.
    Includes bibliographical references.
    ISBN 0-88344-915-3 (pbk.)
    1. Catholic Church—Missions.   2. Mission of the church.
3. Spiritual life—Catholic Church.   I. Title.
BV2180.D66   1993
266'.2—dc20
                                                    93-1613
                                                        CIP

From the fullness of his grace we have all received one blessing after another.

(John the Baptist)

You will receive power when the Holy Spirit comes on you, and you will be my witnesses . . . to the ends of the earth.

(Jesus of Nazareth)

A student is not above his teacher; but every student when he has finished his studies will be on a par with his teacher.

(Jesus of Nazareth)

For we cannot help speaking about what we have seen and heard.

(Simon Peter)

Contents

Part II
Fanning the Flame

CHARGED WITH THE SPIRIT

Kindling the Divine Fire in Us

The Acts of the Apostles is the book about the failures and successes of the first communities formed by people who had met Jesus. A meeting that changed their lives. It tells how those communities sent people throughout their whole world. They also grew locally by attracting the people who lived around them. Luke speaks about that attraction when he — slightly ambiguously — notes:

No one else dared join them, though they were highly regarded by the people. Nevertheless, more and more men and women believed in the Lord and were added to their number (Acts 5:13-14).

The people they sent out did not do any lengthy preaching. Those first missionaries arrived, announced the good news, and shared the Spirit of Jesus (Acts 16:7). As a local community formed itself, the members began to live their newly shared Spirit and immediately began to tackle the religious, domestic, and social issues around them in a new way. They began to worship together, they shared the body and blood of Jesus, but they also started forms of what we would call social care. One community helped another community in economic need. Local communities started a soup kitchen in Jerusalem and a kind of thrift shop in Lydda, near Joppe. The communities had such influence

that in some cities they became a danger to the existing
official and corrupt order.

Why don't our communities send out people in that way?
Why aren't our own communities more attractive? Why is
our mission activity lacking in spirit? What has happened to
us?

Traditional mission activity and heritage has not waned
for lack of studies or analyses. Books about mission
abound, and an ever-growing number of audio and video
tapes accompany them. Not long ago a religious sociologist
gave a paper to a theological faculty in Washington, D.C.
He claimed that by the year 2020 the Catholic community
will be the largest denominational group in the United
States, comprising more than 50 percent of the population.
The tragedy, he said, is that this will make no difference to
the country. It is difficult to judge whether he is right or not,
but why does he think so? Is it true that the Roman Catholic
Church—and the other Christian churches as well—is an
irrelevant presence in a country like the United States? Do
we Catholic Americans, in other words, make no difference
to the world in which we live? Have our symbols lost their
impact on our own lives? Do we fail to offer an alternative to
a torn world that definitely—and desperately—is looking for
one? Have we no mission? Are there any signs left of the
appeal and fascination those first Christian communities
had for so many?

Many of us have experienced entering a church for a
Sunday service and noting that everything in the parish
seems to be dead. There are people, but they all seem gray,
even when dressed in bright colors. The singing seems
muted—booklets are opened, so are some mouths, but no
hymn is raised, no rhythm caught. The organ overpowers
the few small voices. The minister does all he is supposed
to do. The homily is well prepared. The collection baskets
go around. The service is liturgically correct. The members
of the congregation stand, kneel, sit down; they cross them-

selves. The service begins, continues, and ends without a whimper. Symbols are used, the word is spoken, bread broken, but the liturgy falls flat. The young are obviously bored; the older participants yawn behind their hands. After the service everyone moves out, some hands are shaken. The homily—some say—was interesting. Then they are on their way, the door of the church is firmly closed, and after a last look back, it is all over for the week. You decide never to come back if you can help it. You want to find another community. A caricature? Maybe . . .

And then you come into a community where everything breathes joy, hope, and spirit. You notice it when you come in; people welcome you with a smile here and a word there. The singing is taken up by all. The young sit with the old. Young people blow their trumpets and swing their tambourines, while the older solemnly beat their drums. Psalms are sung, and the hymns started by the choir are taken up by all: "Lord, have mercy, Christ have mercy. We share in the Glory of our Lord Jesus Christ, Alleluia!" The organ does not dominate, but is a help. It becomes silent, though perhaps a baby keeps bouncing its first vowels off the vault of the church. The story about God's people and Jesus is read with spirit, and the word is broken open for all in the homily. During the prayers of the faithful the intentions mention healing and sharing, peace and justice, environment and work, far-off lands and members sent out to have a taste of mission and community, perhaps on another continent. Then all turn their attention to the table and commemorate the presence of Jesus in the bread and the wine. People reach for one another's hands as they say the prayer that is going to change the whole of our still so cruel world: "Our Father in heaven . . . . your kingdom come, your will be done . . ." They share a sign of peace; the harm done and the distances created throughout the last week are overcome just before the bread and the wine go around. Every Sunday there are newcomers, and there is a regular list of people who would like to be baptized and confirmed. Those candidates stand near the baptismal font until the day they will publicly and formally share in the Spirit of Jesus present in the community and all its members. Once the service is over, the members divide spontaneously into small groups to discuss issues and tackle problems, which may or may not be solved. Their ministry to each other and the larger community is obvious and clearly collaborative. Tasks are given and received. Appointments are made while children play with each other outside, waiting for their parents to go home. There is laughter and good cheer. Simplicity and utter seriousness seem to go hand in hand. It is a joy to have been there. You decide to join them again when possible. You leave a better and divinely inspired human-divine being. You know again what you are about, living your life and doing your work.

Both types of parishes do exist. We all know about them. It is not difficult to guess the difference. It is not the Spirit of Jesus as such. That Spirit is present in both. It is in the sharing of that Spirit that they differ.

This book is about that sharing. How do we share Jesus' Spirit so that we personally and in our communities become sacraments of Jesus' presence in this world? How do we get coworkers in his mission to realize God's dreams for this world and our common future? To do so, we will have to go far back to the first time that a human couple began to see that future. (Was it from within or was it from without themselves?) We must share in that human/divine vision from its beginning to its fulfillment, sharing in a dynamic that is divine!

Let us, however, not get lost in that enormous upswing. This book also aims to be as practical as possible. It is not only written for personal reading, but also as a workbook for groups of Christians who come together to reconsider their place in the world and its history. Every chapter is followed by suggestions and questions to stimulate individuals and groups to reflect, to discuss, and to react.

Part I

CATCHING THE DEPTH
OF JESUS' SPIRIT

CHAPTER 1

Meeting Jesus of Nazareth

Jesus himself drew near and went with them.
(Luke 24:15)

chance encounter. It happens all the time. You talk to someone, and that stranger changes your life. It happens in planes, buses, waiting rooms, train stations, airport gates.

It happened about two thousand years ago for an Ethiopian minister of finance traveling home by horse-chariot (Acts 8:26). In Jerusalem he got something to read for his long voyage home. Being on a pilgrimage, he chose a sacred text—the Prophecies of Isaiah. The text was more difficult than he expected. It proved to be so difficult that he was reading it aloud, trying to catch the meaning of a particularly hard line:

He was led like a sheep to the slaughter, and as a lamb before the shearers is silent, so he did not open his mouth.

A young man heard what he was reading and asked: "Do you understand what you are reading?" He answered: "How can I unless someone helps me?" He invited the young man, this chance-met stranger who introduced himself as

7

Philip, to come in and sit next to him. It was during the discussion that followed that the government official heard the
good news of Jesus. The conversation must have been a
decisive one, because when they found some water alongside the road later in the day, they stopped and Philip baptized him. Philip engaged the African traveler — right there
alongside the road — in the dynamics of the risen life of
Jesus. We don't know much more about the official. Maybe
he was one of the founders of the still flourishing Ethiopian
Christian community. A chance encounter.

One day on a long flight the place next to me was empty.
A young fellow came from his empty row to the seat next to
mine. He asked me whether he could join me. We talked.
He told me about himself. We compared notes and noted
sympathies for points of view. We spoke about Jesus' place
in human life, and what we thought history would lead to.
We talked about what lies beyond this world, and what we
expected it all would lead to. An unexpected conversation.
Things I had never thought of fell in place. He spoke about
his expectations, and I about mine. A new horizon opened
up before me. The flight was over before I realized it. The
voice of the plane's captain surprised me when he
announced that we were descending to our destination, asking us to fasten our seat belts. I left the plane another person. A chance encounter.

The memory of such meetings doesn't wane. The experience is at times so enlightening that the enthusiasm created
does not fade. Human history is full of stories about such
meetings. No wonder that the Bible sometimes compares
these strangers with angels! A chance encounter — and life
changes forever.

THE ENCOUNTER WITH JESUS

This is how it was for those who encountered Jesus. People met him in the street, along the lake shore, at a well,

during the night, on a boat, on the road from Jerusalem to Emmaus, in the Temple, at their work. They met, and they started to talk. We are inclined to forget that the good news began in such a common way. Women and men, poor and rich, young and old walked up to him; they sat down, dined, wined, and ferried over the lake with him. They talked about their worries, their difficulties and disillusionment, about political rulers and accidents in the city. He in his turn told them his dreams and his hopes. He made them share in his dedication to the love of God. The world of those who listened to him changed. He kindled a fire in their hearts. They found meaning and new hope in their lives.

A chance encounter. No force, no threats, just an occasional meeting, a friendly contact, an open invitation. But the experience changed people completely. Men and women left everything behind to hear more, to be close, to follow him. He gave them self-respect, making them discover themselves, their deepest thoughts, their most daring dreams, the extent of their love. He reminded them of the old promises made by Yahweh to their ancestors. Things hidden were spoken aloud. Old and new dreams turned into reality. They discovered Yahweh — who seemed so far away in their worship and life — in their own hearts and in the hearts and minds of the companions around him. They remembered having heard before that something was happening in human history. They recalled events that had to do with their origin and destiny. They became aware again — though often only vaguely — that they as a people and as persons were taken up in a process. They recognized this process in the Sacred Scriptures read to them: the dreams of their prophets, the expectations of their visionaries, justice and peace, a period of grace to come. Things that too often had remained hidden in mystery and riddle. Here was Jesus, a simple carpenter they easily could relate to, a person of flesh and blood. He was like an artist who provokes sentiments and insights, inspirations and intuitions viewers never, or only vaguely, have been aware of. He made sense not only of the individual, but of the whole of life, marriage, work, children, failures and successes. He connected the person with the past, and opened him or her up to a future hardly dreamed about, even in youth.

The people listened, and they saw. He triggered something in them. He helped them tap into a reality hidden deep in them: the presence of God. The Second Vatican Council *Decree on the Church's Missionary Activity* describes this role of Jesus in our lives pointedly:

> This universal design of God for the salvation of the human race is not carried out exclusively in the soul of a man, with a kind of secrecy. Nor is it merely achieved through those multiple endeavors, including religious ones, by which men search for God, groping for Him that they may by chance find him, (though He is not far from any one of us) (cf. Acts 17:27). . . .
>
> . . .God determined to intervene in human history in a way both new and definitive. For He sent His Son, clothed in our flesh, in order that through this Son He might snatch men from the power of darkness and of Satan (cf. Col 1:13; Acts 10:38) and that in this Son He might reconcile the world to Himself (cf. 2 Cor 5:19).[1]

JESUS' ONGOING STORY

Those who encountered Jesus never forgot. If those meetings with him had not been so memorable his story would have ended. He would have been forgotten. But he is not forgotten. He remains the fascinating person he was to his mother, to men and women, to children in the street, to the academicians and politicians of his time. He showed by word and deed and work how we human beings are taken up in a process that is our common human mission, entrusted to us by God, our common source of existence. His memory has been manipulated at times to the point that many have been alienated from him. Yet people all over the world continue to tell his story and relate their discovery. He did not appear in this world to get lost and forgotten. He remains to millions a faithful companion, a person who roots them in the process of life itself. They cannot keep their story and its richness to themselves if they want to be faithful to that process. They understand that the wisdom of Jesus, the process of life, embraces the whole of humanity and the whole of creation. It is a vision that contains all. That is the reason that those who met him believed him to be divine. This book is about the consequences of that discovery for those who made it long ago, but especially for those of us who are meeting him now in the world in which we live. We will begin by considering the dynamics of such a meeting in the following chapter.

For Reflection

1. Can you recall a coincidental meeting that proved to be influential in your life? What happened to you at that time?

2. Did a chance encounter ever have a spiritual impact on you?

3. Have you ever changed the life of another through a chance encounter? Were you surprised to find that you had?

4. How have you met Jesus in your life?

5. Reread the above quotation from the Second Vatican Council's *Decree on the Church's Missionary Activity*. How does it relate to the kind of chance encounter this

chapter discusses? Can you give examples — physical, psychological, artistic, or spiritual — of potentialities that would have remained undiscovered in you except for a chance encounter with someone?

CHAPTER 2

Aroused by Jesus

A student is not above his teacher; but every
student when he has finished his studies will be
on a par with his teacher.

(Matthew 10:24-25)

W hat happens to us when we meet someone — a teacher, a friend, a guru, a stranger, or someone like Jesus — who moves us so much we are changed? A simple question. A question we should try to answer before we go on speaking about the process that might be the result of such a meeting. Yet we often don't stop to answer simple questions. We think we know the answer, but we don't. Let me try to answer this one by something that happened to me not so long ago.

A LESSON IN THE STREET

It was New Year's day in Melbourne. I walked home from the post office, where I had been mailing late Christmas mail. I heard sirens in the distance. It was difficult to tell whether it was the police, an ambulance, or the fire brigade — or even where the noise was coming from. When I turned the corner, I saw big clouds of smoke billowing out

13

of the windows and the front door of a house. Weeping women were standing in front of the house with children clutching their skirts. Men were shouting nervously to one another. One man put a wet towel over his face and tried to enter the house, but the smoke drove him back into the street.

Along with many others, I stopped to watch the scene. We all looked anxiously at the end of the street as the noise of the sirens became louder and louder. Finally the fire brigade arrived. In no time the firemen had jumped from their vehicle and connected hoses to the fire hydrant. Others unrolled hoses from their truck. They hosed the house down from the front to the back and from the back to the front, quickly bringing the fire under control; it did not even break through the roof.

When the greatest danger was over, the fire brigade commander took a notebook from his pocket and went to the family outside. He asked them the usual questions: "When did it start? Where did it start? Any idea how it started?" (At that question I saw a small boy suddenly hide behind his mother.) "Are you insured? With what company?"

Suddenly a woman who had been standing next to me burst into tears. I asked, "Do you know that family?"

She said: "No!"

"Do you know what happened?" I asked her.

Again she answered, "No!" Then she added, "What does it matter whether I know them or not? Just put yourself for a moment in their position—such a disaster on New Year's day!" Then, still crying, she went over to comfort the distressed family.

Suddenly I understood something that had puzzled and worried me for a long time. For years I had been involved in justice and peace work. For some time I was the Executive Director of the African Faith and Justice Network in Washington, D.C. The main task of our office was to inform its constituency, mainly religious congregations that had missionaries in Africa, about the situation there, and to stimulate them to pick up their phones or pens and to lobby the House of Representatives, the Senate, the president, or church leaders. We collected information from sources on the spot about famines, wars, infringements of human rights in that large continent. We sent that information out in the hope that our members would take action. Often they didn't. We thought perhaps the material we sent out was too long, so we made it shorter. Nothing changed. We made it clearer, longer, more in depth. Nothing helped.

I had been worrying and wondering about that lack of response. The fire in Melbourne was an eye-opener to me. The fire brigade was necessary; it was efficient; it did its job. The commander gathered all the data; when he closed his notebook and put his pencil away, he had an idea what had happened. But the woman next to me had reacted in another way. She sympathized, or better, empathized with the victims. She allowed her heart and mind to vibrate with their hearts and their minds. That is why she wept. That is why she walked over to ask them to come for a cup of coffee in her home.

RESONATING WITH JESUS' SONG

It is that kind of compassion—which means cosuffering—that makes persons take action. Our office on Africa had not been able to evoke that response in its members. Oh, it accumulated all the information, all the data, all the items that the fire brigade commander noted in his booklet. But it did not do what that woman next to me did, and asked me to do: "Just put yourself for a moment in their position." Join for a moment their lament. Sing their sad ballad. Jesus once complained: "I sang a sad song for you and you did not cry!" (Mt 11:17; Lk 7:32). He asks us to *feel* with him.

Paul of Tarsus did this. In one of his many letters he wrote to his friends in the Greek town Philippi: "I long for all of you *with the affection of Jesus*" (Phil 1:8). That is how translators translate the text. They do so to avoid the embarrassment a literal translation of the words would cause. What Paul really writes is that he longs for them with the "guts" of Jesus. Paul had Jesus' gut-level feelings. He reacts in Jesus' way. He wrote to another group of his friends, this time in Galatia: "I no longer live, but Christ lives in me" (Gal 2:20).

Jesus made something happen to Paul, just as he had done to his disciples before, and just as he would do to so many others afterward. He did it to me, and as you are interested in reading this book about him and his dynamics, he must have triggered something in you too. Not many of his disciples would repeat Paul's words about having Jesus' own gut-level feelings, but they do speak about having his spirit, "the Spirit of Jesus" (Acts 17:6), or in more recent times, about having the heart of Jesus. It comes to the same. They are "struck" by Jesus. They reverberate with him. They are on the same wavelength.

An example from the world of music might help to illustrate this point. A grand piano is standing in a spacious and open room. It is well tuned. The lid is open, and the snares and strings of the instrument are visible. You stand some distance from the piano with a tuning fork. You hit the tuning fork on the wood of a table and put it down on its stem. The vibration of the tone fills the whole room. You put your hand on the tuning fork to silence it. And—if all goes well!—the snare on the grand piano that corresponds to the tone of your tuning fork has picked up its vibration and is singing on its own. Something like that happened to Paul. There is something in him that made him react to Jesus. Jesus touched something in him. And he began to resonate with Jesus' own song.

The pain and sadness of the people around that burning

house in Melbourne triggered something in the heart and head of the woman next to me, her compassion. It is from within ourselves that we feel and react, even when stimulated by someone else. Jesus worked on that principle. He teaches us to drink from our own wells. He uses parables and stories to strike values and attitudes in his hearers. Once struck, once brought to life, they vibrate on their own, so to speak.

PLUCKING THE LISTENER'S HEARTSTRINGS

When I was teaching at the University of Nairobi in Kenya and preaching as university chaplain in the university church, one of my African colleagues came to me, obviously embarrassed. After some introductory chitchat he said, "I want to tell you something." I asked him what it was. He said: "I like your teaching and your preaching and so do many others, and yet . . . you do it in an other way than we Kenyans are accustomed to." It was obviously an invitation for me to ask for the nature of the difference. So I did. He explained that an African educator would tell a story, a good story, but he would not—as I tended to do— give an explanation of the story. When he saw that I did not get his point, he gave me an example of what he meant.

One day he discovered that his oldest son, Mungai, had told him a lie. Late in the evening, just before he went to bed, he called his son and told him a story I knew, and you may recognize too.

Once upon a time, a small boy named Kamau was asked to herd some goats for his grandparents. The grass was far from his grandparents' home, so far that Kamau could neither hear the voices of the people at home nor smell the smoke of their fires. One day, when he felt very lonely, he thought, "I know how to get my people here," and he turned toward the village and shouted as loudly as he could: "Lion, lion, help, help!" Everyone in the village who heard him jumped up, took a spear or bow and arrows, and ran to help Kamau. When they found no lion, they went home, telling each other, "Kamau is a liar!"

Some days later Kamau again became lonely in that great African plain, and he thought, "It worked last time, so let me try again." He turned toward the village and shouted, "Lion, lion, help, help!" The people all jumped up, took their spears and bows and arrows and ran to help him. They ran for nothing, for there was no lion. Walking home, they again said to each other, "Kamau is a liar!"

A week later Kamau was in the field with his goats when an enormous lion appeared from behind a bush. Kamau shouted, "Lion, lion, help, help!" But in the village the people did not jump up. They said to each other, "He must think we are crazy; he is a liar!" When Kamau did not return home that evening, they went to look for him. But they only found his stick and one of his sandals.

My friend then said to his son, "Did you hear that story, Mungai? All right, go to bed and sleep well."

And that, my friend told me, is that. You don't explain such a story. If you explain it, you not only suggest that your listeners are stupid, but in a way you steal their conscience away from them and replace it with yours. The wonder of telling a story is that it calls up values in those who listen to you. It makes them recall something that is *in them*. It helps them find out something about themselves.

This is what Jesus must have done to many people around him. They listened to him, they saw him, they touched him, and something in them vibrated. They heard the melody he sang resound in their hearts. That is how they recognized him as someone special, and that is why so many accompanied him. It is the reason they "converted" to him and changed their lives. He—and his stories—awakened something in them. His dynamic became theirs.

There are immense depths in us. There are fantastic possibilities, realities that remain hidden if we are not stimulated by someone else. John once said of Jesus that he came to baptize us with Holy Spirit and fire (Mt 3:11). Jesus himself said,"I have come to bring fire on earth, and how I wish it were already kindled!" (Lk 12:49). What was lighted in those who let themselves be affected? What was the change in their orientation? What was the difference Jesus made? What did they hear in themselves when they listened to him? What does it mean to be taken up in the process he launched here in our world? When and how do we begin to live his energy and his love? To answer those questions, we have to know more about him. One place to start is with his mother.

For Reflection

1. Are there times that others react to you only in a technical and formal way? Are there situations in which that approach is the one you prefer?

2. Why did Jesus prefer to tell parables and stories?

3. Do you ever tell stories in the hope of "striking a chord" in others?

4. Think about a story that has deeply influenced your life. Do you have a favorite gospel story that resonates with something inside you?

5. Here is a story. Does it relate to anything in the chapter?

   A sailing ship had been at sea for months and months. She was now miles out from the coast of Brazil and had been there for weeks. There was no wind; the ship had hardly moved. Rations were gone, and they had finished their drinking water. In the morning the crew could scrape some dew from the sails, but that was all.

The situation was desperate. Then one morning the lookout sees another ship — bigger, better equipped, and making some progress. At the shouts of the lookout, the captain immediately starts signaling to the other ship, "Please, send us some water, we are dying with thirst." The other ship signaled, "Lower your buckets right where you are!" The distressed captain couldn't believe his eyes, and again he signaled, "Please, send us fresh water, we are dying!" He gets the same return message. Those messages go on for quite some time, until the captain — in utter despair — lowers buckets into the ocean. And he draws up sparkling fresh water!

The ship was off the coast of Brazil, where the gigantic Amazon River pushes fresh water into the Atlantic Ocean for miles and miles.[1]

CHAPTER 3

Catching the Depth of Mary's Spirit

I will pour my Spirit on all people. Your sons and daughters will prophesy, your young people will see visions, and your old folks dream dreams.

(Acts 2:17)

Years ago the University of Nairobi in Kenya sponsored a project to interview "wise" people. First, students in the Department of Philosophy and Religious Studies looked in their own communities for men and women considered wise. They did this by finding out whom people consulted when they were in personal or communal difficulties. Once that research was done, they began systematically to interview those men and women. They did not ask them questions, because questions are leading. Rather, they asked them to speak about life, sickness, death, community, the dead, offspring, solidarity, courage, and such issues.

I sometimes joined in these interviews. Though I depended in most cases on interpreters, doing this was an amazing experience—like opening living treasure houses. Most of the wise people put the themes they discussed in contexts that led back into the past for hundreds or thousands of years. That word *past* is not really accurate, because they spoke about those events and experiences as still affecting their present lives. Talking with them was calling up an experience that we in the West are only rarely aware of. It was the vital connection with their past that made them wise in regard to the present and the future.

In a theological course for future ministers in Washington, D.C., a course called "The Practice of Interreligious Dialogue," a group of students listened to a Jewish rabbi. In his lecture he touched on the Holocaust, the destruction of the Jewish people during the Second World War in Nazi Germany. One of the students became impatient. He said that he couldn't understand why Jews could not forget that horror. "It happened more than fifty years ago," he added. The guest lecturer did not seem upset by this interruption. He asked for a Bible, opened it, and read from the book of Exodus. He read of far-off days, when a new pharaoh, who did not know Joseph's story, came to power in the land of Egypt. This pharaoh put slave masters over the Jews, forcing them to build for him the cities of Pithom and Rameses (Ex 1:8-11). The rabbi then put the Bible down and said: "Did Jesus ever forget what happened to his people in Egypt? Do you Christians ever forget it?" He explained the difference between forgiving and forgetting. Only forgiveness can heal the past. We should forgive, but we should never forget what happened, if only to avoid having it happen again.

The last supper Jesus had with his disciples was a Passover meal. During that meal the youngest of the company— was it John?—had to ask the ritual question, "Why are we here tonight together? What does make this night a special night?" Jesus gave the answers to that question the night of his own Passover. He connected the two events, the Passover they were celebrating and the Passover he was engaged in. The whole past of his people echoed that night at his table, together with all the promises made in view of a new future. To sit at that table with Jesus is being in touch with the history and the hopes not only of his people, but with the fate of the whole of humanity, the outcome of the whole of creation. It was to be part of the process, of God's plan.

MARY'S STORY

If we could sit at table with Jesus' mother, Mary, we would also have that kind of experience. If we asked her why she had been willing to bring Jesus into this world, then the same past and future, the same dreams and hopes would open up to us.

We often think of Mary as a simple, young, and pious woman living in a small village, Nazareth. But she was not as simple and naive as all that. That becomes obvious in the story of her meeting with Elizabeth. You remember the story. When an angel came to ask Mary's consent to conceive from the Holy Spirit and to give birth to the one all generations had been waiting for, she did not tell Joseph, the man she was betrothed to. Joseph heard what had happened to his fiancee later from another heavenly messenger. The angel who came to Mary told her also that her relative Elizabeth was pregnant, and that she was already in her sixth month. Elizabeth also had conceived in a miraculous way. She was old, beyond child-bearing age, when an angel appeared to her husband Zechariah during his temple service to tell him that he and his wife would give birth to a son. They were to call him John. Zechariah had never been able to tell Elizabeth; he had been struck dumb. Elizabeth conceived, and she was already in her sixth month when Mary received the news. We don't know what Mary eventually told Joseph, nor do we know what Elizabeth told her husband. What we *do* know is what the two women said to each other when they met. It is at that moment that Mary's world opens to us in her song:

> "My soul glorifies the Lord
> and my spirit glorifies in God, my Savior
> for he has been mindful of the humble state of
>   his servant.
> From now on all generations will call me blessed,
> for the Mighty One has done great things for me
> —holy is his name.
> His mercy extends to those who fear him,
> from generation to generation.
> He has performed mighty deeds with his arm;
> he has scattered those
> who are proud in their inmost thoughts.
> He has brought down rulers from their thrones
> but has lifted up the humble.
> He has filled the hungry with good things
> but he has sent the rich empty away.
> He has helped his servant Israel,
> remembering to be merciful to Abraham
> and his descendants for ever" (Lk 1:46-55).

Mary shows in this song the world in which she lived. It is the reaction of someone keenly aware of what is going on around her—the political intrigues and the power plays. It is the hymn of someone who not only made a kind of social analysis of the world in which she lived, but who was also keen on the role she had to play. It is the response of a woman who reached back to the very beginning of the history of her people and of the whole of humankind. She based her trust and never-ending hope on God's loving promises to her ancestors. She mentioned Abraham and his family by name. The whole history of her people and of the world, and all the promises and hopes ever expressed by them echo in her song, a song that sounds like a battle hymn. No wonder that even in our own world women sing Mary's liberation hymn when they come together to protest injustice and demand change.

Devout Jewish men and women dreamed of being involved in the bringing forth of the Messiah. They considered barrenness a scourge because it precluded the possibility of making a direct genetic contribution to that hoped-for coming. Elizabeth refers to these expectations when she too speaks about "a fulfillment of the things that have been spoken" (Lk 1:45).

GOD'S PLAN

Mary and Elizabeth, and Joseph and Zechariah too, were conscious of being taken up in a process that reached from the beginning of the world's history to its fulfillment. They did not know all the details. But they walked in faith. They walked faithfully according to the promises made to them. They were aware that something was going to happen, and they were willing to involve themselves in the dynamics of God's plans for this world. According to Mary's own words, that divine project had something to do with a promise of long ago, a promise made to Abraham, a promise that had made him and his wife Sarah "strangers in a strange land."

The things Abraham and Sarah only saw and welcomed from a distance (Heb 11:13) still had the power to make them move. Mary's and Elizabeth's awareness of being taken up in a process came from that earlier promise. So, if we want to understand better what made Mary agree so enthusiastically to become involved, we have to know what happened to Abram and his family.

For Reflection

1. Do you consider yourself to be taken up — as a Christian — in the dynamic process of the world's history?

2. Mary played a critical role in God's plan. How would you have reacted to what happened to Mary? Do you see yourself as invited to take part in her role in this world?

3. What promises help you to continue your journey?

4. Do you "echo with the past" in your view of the future?

5. Reread Mary's song. Does it strike you as having implications other than the religious and pious ones we usually associate with it — and with Mary?

6. How does Mary's story resonate with your own?

CHAPTER 4

Beginning with Abram and Sarai

*For he was looking forward to the city with
foundations, whose architect and builder is God.*
(Hebrews 11:10)

A bram and his wife Sarai are the first traceable people mentioned in the Bible. By traceable we mean that we have material evidence of their existence; we can find their footprints; they left things behind we can lay our hands on. This is not to say that the persons who are mentioned in the Bible before them did not exist. They did, but we can't trace them. They have disappeared into a kind of mythical mist. We don't know where paradise was. And despite the efforts of many explorers, the ark of Noah remains hidden.

Abram and Sarai are different. We know they lived about four thousand years ago, and we know where. Abram lived in two cities, Ur and Haran, both situated in the land of the Chaldees and both excavated in recent years. Ur and Haran were similar in their worship; they worshiped a moon god named Sin. Excavation of their temples revealed that they sacrificed children to their moon god, probably their first-born in order to assure further fertility. Abram and Sarai—as they are called in the beginning of their story—decided to leave that environment. The Bible tells us that Yahweh asked them to do so (Gn 12:1-3). They could not agree with what was going on in Ur, so they moved to Haran, but finding the same difficulties, they left that city, too.

How they heard Yahweh's command to leave we don't know. Whether they heard it from God's presence in their own hearts or from a divine appearance we can only guess, but they did leave. That departure can't have been easy for them. Others must have thought they had lost their faith. They became nomads in the desert; Abram, Sarai, and their extended family had many adventures.

TO WALK WITH GOD

The point is that they walked their way and faithfully fulfilled their mission. The Bible often gives them as examples of how to walk with God. Mary followed the example of their faithfulness when she responded to the angel. Yet that is not the reason that Mary thinks of them when she sings her song in the company of Elizabeth. At that moment something else in the life of Abram and Sarai is in her mind—the promise made to them at the moment that Yahweh changes their names from Abram and Sarai to Abraham and Sarah (Gn 17:1-8). Yahweh promises them that Abraham will be "the father of the nations." The Judaic Holy Scriptures never mention Abraham without a reference to all nations. That is the promise Mary has in mind.

Take the night that Yahweh called them out of their tent in the desert and asked them to look into the sky at the stars. Abram, and most probably Sarai too, must have been amazed that they were asked to do so. They had left Ur and Haran because they felt that they should not stare at the moon and the stars any more (Jdt 5:3-9). Now Yahweh asked them to do so, and they did. Looking in the bright star-studded sky they saw for the first time something in between those stars that became the leading vision all through Judaic and Christian literature. As the letter to the Hebrews so much later will recount, they didn't see it clearly yet. They only had an inkling. They saw "from a distance" (Heb 11:13) and from afar "the city, with foundations, whose architect and builder is God" (Heb 11:10). This image is fully worked out in the last book of the Bible, the book of Revelation. John describes the end, when there will be one city. God will dwell in that city, and Jesus Christ, the Lamb, will be enthroned in it. All nations will come together to the city, each one bringing its own glory and honor (Rv 21:24-27). It is the final outcome of God's love project for the human family. It is our destiny, and our mission.

Abraham and Sarah did not see all that. They were just beginners. But they started to move in the direction of the promise, leaving Ur and then Haran, and journeying on. They endured all kinds of complications: the initial barrenness of Sarah; Abram's relation to his second wife, Hagar; Sarah's envy at the birth of Hagar's son Ishmael; and too many other adventures to mention. It was the beginning of a divinely inspired initiative, a new process that ultimately will lead to the gathering of the nations and the final peace, justice, and fulfillment the whole of humanity always has hoped for. This is a hope based on a contract: "I am God Almighty; walk before me and be blameless. I will confirm my covenant between me and you" (Gn 17:1-2). God signed this new pact by sending a torch of fire to scorch the sacrifices Abram and his family had put down on the earth as their part of the new human/divine covenant.

This covenant was not the first between God and the human family. Earlier the rainbow was given as a sign of God's covenant with Noah and his family. It would not be the last covenant either. Later Moses would come down from the mountain with his stone tablets. The later covenants did not replace or cancel the earlier. They clarified one another. The overall picture became clearer and clearer until finally it was no longer a picture but the living reality of Jesus Christ, Immanuel, "God with us."

But we are running ahead. Let us get back to Abraham and Sarah. It was on the occasion of this new covenant that Yahweh changed Abram's and Sarai's names, as we mentioned before. God added a vowel to Abram. God added something to the original, as if to indicate that what happened to Abram and to his family should happen to every one and to every family, clan, and ethnic group in the world. That is, we have to leave our old set-up, and remaining faithful to ourselves, enter the march toward that future that will bring us all together, each one carrying his or her own gift.

FAITHFUL TO THE VISION

We have still a long way to walk before we will reach that city described in Revelation. The rest of Abraham's story — Abraham, who was also the first person to be called a Hebrew (Gn 14:13) — and the story of his offspring makes that very clear. That story is at times so violent that we wonder just how the vision was carried on to the time of Mary and Elizabeth. How is it that the book containing the vision of that ultimate human/divine city at the same time tells of so many terrible battles? How is it that the descendants of the visionary Abraham tell about the gruesome battles they fought against others, even claiming that they were ordered to do so by Yahweh?

> Now go, and attack the Amalekites and totally destroy everything that belongs to them, put to death men and women, children and infants, cattle and sheep, camels and donkeys (1 Sm 15:3).

It is even more amazing that these kinds of texts were not censored away by later editors. They could report and keep them, however, because they always read them against the background of prophets like Isaiah, who remained faithful to the vision. The events always were contained in the context of the promise, that the time would come when Abraham and Sarah's vision would be realized.

The final editors of the Hebrew Bible expressed that same conviction in the way they edited the Bible's final edition, in the way it came to us. They did that during the Babylonian exile, a terrible time for the Jews, surrounded as they were by enemies who often laughed at their humiliation—a time so terrible that they did not even find the courage to sing their own songs. They did, however, edit their Bible. In the midst of an alien people they remained faithful to their vision. They did not put Abram's story, the beginning of their own people, as the first chapter in their collection of books. Rather, they began with some creation stories, each conveying in its own way how the whole of humanity is born from one and the same womb. What Abraham and Sarah had seen as the final outcome, they projected as the beginning.

They even used a third approach to save the overall vision that the peoples belong together and should not use violence against one another. It is not a persuasive approach—some would say it is just an evasion—but nevertheless it has its merit. Instead of blaming themselves for the disasters they wrought, they told how Yahweh waged their wars for them. Just think of the description of the conquest of Jericho. *They* did not do anything. They just marched around the town seven times, blasting their trumpets and chanting their war slogans. They did not throw a stone. They did not fire a shot. It was at the seventh turn around the town that the whole city and all its ramparts and walls fell apart and turned into dust. It was *Yahweh* who was the warrior, who could be the warrior because Yahweh was the creator of all human beings, a God who sends rain over the good and the bad. God had given them a vision that one day the whole of humanity and the whole of creation would be together, though the path was long and often violent and the difficulties almost insurmountable.

THE VISIONARY SONG OF THE PROPHETS

The prophetic voice remained sure in all those difficulties. Just listen to Isaiah, a prophet Mary and Jesus would later quote:

> It will happen in the final days,
> that the mountain of Yahweh's house
> will rise higher than the mountains
> and tower above the heights.
> Then all the nations will stream to it,
> many peoples will come to it and say:
> Come, let us go up to the mountain of Yahweh,
> to the house of the God of Jacob. . . .
> They will hammer their swords into plowshares
> and their spears into sickles.
> Nation will not lift sword against nation,
> no longer will they learn how to make war
>   (Is 2:1-4).

The prophets remained firmly convinced of Abraham's vision and Yahweh's promise to him and his family. They were also conscious of the difficulties that had to be overcome to fulfill that vision. They wondered how the promise ever would be fulfilled in the world as they knew it and as it is described in the Bible from the murder of Abel by Cain to their own exile in Babylon. That is how they received the inspiration that someone—a Messiah sent by Yahweh—would come to this world, to make a new beginning. This is the one Mary was willing and eager to bring into this world.

For Reflection

1. Can you see your own life in the light of the promises made to Abram and Sarai? What does that mean to you?

2. Would it be fair to say that Christians have reduced the Abrahamic vision of reaching the city of God to something that is almost exclusively personal?

3. How is Abraham and Sarah's vision significant for our time and age?

4. How can their vision counteract the meaninglessness so many seem to experience in their lives?

5. Can you appreciate Mary's eagerness to be involved in the Abrahamic dynamics?

CHAPTER 5

Prophetic and Messianic Imagery

My eyes have seen the king, the Lord Almighty.
(Isaiah 6:5)

It seems to me that we often overlook what really happened to people in the Bible, because we think they are different from us. Not different because they lived in another time and age or in another region of the world. From that point of view they *do* differ from us. What I mean is that we make super-human beings of them. We make Mary so holy and precious that she is out of our reach; we can hardly compare ourselves with her. When we hear Paul say that he does not live anymore but that Christ lives in him, we think of Paul as very privileged and special. We risk not applying what he says to ourselves.

THE VOICE OF INSPIRATION

In the last chapter we spoke of how the prophets, and especially Isaiah, were inspired to think that God would send someone to help humanity forward on its way to the realization of Abraham's vision. It might be that those prophets were inspired by a voice from heaven. That is quite possible. But there is also another possibility. The voice of inspiration may have come from within themselves. They believed passionately in the force of God's promise to their ancestors—just as Mary did years later. They were well aware of how difficult the road to the fulfillment of that vision was. They saw around them a human behavior that wasn't too promising, to say the least. They reported one disaster after another. Yet they maintained their belief in the promise from God. It was the combination of those two things, their belief in that final outcome and the difficulties they experienced, that convinced them that God was going to send someone to help.

It was not a difficult conclusion to reach. We often use the same kind of reasoning. Coming out of church one day, I met an older woman standing at the door. Practically all the parishioners had gone. The last ones said goodbye to one another and dispersed in different directions. The woman stood there alone. I asked whether I could help her, whether she had been left by someone, whether I could take her somewhere. She thanked me for my offer, but said her son had promised to come to bring her home. I need not bother about her. So I left. About half an hour later I came back to the church, and she was still standing there. Again I asked her whether I could help her. Again she refused. I pointed out that something might have happened to keep her son from coming. In that case, she told me with a wide smile, he will send someone else to pick me up. At that moment a car came around the corner to pick her up, as she had believed it would.

FAITH IN GOD'S PROMISE

A prophet like Isaiah was convinced that Yahweh would be faithful and lead God's people to the New Jerusalem, that city of the promise. God's love is reliable. Isaiah was also sure that something had to happen to make this possible, for he was convinced that it would be very difficult if not impossible for humanity to reach that aim as things were. How could the disastrous harm individuals and nations did — and do — to each other be stopped? Besides, even if it was possible to end that violence, how could people be reconciled after the terrible things they did — and we do — to each other? Would it ever be possible to bring together what was torn apart? Yet, there was the promise! As a consequence of his pondering on these issues Isaiah began to foresee and to foretell that one day Yahweh would send a savior, a redeemer, a liberator to rally the world and its population. That is how he and other prophets began to sing the song of a helper, a servant of Yahweh, a Messiah, who would come to the aid of his people, of all peoples in the world. A savior who would make the final breakthrough possible. Isaiah sang about that future event as if it had happened already:

> Every warrior's boot in battle
> and every garment rolled in blood
> will be destined for burning,
> will be fuel for the fire.
> For to us a child is born,
> to us a son is given,
> and the government will be on his shoulders.
> And he will be called Wonderful Counselor,
> Mighty God, Everlasting Father,
> Prince of Peace (Is 9:5-6).

THE SUFFERING SERVANT

Isaiah foresees that this new human beginning, the Messiah, will be called Immanuel ("God with us"). He knows intuitively that this new beginning must be untouched by the past and yet rooted in the past, virginal. Touching the great mythic stories he foretells that even by his birth the great one, the Messiah, will be distinguished from other human beings. In short, it becomes clear to Isaiah as he ponders all this that the Messiah will be born of a virgin (Is 7:14). He also draws another conclusion. The Messiah will suffer dreadfully. He could, of course, come with divine power to force Israel and the nations to march toward their goal. The promise, however, was that humanity itself would decide to move in that direction; in the end we would be able to say Yahweh and we arrived at our destination. The promise to Abraham excluded force. The journey would remain a human one, one freely willed. The Messiah would operate within the context of our human world. Isaiah fore-saw that he would be welcomed by many, but also that many others would turn against him, and that he would lose his life in the process. But he would not be forsaken by God and would rise from the dead.

> He was oppressed and afflicted,
> yet he did not open his mouth,
> he was led like a lamb to the slaughter,
> and as a sheep before her shearers is silent,
> so he did not open his mouth (Is 53:7).

It is not disrespectful to say that one didn't have to be a great prophet to prophesy the suffering and death of the Messiah. Anyone who came to help humanity break through its resistance in fulfilling God's plan would meet that fate. That is still true of the world in which we live today. Anyone who wants to bring humanity a step nearer to the ideal of one human family meets resistance. Too many people don't want that gathering of the whole of humanity in justice and peace as yet.

THE PROPHETIC LOGIC

Do we want to see in fulfillment that vision Abraham and Sarah first glimpsed so dimly? We might think that we are in favor of it, but that often is because we have never really been put to the test. So many among us are rejected or attacked when they put themselves on the line for justice and peace — from a coach who wants to make a team inter-racial, to someone like Reverend Martin Luther King, Jr., who wanted to assure the rights of the communities we often call minorities.

Of course the Messiah would get into difficulty! Isaiah foresaw that his appearance would be disfigured beyond that of any human being, and his form would be marred beyond any human likeness (Is 52:14), but he would see his offspring and the intention of Yahweh would prosper in his hands (Is 53:10). His confidence in Yahweh's faithfulness to the promise made to Abraham's family combined with his insight into the actual sinful state of humanity made him expect God to send a Messiah. The same logic made him know that the Messiah would suffer and even be killed. But the promise would be kept, the Messiah would rise from destruction and death, and humanity's journey would continue into its last stage. Mary and Jesus were aware of this prophetic logic. They both quote Isaiah when they explain to themselves and to others their mission, as we will see in the next chapter.

For Reflection

1. Do you agree with Isaiah's prophetic logic that if the promise made by Yahweh to Abraham is valid in a world like ours, then a Messiah should come to us?

2. Can you remember a situation in your life when you had absolute confidence in a promise?

3. Why did Isaiah expect the Messiah to suffer? Discuss that expectation in relation to a contemporary martyr for the cause of justice and peace.

4. Have you ever acted for the cause of "gathering the nations" into God's friendly family by attempting to open your family, circle, club, community, or organization to "strangers"? What was the result?

===

CHAPTER 6

Mary and Her Circle

*Look! The virgin is with child and will give birth
to a son whom they will call Immanuel.*
(Matthew 1:23; Isaiah 7:14)

T he information about the person of Mary is
sparse. We have no idea what she looked like or
how old she was when the angel addressed her,
though we might have a good guess. We do
have information about her spiritual life, about what moved
her. For example, when the angel invited her to be the
mother of the savior, she did not ask her heavenly guest
what his message was about; she knew that. Later, she
showed that she understood what was at stake when she
sang her song upon meeting Elizabeth. Speaking about herself she quotes the prophet Isaiah: "My soul proclaims the
greatness of the Lord" (Is 61:10), and speaking about her
future son, she quotes Isaiah again, saying that her son is
"coming to the help of Israel" (Is 41:9). She must have
known that Isaiah foresaw that the Messiah would be born
of a virgin (Is 7:14). What she did not know was how this
would happen, how it would come about. So that was her
question to the angel. The angel answered her question:
she will conceive from the Holy Spirit. Once the angel had
clarified that, Mary had no further difficulty. On the contrary,

she sang — quoting Isaiah. She rejoiced in her call, not only because of herself, but because of her people and the whole of humanity. She had hoped and prayed for this event. She carried in herself all the expectations of her people. She was the best expression of humanity's longings. Using an image from our first chapter, she resonated with all the hopes of those who went before her.

REJOICING IN THE PROMISE

Yet, according to Luke, Mary was not the only one who thrived on those hopes and expectations. Once Zechariah, Elizabeth's husband, could speak again (after the birth of their son, John), Luke reports that he also sang a song describing not only what happened to him and his family, but also how he saw the role of his son. Like Mary in her song, he went all the way back to the promise Yahweh made to Abraham and his family. He alluded three times to Isaiah when relating his son, John, to the fulfillment of that promise and to the dynamics that further it. He sang that people would call John Prophet of the Most High, and that he would prepare a way for the Lord (Is 40:3), who will give light to those who live in darkness and the shadow of death (Is 42:7), and will guide their feet into the way of peace (Is 11:6).

There are others in Mary's circle who were aware of what was happening. They didn't see her and her child as just another mother and child. They tuned in to the energy that could be felt in her and in Jesus. They were aware of the dynamics that were at work. When Mary and Joseph went to the Temple to present their child, two other prophetic people came out of the Temple's shadow: Simeon and Anna. Simeon asked them to allow him to hold the child Jesus, and he said:

Now, Master, you are letting your servant go in
   peace
as you promised;
for my eyes have seen your salvation
which you have prepared in the sight of the
   nations,
a light for revelation to the gentiles
and for glory for your people Israel (Lk 2:29-32).

In this short blessing of himself he quotes Isaiah four times! No one in Mary's circle expressed the reason for Jesus' coming more clearly: *all the nations are going to be blessed because of the one who is born here.* He is going to assure salvation to all. He is going help the whole of humanity on its way to the common goal. Because he sees this so well, he is also the one who sees best what this is going to mean for the baby he has in his arms and for his mother: "Look, he is destined for the fall and the rise of many in Israel, destined to be a sign that is opposed," and looking at Mary he adds, "and a sword will pierce your heart too" (Lk 2:34). Mary and Joseph did not need much proof of that—very soon afterward they are on their way to Egypt, fleeing from Herod's terror. Refugees in Africa! When they come back, they are not allowed to return to Bethlehem as they had hoped to do. They live as refugees in Nazareth, a little settlement of no importance.

JOHN THE BAPTIZER

Among Mary's family there is another person alive to what is happening: John the Baptizer. Out in the desert and baptizing masses of people, priests and other officials come to ask him to give account of what he is trying to do. They ask him who he is. They try to place him in what they know of Messianic dynamics. Is he the Christ? Is he Elijah? Who is he? John replies, again quoting—in his turn—Isaiah:

A voice of one that cries in the desert:
prepare a way for the Lord.
Make *his* paths straight (Jn 1:23).

Using the words "make his paths straight," John connects what he is doing in the River Jordan to a journey. His
words recall what Abraham and Sarah first glimpsed when
looking at the stars in the sky—the new city of God and
humanity. John refers to a trek that will lead to the great
gathering at the end of these days. His words echo what
Isaiah prophesied, that in the last days all nations will
stream together, affirming Yahweh's promise to Abraham, a
gathering that assures the salvation of the whole of the
human family and of every individual person willing to walk
that way.

BROUGHT TOGETHER IN GOD

It is this path Mary wanted to walk. We too often think of
salvation as something personal. But that kind of salvation
was not Mary's only concern. Her personal destiny definitely
is included in her vision; she is very aware of her personal
role and vocation. But, as all the prophets do, she sees her
personal destiny linked to a salvation that is much larger in
scope, a salvation by which the whole of humanity, the peoples of all times and the whole of creation, will find the fullness of life. Personal conversion is a basic part of it. John
the Baptizer makes that clear when he asks the people to
convert and be baptized. But that is not all. John asks them
to do so within a wider context—that of the whole of
humanity:

Let every valley be filled in,
every mountain and hill be leveled,
winding ways be straightened

and rough paths made smooth,
and all humanity will see the salvation of God
(Lk 3:5-6).

The whole of existence is connected and should be brought together in God. That is God's promise and the vision of Abraham and Sarah, Isaiah, John the Baptizer, Mary, Zechariah, Elizabeth, Simeon, and especially Mary's son, Jesus! Would that the human family saw it more clearly!

For Reflection

1. Does this prophetic vision of God's plan and promise play any role in your life?

2. Do you see Mary as one who shared the vision of the prophets? Discuss.

3. Do you see your personal life journey in the context of a movement of all humanity? Explain.

4. How has the common Christian understanding of salvation broadened in recent times beyond the personal? Are you expressing that new understanding in the practice of your life?

5. Do you relate Jesus' mission to your life? Discuss this issue in your community.

CHAPTER 7

Jesus' Self-Image

1 is on me, because he has
ch the good news to the

(Luke 4:18; Isaiah 61:1)

ιzareth was humming with
who had left some months
ck in town for the weekend. The
red that he had joined some oth-
d by John the Baptizer. Some-
ι at that baptism that had
something about heaven break-
own, and a voice being heard.
ιat, so nobody could ask him
ιvas in the desert for forty days,
ed him. He had come out of
ιming back to Nazareth, he had
ιlilee, preaching in synagogues.
use in Capernaum, where he
s in the streets. There were
lings and the driving away of

SABBATH IN NAZARETH

Now he is home. It is time for him to explain what happened to him, why he did not settle at home after discovering his powers. He should account for his behavior.

The people of Nazareth knew that they could expect him to come to the synagogue service. Luke notes that it was his custom to do so. That Sabbath day the whole of Nazareth must have been there. When the time came for someone to do the reading, they all remained sitting. Nobody volunteered. They did not look at him, but they were waiting for him. They expected him to do the reading. He obliged. Luke does not explain whether he asked for the scroll of Isaiah, or whether they gave it to him. Whatever was the case, he ended with the book of Isaiah in his hands. He rolled it down until he had found the text he wanted to read:

> The Spirit of the Lord is on me,
> because he has anointed me
> to preach good news to the poor.
> He has sent me to proclaim freedom for the
>   prisoners
> and recovery of sight for the blind,
> to release the oppressed,
> to proclaim the year of God's favor
>   (Lk 4:18-19; Is 61:1-2).

Those who knew the text well must have been surprised that he ended his reading like that, for he did not finish the second verse. He stopped in the middle of it. He mentioned the proclamation of the year of God's favor, but he did not quote the continuation of that verse: "to proclaim the year of God's favor, *and the day of vengeance of our God* . . ." Not finishing the sentence from Isaiah, he sat down, a sign that he was going to speak and to teach. The tension in the synagogue became almost unbearable. Luke writes: "The eyes of everyone in the synagogue were fastened on him." Jesus looked at them, and said: "Today this scripture is fulfilled in your hearing." They all were delighted. This was more than they had been hoping for. He had announced that he was the one who was going to do the things Isaiah had prophesied for the last days. He announced that he was going to begin the final year of grace—the year of the Jubilee, as they sometimes called it.

This was the time that all wrongs would be straightened out, all wounds would be healed, and Israel restored in its full glory. They were enthusiastic about "the gracious words" that came from his lips. They wondered how this could happen to Joseph's son, whom they knew so well, but they were quite willing to accept what he said. The rumors they had heard proved to be true after all.

A YEAR OF GRACE FOR ALL

Jesus then tackled directly the problem they had with him: "Surely you will quote this proverb to me: 'Physician, heal yourself! Do here in your hometown what we have heard that you did in Capernaum' "(Lk 4:2). He explained that this year of grace was not for them or for Israel alone. He gave the examples of a non-Jewish widow in Zeraphat and a Syrian army commander to illustrate that what he came to do would touch the whole of the world and all its population. At that moment the mood in the synagogue changed completely. If the year of grace was not for them alone, they did not want it. They could not bear the idea of having to share with aliens and pagans. If that was what he wanted, away with him. They became so angry that they jumped up, threw him out of their synagogue, pushed and pulled him out of town to the brow of the hill on which their town was built in order to throw him down the cliff. Jesus did what anyone should do in such a situation. Don't show an angry crowd your back, but face them. That is what he did. He turned around, faced them, and walked right through the crowd and went on his way (Lk 4:25-30).

It is easy to blame those villagers. But we should not do so before making sure that we ourselves are free from that kind of envy! We meet their refusal to share in the reluctance of so many to receive refugees and immigrants, to be with the poor and sick, to take care of the young and the old, to accept strangers and those who don't share our beliefs and customs. We hope for yet fear and resist God's promise of oneness.

Jesus went back to Capernaum. The people of Nazareth must have been wondering about Capernaum, a harbor and bordertown full of sailors, smugglers, minorities, and aliens from all over. It had a bad reputation. It was — though in a modest way — the most cosmopolitan town in the region Jesus covered. Galilee was the least Jewish region of Palestine, and Capernaum was the least Galilean town in the neighborhood. It was in the streets, on the squares, and in the synagogues of that town, a gathering point of all kinds of people and nations, that Jesus preached for the first time the coming of God's kingdom.

The incident in Nazareth shows that from the beginning of his preaching and healing Jesus saw his mission as universal, touching the whole of the world. He had come to help humanity on its way to the fulfillment of Abraham and Sarah's vision; he had come to honor the promises made to Abraham and Sarah and their family, and through them to all the nations of the earth. That is what he told them in Nazareth when he applied Isaiah's prophecies to himself, when he told them that he had not come only for them but for the whole world. Jesus lived those words in his deeds. He moved from Nazareth to Capernaum, a move from the province into the world. It is from Capernaum that he starts his mission, full of the divine dynamics of God's Spirit. He had come to gather the nations, to fulfill God's dream about humanity. This was the dynamic he wanted to share. He began to look around for company.

For Reflection

1. Discuss some contemporary situations that mirror Nazareth's refusal to share salvation. Is the reluctance to accept immigrants and refugees, mentioned in the chapter, a valid comparison?

2. Liberation theologians often take Jesus' reading of Isaiah at Nazareth as the starting point for their theology. Why would they do this?

3. Is it correct to say that Jesus "opts for the poor" in the incident in the synagogue at Nazareth?

4. Humanity's journey to the new city began with Abraham and Sarah, who moved from Ur and Haran because of their beliefs. Now we see Jesus acting on his beliefs by moving from Nazareth to Capernaum. A journey begins with movement. Do you know of anyone who moved from one place to another because of his or her convictions?

CHAPTER 8

Gatherer of the Nations

He who does not gather with me, scatters.
(Luke 11:23)

J esus' weekend appearance in Nazareth was a failure. It is interesting to look at the nature of that fiasco. It was a portent of what his difficulty would be. It was the first time that he faced a death threat, a threat uttered because he wanted to move the whole of humanity on its way to fulfillment. The people in the synagogue in Nazareth were eager to enter that fulfillment and period of grace for themselves, but they were unwilling to do so with others. They had difficulties opening their circle; they hesitated to live in a larger tent than they were accustomed to, to sit together with others at an expanded common table. They had been dreaming about Yahweh's promise to Abraham and Sarah and thus to them. They knew about Isaiah's prophecies, but they were not prepared to begin living that dream in the reality of their lives.

Every time Jesus opens the circle of the people around him, every time he breaks their restrictive taboos, he encounters resistance. It is not only in Nazareth that he gets death threats. The first time his life is threatened by priests in the gospel of Mark—considered by many as being the first gospel written—is during the so-called purification of the Temple. This is the story.

THE PURIFICATION OF THE TEMPLE

Jesus had been to the Temple the evening before. He had looked at everything, Mark notes, but since it was already late, he and his company had gone to Bethany for the night (Mk 11:11). The next morning they return to the Temple. Jesus interrupts the business done in the Temple. He throws over the bankers' stalls, and money rolls everywhere. He kicks over the stools of the sellers of sacrificial animals, and clouds of pigeons and doves fly up. He does more. He does not allow people to pass over the Temple square, which means that he essentially stopped the Temple service. The priests waiting in the back of the Temple for the next animal to be sacrificed wait in vain. Nobody turns up. They hear a man preaching at the entrance of the Temple: "Is it not written: 'My house will be called a house of prayer *for all nations!*' " (Mk 11:15). What he says echoes the promise to Abraham and Sarah. It is a realization of Isaiah's prophecy, the very mission of the Messiah in this world. It is then, Mark notes, that the priests and scribes came and "began looking for a way to kill him" (Mk 11:18). Mark doesn't mince words. He also mentions the reason they wanted to kill him: fear. They were afraid of the consequences of that gathering of all those nations.

We find the same fear among his own disciples. John tells a story about their hesitation. According to some biblical scholars the incident is the turning point in the gospel of John. Just before this story starts, John briefs us that the Pharisees told each other, "Look how *the whole world* is going after him!" (Jn 12:19). How right they were! This report follows that remark.

"MY HOUR HAS COME"

Some Greeks had come to the celebrations in Jerusalem. They approach Philip, the only one among the twelve with a

Greek-sounding name, and they tell him, "Sir, we would like
to see Jesus" (Jn 12:21). It is obvious from the way John
tells his story that Philip does not know what to do with this.
He goes to Andrew, as he does often when he is in doubt,
to ask his advice. We don't know what they discussed. Did
they hesitate because they did not like to introduce Greeks
at their common table? That would not be surprising; in
those days the Greeks were a cultural threat to the Jewish
traditions. The two, Philip and Andrew, decide to see Jesus
about it. They tell him some Greeks would like to see him.
Jesus' response must have been a surprise to them. Jesus
says, "The hour has come for the Son of Man to be glorified." It is as if he is saying, "This is what I have been waiting for. Finally, things are starting to fall in place."

Earlier, at the wedding feast at Cana, Jesus said the hour
"had not yet come." You remember the story. Jesus'
mother was there together with the guests, family members,
and their acquaintances—a very homogeneous group.
Jesus and the disciples had been invited. It is difficult to
know what went on in the heart and mind of Mary when she
went to Jesus to tell him the wine was gone. Was Mary
thinking of those passages in Sacred Scripture that describe
the final outcome of our human journey toward God as a
wedding feast—a wedding feast with plenty of food and
plenty of wine? Did she get somewhat over-enthusiastic
when she saw her son arrive at this wedding? Some exe-
getes, and many mystics, think so. There are good reasons
for their opinion. Jesus himself often used the image of a
wedding feast to describe the final outcome of the human
pilgrimage toward God. Seeing her son at the wedding
feast, Mary might have thought, "it might all start today, the
hour has come, *his* hour has come!" She then went to
Jesus to give him a hint of her guess. She tells him, "They
have no wine," meaning they are waiting for the definite
wine, the wine of the end, the wine of the kingdom, the
wine of the New Jerusalem. Jesus answers, "Woman, what

have I to do with you? My hour has not yet come!"

At Cana the hour had not come. When Philip and Andrew announce the arrival of the Greeks, Jesus says, "My hour has come." What is the difference between these two occasions? One difference is that at Cana only one sort of people were present, a homogeneous group of family members, friends, acquaintances, and neighbors closely related to one another. The gathering at Cana could not be seen as a fulfillment of either Abraham's vision or of Isaiah's prophecy of "all nations coming together." It was too restricted a group.

But when Philip and Andrew come to Jesus with their message that some Greeks want to see him, the situation is different. The Jewish contemporaries of Jesus' Greeks were not only strangers and outsiders. They were their diametrical opposites. The Romans were a military and political danger, a danger the Jews knew what to do about. The Greeks were a danger that rooted more deeply. They were a threat to Jewish civilization and culture. The ways Greeks dressed, ate, philosophized, socialized, and organized themselves were a constant temptation to the Jewish nation. Greeks were the most unlikely people to join a Jewish movement like the one growing around Jesus. No wonder Philip did not decide on his own what to do when he was approached by some of them! He goes to his friend Andrew, and together they go to Jesus with their message. They had seen that Jesus did not mind relating to strangers. They had seen him deal with a Roman officer, a Samaritan woman, a Syro-Phoenician woman, and all kinds of other people, but what about those Greeks? What would the end be of all this socializing? As the alarmed Pharisees had been telling each other, "The whole world has gone after him!"

REALIZATION OF THE VISION

For Jesus, this was the realization of Abraham's vision. His hour had really come. Humanity had begun to gather as

God's one family. Philip and Andrew don't seem to have reacted too eagerly to Jesus' response. They needed further explanation, so Jesus tells them:

> I tell you the truth, unless a kernel of wheat falls to the ground and dies, it remains only a single seed. But if it dies it produces many seeds (Jn 12:24).

In other words, if the circle does not open up, it will remain fruitless. Open your circle, expand your tent, add places to your table!

All through the gospels Jesus exemplifies this attitude. He talks in public to women he should not have talked to. He was interested in children neglected by almost everyone. He wasn't afraid when lepers and other people considered impure approached him. He sat down with sinners and strangers. He asked his disciples again and again to get to the other side of the lake, the side they don't want to go to because it is foreign country to them, full of strangers. He uses signs and symbols to explain the universality of his mission. Once he sends the twelve out on their mission, indicating that they should cover the twelve tribes of Israel.

Another time he commissions seventy-two of them, probably with a reference to the seventy-two grandsons of Noah, who one day were sent out from the homestead of their grandfather to be the beginning of all the nations on earth (Gn 10:32). The number seventy-two, then, indicates that Jesus' disciples are being sent out to the whole of humanity. He is preparing them for the moment that he will send them and all his followers to the ends of the earth!

Jesus describes himself as someone who came to bring the harvest together, as a fisherman who brings the fish together in his nets, as a hen who gathers her chickens under her wings. At his last breakfast with his disciples he lets Peter and his companions catch 153 sizable fish. According to Saint Jerome, that number 153 was the com-

plete list of different types of fish known in that region at
that time. If that is true, it is another indication that he was
to bring all of us together. He speaks about the final homecoming of the human family—Yahweh's promise to Abraham—as a great banquet. He loves to organize gigantic
picnics in the open where thousands of people come
together and are fed. He will die—as the high priest Caia-
phas unwittingly attests—"for the scattered children of God,
to bring them together and make them one" (Jn 11:52).

JESUS THE GATHERER

Mark tells a story in which Jesus' outreach to absolutely
every human being is perhaps best illustrated. It is the story
about a possessed man in the land of the Gerasenes. Mark
could not have put that man any further away from normal-
ity. He lived at the other, the pagan side of the lake. He
lived in a cemetery, an unclean place for a Jew. People
chained his hands and his feet, but he tore everything apart.
No one dared to approach him anymore. He behaved as a
wild man, shouting among the tombs at night and cutting
himself with stones. He lived with pigs nearby, for a Jew
another horror. He was possessed not by one, but by a
legion of evil spirits. Mark did everything possible to
describe the man and his world as alien. He even adds that
the people in the villages around did not take kindly to
Jesus. If there was ever a marginalized human being it was
this man in Gerasa. Everyone in the region was deadly
afraid of him; he was a non-person. Yet Jesus asks his disciples to bring him to that side of the lake, where the man
is raging around. When the man comes to him, he meets
him, chases the demons out of him, and heals him. In the
end of the story Jesus sends him home to his family to tell
them what the Lord had done for him.

Jesus' outreach as a gatherer is all-embracing. He does

not exclude anyone; he is divine in his approach. He displays the attitude of God, who lets his rain fall over the good ones and the evil ones. He tells his followers to love their enemies, that we belong together. We are invited not only to listen to what he says but to live as he lives, to be as he is. Those who refuse to follow his example, those who divide humanity, considering themselves as the only chosen ones, fear him. For their exclusive attitude Jesus had no good word. When he met them, he spoke in terms of vipers and whitewashed tombs, of hypocrites who falsely called themselves sons and daughters of Abraham. In his vision the whole of humanity was blessed and vivified by the same call and mission. Bringing us together would heal all of us. It is the reason he called himself a physician, a healer, as we will see in the next chapter.

For Reflection

1. In 1948 the Nobel Prize-winning astronomer Sir Fred Hoyle said: "Once a photograph of the earth, taken from the outside, is available . . . a new idea as powerful as any in history will be let loose." Discuss.

2. The photographs Hoyle asked for have since been taken. How do they compare with what Abraham and Sarah saw when they were asked by God to look at the stars?

3. Philosopher Karl Popper once wrote that the norm to test a society is its care for its weakest members. What do you think of that norm from Jesus' point of view?

4. We say that "God listens to the cries of the poor." Has this something to do with Jesus' outreach to the marginalized?

CHAPTER 9

Empowering and Liberating Healer

And he said to her, "Daughter, your faith has made you whole; go in peace."

(Luke 8:48)

L uke was most likely a medical doctor. There are many reasons for this traditional belief. One is that he has Jesus introduce himself as a doctor to the villagers in Nazareth. At another time in Luke's gospel Jesus says that he did not come for the healthy, but for the sick. He says this when he is blamed for eating and drinking with sinners. His healing reaches beyond physical and psychological sickness to spiritual defects, addictions, aberrations, and sinfulness. When he sends his disciples out, he gives them his healing power. He sends them out to announce the kingdom, to convert people, to chase evil spirits, and to heal the sick. The gospel is full of his healings. Sometimes he touches people; at other times people touch him. In most of the cases Jesus rounds off his healing by telling the healed ones, "Your faith has healed you." It is something in the sick persons that makes them whole again. This does not mean that he does not do anything to them. He does, but the healing he brings about also has something to do with the sick person in question, or sometimes with people related to them. It always has.

THE POWER OF FAITH

Healing comes from a power within. The doctor plays the role of a midwife, trying to help us give birth to the energy and the life power that will overcome our illness. Healing differs from chasing something away. You can chase away an evil spirit, but you can't chase away a physical sickness. It has to be healed from within. When that inner restorative power is not present there can be no healing. Jesus often calls that power faith. Mark tell us that once in his own region Jesus could not work any "mighty work" (Mk 6:5), because the people in question refused to tap that power in themselves. It is a power he finds in people written off by their fellow citizens and their religious leaders, in lepers and people born blind, deaf, and mute. He finds it in a Roman officer, a Samaritan woman, a Syro-Phoenician mother. He is a healer to them all, empowering them to stand up, walk, see, hear, speak, and react. He not only prompts physical healing in this way, but he helps victims to overcome their addictions.

ZACCHAEUS

Luke gives us a case study of this in the story of Zacchaeus, the money-addicted tax collector. Before he left his house he carefully locked his money box, the drawer in which he kept his money box, the door of his office, and finally the door of the building. He was rich, a chief tax collector, and small of stature. His smallness was not only of body. Between the lines of the story we can read that his self-esteem was not much bigger. Maybe he even hated himself; people who are only after money often do. No wonder that the people in town considered him to be just plain mean.

Zacchaeus knows that he will have no chance to see Jesus, being so small and hated. Nobody is going to make room for him in the front row. So he climbs up into a tree to see Jesus. And Jesus looks up and calls Zacchaeus down, saying, "Today I am going to stay in your house." Zacchaeus came down as quickly as he could; he practically fell out of the tree in his haste to receive Jesus well. At once the people around begin to murmur, "He is staying with a man who is no good." Jesus responds, "He is also a son of Abraham!" By saying this he touches in the addict Zacchaeus his real worth, the old vision, which he has lost in his life. Stimulating that vision, teasing it out, he makes Zacchaeus alive to himself, so that he even reevaluates his view of money, "Lord, half of my goods I give to the poor, and if I have wrongfully exacted anything from anyone, I will restore it fourfold." Zacchaeus is himself again and on his way to Abraham's vision!

THE GOOD NEWS FROM WITHIN

Jesus often speaks about the fish that has to be caught, the pearl that has to be found, the treasure that has to be dug out, or producing things from a cupboard that holds all kinds of things, old and new. He is constantly helping others to do that fishing, finding, digging, and producing from within themselves. He is a passionate believer in the good work God did when putting us together. The good news he brings reminds us of our often forgotten common divine origin. Notwithstanding all that has happened to the human family and its world, God remains faithful. The divine breath blown into all of us from the very beginning never has left us. The divine spark might be smoldering almost invisibly under piles of ashes, but the spark is still there. One of the most touching descriptions of Jesus' renewing activity is when Matthew applies to him this old prophecy of Isaiah:

> He will not shout or cry out, or raise his voice in the streets. A bruised reed he will not break, and a smoldering wick he will not snuff out, till he leads justice to victory (Mt 12:20; Is 42:3).

THE ADULTEROUS WOMAN

Another occurrence, this one in the gospel of John, also illustrates Jesus' approach well. It is the incident of the adulterous woman. Let us analyze what happens in this story. It is early in the morning when Jesus comes to the Temple. He does not enter it but sits down somewhere near by. Some people surround him, and he begins teaching them, telling stories and asking questions. At some point they hear noise in the distance, a threatening noise, the noise of an excited crowd. Then they see a group of men with stones and sticks in their hands surrounding someone whom they push and pull about. As the group gets nearer, the people around Jesus can see what is going on. A riotous group of men are manhandling a woman, who hardly manages to keep herself upright. She obviously has had no time to get properly dressed. Her husband had come home unexpectedly and caught her with another man, who escaped. She was caught. Neighbors joined the commotion, elders and some Pharisees were called in, and the mob decided to stone her outside the city. Then one of the Pharisees got an idea. Why not use this woman to trap Jesus? He proposed to the others that they take her to Jesus to ask whether they should stone her to death. Whatever answer Jesus would give, he reckoned, could afterward be used against him. If he said, "Yes, stone her!" that story could be told all over

the country. If he said, "No, don't stone her!" the story
would be that Jesus did not obey God's law given to Moses,
to stone such a woman.

The group arrives before Jesus, who hardly looks up.
They tell him what happened and ask him what he suggests
they do. Jesus remains sitting while he doodles with his finger in the sand before him. They don't let him off so easily.
They insist. They want an answer. Finally he stands up. He
then looks at the men, some of whom already have stones
in their hands. He says, "Let him who is without sin throw
the first stone." It is silent for a moment. They are caught
by surprise. They had not expected this answer. The oldest
one in the group walks away, dropping his stone alongside
the road. Another one follows him. Then several walk out of
the group at the same time. More and more of them leave,
and finally Jesus is standing there with only the woman,
disheveled, debased, scared to death, and visibly in shock.
He looks at her and asks, "Did anyone condemn you? Did
anyone throw a stone?" She answers, "No, Sir." He then
says, "I won't condemn you either, go home and don't sin
anymore."

Jesus does the same thing to both the woman and the
men. He tells the woman not only to go, but also to change
her life. While she must have loathed herself, standing there
in her shame before Jesus, Jesus touches in her the possibility to be good and do better. He does the same to the
men around her. Why did the oldest one leave first? It might
be that he remembered that he too had sinned; maybe he
too had committed adultery during his life. It might also be
that he reasoned differently. Jesus said, "If any one of you
is without sin—if any one of you is good, just, and righteous—let him throw the first stone." If a person is really
good and righteous, would he be able to take up a stone
and throw it at the soft face, the eye, the head, the breast,
the belly, or the mouth of that woman? He couldn't, could
he? Jesus appealed to the goodness in the men, just as he
did for the woman. They understood, and they left.

ENKINDLING THE DIVINE SPARK

However high the ashes of sins and mistakes are piled in a person's life, Jesus always discovers under those ashes the original fire put there by God. He not only sees it, but he remains faithful to it and tries to rekindle it by blowing new spirit into it. He does what Isaiah foretold he would do:

Forget the former things, do not dwell on the past.
See, I am doing a new thing! Now it springs up, do
you not perceive it? I am making a way in the desert
and streams in the wasteland (Is 43:18).

The healer Jesus finds sufficient divine spark in all of us to activate our healing from within. He is an empowering healer. He does not write off anyone; he is not able to do so. His vision, the same vision Abraham and Sarah began to perceive, did not permit that. Everyone created is charged with the same divine breath, the same fire, the same hope. We all belong to the same reality; it is together that we form the full picture. Jesus did not come only to heal us as individuals. He came to empower everyone to be together. We belong together. We are like pieces in a puzzle. From one piece it is difficult or impossible to see the final picture. It is only when all the pieces are together that the picture shows. We form one family, one city, one kingdom, one offspring, one body, one spirit. Yet we are broken and divided against each other as persons, nations, races, tribes, classes, sexes, generations, in our policies and beliefs. Being a gatherer and an empowering healer in this imperfect world means being at the same time a reconciling peace-maker. Considering Jesus' role, our personal mission and that of our community becomes more and more clear.

For Reflection

1. Share an experience from your life in which someone affirmed you exactly when you needed that affirmation. Have you ever encountered Jesus in such a way?

2. Have you ever empowered someone in a difficult situation?

3. Have you ever been "written off" because of your color, class, education, sex, or religion? How did you react? Did you ever feel you interiorized what those others said to some extent?

4. Frantz Fanon, a West Indian psychiatrist who worked in Algeria during the independence struggle in that North African country, treated both victims and their torturers. He noted that human beings could not begin torturing people before calling them "pigs," "vermin," "dogs," or something similar. Can you explain this? Have you ever encountered such a situation?

CHAPTER 10

Reconciling Peace-Maker

Peace be with you! As the Father has sent me, I am sending you.

(John 20:21)

I t is evening. The disciples are sitting in an upper room in Jerusalem — an upper room is always just a bit safer than a room on the first floor. They have locked the doors. They are scared; and they have good reasons for their fears. Certainly they are worried about the people who condemned Jesus. But they are not too sure about Jesus either. From early in the morning of the third day after Jesus' death and hasty burial, women have come to tell them that they have seen Jesus, that the tomb is empty. Some of them have gone to the tomb to check the women's story. They found the tomb empty, but they did not see Jesus (Lk 24:24). Why hasn't he appeared to them? Has he written them off because of their betrayal? Is it over for them as far as Jesus is concerned?

While they are discussing all this, recounting their stories again and again, Jesus comes. He stands in their midst saying to them, "Peace be with you." To identify himself, he shows his hands and feet. He repeats, "Peace be with you" (Jn 20:20-21). By saying this, he overcomes any feelings of rejection or separation they might have felt. In the same breath Jesus gives them the same task, "As the Father has sent me, I am sending you!"

THE WHOLENESS OF THE KINGDOM

When Jewish scholars finalized the Sacred Scriptures, they did not put the story of Abraham and Sarah at the beginning of their book. Instead, they began with the stories about Adam and Eve. Though different, both stories tell that humanity comes from the same womb, that God created all of us in God's image, that we all live from the same divine breath blown into us, and that we—having the same origin—form one family (Gn 1:26-27). The human family forms, together with God and with the rest of creation, one "piece," and that one piece is called "peace" or "shalom."

All through biblical and human history this wholeness has been threatened. The human family broke the original shalom in its world in many ways. Yet the fundamental unity of creation remains intact. God's Word has not returned in vain. God's work cannot be undone. The vision is never lost. Abram and Sarai—the beginnings of the Jewish people—see it; prophets preach it; Mary expects it; Jesus brings it. This wholeness is the basic nature of the kingdom of God.

This is the dynamic we see at work in the life of Jesus, who simply cannot see anyone as separated from him. Even in his most difficult personal moments he sincerely and with all his heart and mind prays for those who are nailing him to the cross, "Father, forgive them, for they do not know what they are doing" (Lk 23:34). This is the reason Jesus tells us to love our enemies. He does not suggest that we won't have any enemies. He had enemies, and we will have them too, but those enemies belong to the wholeness of the human family.

I tell you, love your enemies and pray for those who
persecute you, that you may be children of your
Father in heaven. He causes the sun to rise on the evil
and the good, and sends rain on the righteous and the
unrighteous (Mt 5:44-45; cf. Lk 6:5).

The unjust, too, relate to God, and God relates to them.
Without that relation they would not even get rain—they
would not be able to exist. It is the same dynamic that
makes Jesus sit down with sinners, prostitutes, tax collec-
tors, children, women, pagans, lepers, and all other disen-
franchised people within his reach. He can't help doing it,
aware as he is of how all relate to God and to each other.
He is referring to the same underlying truth about the
human family when he states:

"Love the Lord your God with all your heart and with
all your soul and with all your mind." This is the first
and greatest commandment. And the second is like it:
"Love your neighbor as yourself" (Mt 22:37-38).

THE LIFE OF COMMUNITY

Luke describes this dynamic as reigning in the Christian
communities throughout the Middle East of his time. Such
communities are composed out of all sorts of people. They
organize an interracial soup kitchen in Jerusalem, an economic revision of the way they own their goods to bridge
the gap between rich and the poor, a fund drive among the
well-to-do in Antioch for the poor in Jerusalem, and reconciling, gathering and peace-making missions to the whole of
their world. The same activities we find today in so many
forms in our own communities, activities that make the
Spirit of Jesus the life principle of the community.
Luke was not the only one to be impressed by this

aspect of Jesus' dynamic at work. So was Paul. Paul saw reconciliation as the main role Jesus plays in our world and as the reality we have to work out in the world.

All this is from God, who through Christ reconciled us to himself, and gave us the ministry of reconciliation (2 Cor 5:18-20).

Reconciliation here does not mean a simple mutual agreement after a fight or a difficulty. It is about the peace, the wholeness, the shalom Jesus left us. Paul writes that he has only one message, good news hidden up to then. That good news is that we are one:

There is neither Jew nor Greek, slave nor free, male nor female, for you are all one in Christ Jesus (Gal 3:28).

There is no Greek or Jew, circumcised or uncircumcised, barbarian, Scythian, slave or free, but Christ is all, and is in all (Col 3:11).

Is this the realization of Abram and Sarai's vision, the fulfillment of Isaiah's prophecies and Mary's hope? It is, and at the same time it is not. The dynamism in our Christian communities, and in our own personal spirituality, is caused by that discrepancy. The reality of our reconciled and restored original oneness has not yet fully unfolded. It is the mystery of the kingdom, which is already here and is not yet here. We are reconciled, we are restored, but the effect of all this has still to be applied in our concrete human situations. Humanity has been breaking the original shalom in this world in many ways, but for God the fundamental unity of creation has never been broken. Jesus lived that original unity of the whole human family and of all creation. He realized Abraham and Sarah's vision, the expectation of Isaiah and the other prophets, and he fulfilled the hope of his mother Mary. His followers were not so advanced. Their journey—and ours—is not yet over.

Driven by Jesus' dynamics at work in them, they started the soup kitchen in Jerusalem. His dynamism led them to organize their new ministry to the poor, but within a few weeks they failed. The best of the soup was given to Hebrew widows, while the Gentile ones got the thin of the soup (Acts 6:1). Discrimination crept in. Driven by the same spirit of Jesus they tried to overcome the problem by a reorganization of the service. They chose deacons, with Stephen as their director.

The Corinthians received the good news about their oneness from no one less than Paul. But in no time they had to face up to the fact that they were divided (1 Cor 1:12). They could not even celebrate the breaking of the bread and the sharing of the wine in an orderly way (1 Cor 11:20-23). Paul has to write them to be faithful to the spirit of Jesus.

Even Paul does not succeed in realizing the oneness he preaches. Jesus' dynamic makes him write that men and women are equal, but then he adds, "Women should keep their heads covered and their mouths shut." He notes that the time of masters and slaves is over, yet he states, "Slaves should submit to their masters."

BUT SUCCESS IS ASSURED

Our own communities are full of the same discrepancies. We believe in the unity of all people, and yet in our political and economic structures we hardly take it into account. We confess that all people are equal, yet in our relations to the poor and the wretched in this world that belief often falls flat. Jesus' reconciling peace-making smolders in our hearts, but it seems to get covered under the ashes of personal or communal war and strife.

It is difficult to find a fitting comparison for this tension between the "already" and "not yet" of this shalom, of Jesus' reconciling peace-making, of the kingdom of God. Perhaps it can be compared to a choir wrestling with a difficult piece of music, rehearsing and repeating, failing and trying, stumbling and impatient. The music is there. The singing is not yet what it should be, but because the melody is set and on paper, the stumbling will end and final success is assured.

Others also struggle to express the same reality. A Hindu guru will try to overcome the difference between what is and what is not yet by using the image of the unfolding of a lotus flower. Or the already and not yet of the kingdom can perhaps be compared to what Jacques Rivette, a film maker, once said of a good film, "A film is interesting only if you have this feeling that the film pre-exists and that you are trying to reach it." The essence is in us, and it is not. We have to be helped from outside to find it in ourselves.

Something of the kind happened at Pentecost when the international crowd in the streets of Jerusalem listened to Peter and said, "How is it that we understand what he says each one in his own language?" It was not only that they heard him in their own vernacular or dialect, but that he spoke their language in the sense that they recognized things that now seemed always to have been hidden in the recesses of their own hearts and minds.

Do these examples and analogies help clarify the dynamic tension between the already and not yet of the kingdom of God? Maybe. Jesus struggled with the same difficulty. He left us a multitude of analogies, parables, stories, examples, and signs to express his intentions, his spirit, and his dynamism. Finally, he put his life on the line to bridge the difference, to realize his vision, that vision that had sustained his people from Abraham to his mother Mary.

For Reflection

1. Why did Jesus say:

"When you are bringing your offering to the altar and there remember that your brother or sister has something against you, leave your offering there before the altar, go and be reconciled with your brother or sister first and then come and present your offerings" (Mt 5:23-25)?

2. Is there any reason to stress the peace-making aspects of our mission as Christians in our world? What organizations specialize in this task?

3. Some parishes organize reconciliation or mediation teams to help people avoid legal procedures against each other. Has your Christian community—your family, your religious community, or your parish—ever entered the work of reconciliation? Why? What was the outcome?

4. Comment on Corrie ten Boom's story about meeting after a church service she had led one of the SS guards who had terrorized her in a concentration camp:

He came up to me as the church was emptying, beaming and bowing. "How grateful I am for your message, Fraulein," he said. "To think that as you say, He washed my sins away!" His hand was thrust out to shake mine. And I, who had preached so often to the people in Bloemendaal the need to forgive, kept my hand at my side. Even as the angry, vengeful thoughts boiled through me, I saw the sin of them . . . I prayed, forgive me and help me to forgive him. I tried to smile, I struggled to raise my hand. I could not. I felt nothing, not the slightest spark of warmth or charity. And so again I breathed a prayer. "Jesus, I cannot forgive him. Give me your forgiveness."

As I took his hand the most incredible thing happened. From my shoulder along my arm and through my hand a current seemed to pass from me to him, whole into my heart sprang a love for this stranger that almost overwhelmed me.

And so I discovered that it is not on our forgiveness any more than on our goodness that the world's healing hinges, but on His. When he tells us love our enemies, He gives, along with the command, the love itself.[1]

5. Comment on the following:

Most of the time, we bypass forgiveness. Most of the time . . . we race with lightning speed from our hurts to reconciliation without taking a look at what must be forgiven before lasting healing can take place.[2]

CHAPTER 11

Signs, Symbols, and Reality

Interpret the signs of the times.

(Matthew 16:3)

T he crowds around Jesus constantly asked, "Tell us, when will these things happen? What will be the sign that they are about to be fulfilled?" (Mk 13:4). "Teacher, we want to see a miraculous sign from you!" (Mt 12:8). His disciples also ask at moments when they are alone with him, " 'Tell us,' they said, 'when will this happen, and what will be the sign of your coming and the end of the age?' " (Mt 24:3). Understandable questions. Jesus promised them the kingdom of God, the year of grace, but not much seemed to happen. Jesus faced the same difficulty. He could point to himself as the fulfillment of the kingdom, but the world at large seemed to remain unchanged. His whole life was a sign of things to come. He overcame in his own life the paradox between the already and not yet of God's reign in a world that still has to overcome that tension.

JESUS—FAITHFUL TO THE VISION

After living thirty years as a carpenter in the village of Nazareth, he heard a voice calling him to be baptized by

John at the River Jordan. The Holy Spirit activated in him the fullness of God's vision for the whole of creation. What Abraham and Sarah had vaguely foreseen, what the prophets had foretold, and what his mother Mary and the group around her had firmly expected, found its fulfillment in him. He fought the temptation to live this fullness only for himself—a temptation any one of us has when discovering a special gift or skill of any significance. He overcame the temptation, came out of the desert, and turned to the others in his world, faithful to the vision. Healing the sick; curing the afflicted; addressing crowds and telling fascinating stories; capturing the attention of thousands and thousands; speaking to women; hailing street children; sitting at table with the rich and the poor; listening to young and old; making the blind see, the deaf hear, the dumb speak, the lame walk; raising the dead; liberating the addicted; returning Lazarus to his family and an only son to a widow; cleaning out the Temple, declaring it a place of prayer for all nations; expressing his amazement at the faith of Jews and Gentiles alike; not only caring for the powerless but empowering them; straightening out the bent-over woman; helping an adolescent girl through her crisis; appreciating and praising the old widow; promoting the human/divine dignity of all; gathering around himself people from all over his world, Jews, Greeks, Romans, and Gentiles of all sorts; praying the Our Father; accepting invitations to banquets and weddings; befriending the outcasts; teaching in synagogues and marketplaces; saving the lives of those harassed; weeping and laughing; forming support groups of twelve, of seventy-two, of hundreds and thousands; meeting people afraid of daylight and publicity in the middle of the night; calming storms and making water blush into wine; organizing outings and picnics; traveling to pagan lands; climbing mountains and hills; going to "the other side"; sailing the sea; and finally, walking to the center of it all—Jerusalem. It was a long journey leading him from the hills of Galilee to the

River Jordan, and on to a hill outside Jerusalem called Golgotha.

The journey led even further. It led to the promised New Jerusalem itself. He laid down his life to attest that he was absolutely sure of the fulfillment of that vision. His willingness to die for his cause in the certainty that he would rise from the tomb is the ultimate and absolute sign he gave. He was willing to die for what he believed in, because he was so sure of God's loving promise that he would not remain dead. His willingness to accept his Passover is his answer to all their pleas for a sign.

> None will be given it except the sign of the prophet Jonah. For as Jonah was three days in the belly of a huge fish, so the son of Man will be three days and three nights in the heart of the earth (Mt 12:39-40; Mt 16:4).

He does not give that answer only once. In both the gospels of Matthew and Luke Jesus gives the answer twice, mentioning the sign of Jonah and applying it to himself. In John's gospel Jesus is more direct. Asked what sign he will give to prove his insight and authority, he speaks of his own body: "Destroy this temple, and I will raise it again in three days" (Jn 2:19). Answering them, he betrays at the same time his exasperation with their blindness to the sign he gave by his life itself by telling them, "A wicked and adulterous generation asks for a miraculous sign!" (Mt 12:39).

JESUS' DYNAMISM

The dynamism in Jesus' life can be explained by his living *here* and *now* the final fulfillment to come. It is more than living ahead of his time. It is living the vision now, at this very moment. It is the dynamism he wants to spark off in his disciples. How could he explain what made his heart burn? How could he explain to those around him that the same love and the consequent reaching out to the New City, the great Gathering, the final Homecoming, the ultimate Healing, the promised Peace and Justice, and the complete Fulfillment could be found within them? How could he rouse in them—from within themselves—the dynamic tension that made him the one he was, is, and always will be? He had to awaken the presence of this dynamism and its effects in the human family.

Jesus' eagerness to make himself understood led to an abundance of creative imagery. The images almost tumble over each other. In the gospels he calls the New Jerusalem that Abraham and Sarah saw, the prophets foretold, and Mary expected, the kingdom of God or the kingdom of heaven. He does that over a hundred times. He compares it to a treasure found in a piece of land. He tells how the finder hid it again, and then, full of joy, went and sold all he had to buy the land with the treasure. The kingdom of God is like a fish swimming in the dark of our subconscious, waiting to be caught and brought into the light of day. It is a pearl found by a merchant, who sells all he has to obtain it. It is like a fishing net thrown out in the ocean and bringing together all its fish. It is like the seed sowed in a field. It is like a tiny mustard seed, which grows into the largest of garden plants. It is like yeast working its way all through a large amount of flour. The one who hears about the kingdom of God is like a householder who brings out of his storeroom new treasures as well as old. The kingdom is like a landowner hiring people to bring in the harvest, a king inviting guests for a feast, a bridegroom waiting for the bride, bridesmaids waiting for the arrival of the bride and bridegroom, a whole party waiting for the wedding party to begin—as Mary once did at Cana!

THE ALREADY AND NOT YET

In those analogies and examples Jesus speaks about a reality that is present—the treasure, the pearl, the fish, the harvest, the seed, the provisions in the pantry. At the same time it is not yet present. It has to be found, dug out, bought, caught, gathered, developed. All these examples point at an already and a not yet! They all indicate a dynamic tension, something to be done, a process spread out over time, a goal to be reached, a journey to be made, a mission to be accomplished. They explain his own dynamism and his own life. They explain why he said of himself — at the peak of his activity —

"As long as it is day, we must do the work of him who sent me. Night is coming, when no one can work. While I am in the world I am the light of the world" (Jn 9:4-5).

He lived the kingdom to the full in his life; he was the Light. The dynamism that charged his life had to be made active in the whole of the human family. God remained faithful to the original nature of the covenants made between Yahweh and the human family. The outcome would be the result of a process in which both God and humanity continued to be involved. Jesus was not going to take over the process. In him the kingdom of God definitely broke into this world. But humanity would have to join the process to make it its own.

To explain this to people who expected him to start the kingdom of God once and for all among them remained a problem, notwithstanding all his parables and stories. His listeners simply did not understand, or they did not want what he offered. He must have felt especially frustrated at his last gathering with them — the last supper. How could he explain his personal feelings and insights to his confused and mistaken friends during a meal that he knew would be their last one before his Passover?

Just imagine yourself in that situation. Don't be afraid to compare yourself to Jesus. The author of the letter to the

Hebrews wrote that Jesus is "just as we are, except for sin" (Heb 4:15). Remember the story about the woman in front of that burning house in Melbourne, the one who said, "Just put yourself for a moment in their—in this case, in his—position." Just put yourself for a moment in Jesus' position at the last supper. What would you do? We know what he did.

After having washed their feet to show his love and to give them an example of how to relate to each other, he gives a second farewell gesture after the Passover meal is over. In Mark's and in Luke's versions he takes some bread, gives thanks, breaks it, passes it around and says, "Take and eat, this is my body"; he then takes the cup, gives thanks and passes it to his friends, saying, "Drink from it all of you, this is my blood of the covenant that is poured for many" (Mk 14:22-23). In Matthew's gospel Jesus adds to these last words "for the forgiveness of sins" (Mt 26:28). In Luke's version he adds "do this in remembrance of me" (Lk 22:19).

By doing this, Jesus expresses his divine/human love for them. He gives himself to them and for them, and he asks them to do the same. He asks them to *"eat and drink him,"* to share his vision and dedication to God's dream for the human family and the whole of creation. He asks them—and us—to live his life, to set out on our journey to the New Jerusalem, healing, gathering, reconciling, and peace-making.

At the last supper Jesus lived the kingdom of God to the full, as he always had done. For a moment his disciples did so as well. When they ate that bread, and drank that wine, they shared in that fullness. They formed the one body, not mystically but really, concretely, though in a sign. During the eucharist the sign of the kingdom of God is at the same time reality and fulfillment. It still is, when we celebrate it. During its celebration we are one body, one blood, one spirit—his body, his blood, his spirit. Every one of us is able to witness to that reality. For a moment the fights are over, the differences healed, the past overcome.

ONE BRIEF GLIMPSE

My most vivid memory of this sharing recalls a Christmas night during the Second World War in the occupied Netherlands. The military commander of the town where I lived lifted the curfew to allow us to go to Midnight Mass. Just before the eucharist a group of German soldiers marched into the church to celebrate with us. No upright Dutch man or woman would ever associate, let alone eat, with them. As kids we stole from them whatever we could, but when they offered us some candy, remembering their own children at home, we would never accept anything, preferring to spit in their faces. At communion time they came to kneel with us at the communion rail—as we did in those days—and nobody objected to those soldiers being there. For a moment all was as it one day will be. We were not enemies. We were interconnected. We were, for a brief moment, at the end of our common journey.

The final gathering, the ultimate reconciliation, the definitive shalom were all realized "already." The future had become real and present just for a moment, just as it always had been in the life of Jesus.

> Clearly he didn't just believe in it [the Kingdom of God] or wish for it. He "knew" it, and spoke with the authority that only direct experience can give. For Jesus the absent, the far off had become real and present—present enough for him to stake his life on it.[1]

THE OTHER SIDE OF GOODNESS

Jesus put his life on the line to prove that he was right in his vision, that God guaranteed it. Many of the people under his cross understood that his vision was at stake. They wanted to kill it; they wanted to kill him. It was not the first time they wanted to do this. In his own village they had wanted to kill him two or three years before.

It is not difficult to guess why so many reacted in such a negative way. There is always a kind of "flip side" to any manifestation of goodness, whether it is the goodness of someone like Mother Teresa or the integrity of someone you work with. There is a flip side to the goodness manifest in Jesus too, a serious one, a sinful one. His very goodness can be an obstacle to accepting him. The people who applauded him at his triumphant entry into Jerusalem condemned him some days later. Jesus shows us who we can be, if we want to. He is a challenge to our integrity and to our life—a challenge that is not always and to everyone welcome. He is, as John already wrote, light in our darkness. But not all darkness is willing to accept the light!

That is why they wanted to undo him. They desperately wanted to prove to themselves that he was wrong in his vision and his expectation. It was the only thing they could do to him, their ultimate test. At the peak of his agony he shouted, "My God, my God, why have you forsaken me?" But God did not forsake him or the reality he stood for. He passed the test. Peter was the first one to put into words what happened, when he said at Pentecost:

> With the help of wicked men you put him to death, by nailing him to the cross. But God raised him from the dead, freeing him from the agony of death, because it was impossible for death to keep its hold on him (Acts 2:24).

VINDICATION OF A DREAM

Jesus is not the only one vindicated at the moment of his resurrection. So were Abraham and Sarah, in beginning their journey to the New Jerusalem, the Jerusalem of the Nations. So were the prophets, with their vision of a kingdom of justice and peace. So was his mother Mary, in her willingness to give birth to him. So were so many others, who had been waiting for him. Death did not overcome what lived in their hearts and their minds. Death could not overcome the dynamism of God's project, the dynamism that is present in the communities in which his Spirit lives on. The Spirit makes him present among us, while he himself is absent. The Spirit lives in the hearts and minds of all who have a sense of justice, peace, and love, and who yearn for the newness to come. The Spirit overcomes the temptation to leave things as they are. The Spirit moves us on. Jesus himself was tempted to leave things as they were. He did not give in. He remained faithful to the vision. So should we.

For Reflection

1. Can you think of any place where the reality of the kingdom of God is transparent in our world? Can you name any persons who are examples of this transparency?

2. Do you consider yourself as living a covenant with God? If so, what does that mean in your life?

3. Discuss the following story:

   While distributing communion I noticed that one of the eucharistic ministers walked away. After some time she came back. After the service she asked, "Did you see me walking away?" When I answered that I had noticed, she told me that she and her teenage daughter had had a terrible week. They had offended each other and had not spoken since.
   That morning the daughter had stayed in bed when the mother came to church. At least that is what she thought. But when she was distributing holy commun-

ion, she saw her daughter lining up in front of her to receive the sacrament. Her daughter could have lined up in front of any of the other eucharistic ministers, but she chose her line. When she gave her daughter the host, she was so moved that she began to cry and had to walk away for a while to regain her composure. The eucharist brought them together again.

4. What do you think of the following argument?

In the '60s a Latin American Catholic priest, Camillo Torres, decided that he could not celebrate the eucharist anymore in a country where people were divided, the rich oppressing the poor, while the church was not willing to tackle this issue. He joined the guerrilla fighters. After having made his decision, he met liberation theologian Gustavo Gutiérrez, who told Camillo that he was not a good theologian, that he misunderstood the significance of the celebration of the eucharist. "In a time like this," Gutiérrez reasoned, "the eucharist is all we have, it is the model of all to come." He apparently did not convince Camillo Torres, who was killed as a freedom fighter some time later.

5. Answer the question at the end of the following quotation: If a person could pass through paradise in a dream, and have a flower presented to him as a pledge that he had already been there, and if he found that flower in his hand when he awoke—'Ay! and what then?[2]

CHAPTER 12

Initiation, Spirit, and Mission

*Go and make disciples of all nations, baptizing
them in the name of the Father, the Son, and of
the Holy Spirit . . . and surely I am with you
always, to the very end of the age.*
                                        (Matthew 28:19-20)

T here are several versions of what happened when
Jesus was baptized by John the Baptist. Matthew
and Mark note that the event occurred "when he
came up out of the water" (Mt 3:16; Mk 1:10).
Luke writes that it happened after his baptism while he was
praying (Lk 3:21). In John's gospel we read that John the
Baptist saw "the Spirit come down from heaven and remain
on him" (Jn 1:32-34). Then there was the voice that said,
"You are my beloved son," indicating God's absolute near-
ness.

REALIZATION OF THE VISION

However and whenever it happened, Jesus' baptism by
John changed his life. It did not change his person, but it
definitely changed his self-awareness—a change so formida-
ble that he needed forty days to get settled and consoli-

dated in this newness. It was an initiation in living the fullness of God's Spirit. Coming out of the desert, he is the presence of God's kingdom in this world. He is the realization of all Abraham and Sarah, the prophets, his mother, Mary, John the Baptist's mother, Elizabeth, and all the poor in spirit, had been hoping and living for. The fullness of the divine dynamism, so openly revealed in him, had to be sparked off in his disciples. They, too, had to find the treasure, the pearl, the fish, the yeast, the salt, the fire, the seed, life, spirit, and God in themselves. They had to see, to hear, to speak, to walk, to smell, and to touch it for themselves. They had to change, to grow up, to turn around, to convert. The kingdom of God had to begin in them, too. To enable them in this was his mission and task, the intention of his life, death, and resurrection. That is why he had come. It was the lesson of all his stories, parables, and examples.

It is also the main topic in the long and repetitive conversations he has with his disciples during the last days of his life. They are upset when he tells them that he is going to leave. What are they going to do without him? He assures them that he will not leave them alone. He insists that it is good for them that he goes. If he doesn't go, they will remain staring at him, like children at their parents. They will never experience and realize that they themselves are empowered by his Spirit. "It is good for you that I go!" (Jn 16:7). He promises them "another advocate," the Holy Spirit, who will be with them while he is physically away (Jn 16:13-15). He assures them that they will be able to do what he himself has been doing and "even greater things than these" (Jn 14:12).

THE VISION WITHIN US

What happened to Jesus during his baptism by John should happen to us during our baptism. That is what he meant when he told his disciples that they would be baptized with the Holy Spirit (Acts 1:5). He wants us to do what he did. He wants us to share in his experience of the Holy Spirit, who always had been present in his life but became visible to all after his baptism. We have to help others share in what Jesus himself experienced in his own life, the realization that the divine longing for the justice, peace, and love of the kingdom of God is living in all and everyone. He put this experience in words when he prayed with his disciples, "Our Abba in heaven . . . your kingdom come, your will be done" (Mt 6:9). This prayer introduced a new covenant between God and humanity.

OUR MISSION — TOGETHER

The disciples are charged with a mission, his mission. They are sent as he was sent (Jn 20:21). They had to begin in the whole of the world what he had begun in them by his deeds and his words (Jn 15:3). They are to help others flush out in themselves their deepest longing, the treasure, the pearl, their value, their worth, their dignity, their center, the kingdom of God — the vision. At the end of the gospel of Matthew Jesus makes that mission explicit at his last meeting with them before he ascends to heaven:

> Go and make disciples of all nations, baptizing them in the name of the Father, the Son, and of the Holy Spirit (Mt 28:19).

The whole of the human family has to be initiated in the reality that all have one and the same divine Parent, that we are created in one and the same Offspring, and that we are all vivified by one and the same Spirit. The Trinitarian formula Matthew reports tells us about the life of God. It tells us also how God relates to us and how we relate to God.

Anyone among us is of divine origin (Gn 1:27). We are all created together as God's offspring in the Son (Jn 1:1-4); we are living from the same divine Spirit breathed in us from the beginning (Gn 2:7). It is a relationship that not only defines us, but it is at the same time a reality we have to work out in our world. As Catholic African President Julius Nyerere of Tanzania once said:

> We say the human being was created in the image of God. I refuse to imagine a God who is miserable, poor, ignorant, superstitious, fearful, oppressed and wretched. If a human being is really the temple of God, we have to do something about the flies in the eyes of a child, as those flies are ruining God's temple.[1]

The baptismal formula is — like the eucharistic breaking of the bread and sharing of the wine — an action program. It is a political issue. It is an economic task. It is a spiritual issue. It is a social plan. It is the charter of the kingdom of God. It is what empowers us. It is the reality Jesus lived in his life. It is the kind of life he led his disciples to discover in themselves. It is the life he asked them to witness to in such a way that others would feel it vibrate within them too. It is the kingdom of God in and among us. It is a life to be actualized in everyone. It is the reason we are equipped with his Spirit:

> What was once preached by the Lord, or what was once wrought in Him for the saving of the human race, must be proclaimed and spread abroad to the ends of the earth (Acts 1:8), beginning from Jerusalem (cf. Lk 24:47). Thus, what He once accomplished for the salvation of all may in the course of time come to achieve its effect in all.
>   To accomplish this goal, Christ sent the Holy Spirit

from the Father. The Spirit was to carry out His saving
work inwardly and to impel the Church toward her
proper expansion. Doubtless, the Holy Spirit was
already at work in the world before Christ was glorified.
Yet on the day of Pentecost, He came down upon the
disciples to remain with them forever (cf. Jn 14:16).
On that day the Church was publicly revealed to the
multitude, the gospel began to spread among the
nations by means of preaching, and finally there
occurred a foreshadowing of that union of all peoples
in a universal faith.[2]

THE ORIGINS OF MISSION

Jesus gave us that assignment. But we aren't only "in
mission" because Jesus commanded it. There is another
dynamism at work—the dynamism of people who are aware
of the Spirit of Jesus in themselves and in their communities. To be "charged" with Jesus' Spirit means being taken
up in a process, a process of a cross-cultural gathering of
all the nations and the whole of creation, a process that
reaches from the vision of Abraham and Sarah to the fulfillment at the end of time.

When the Second Vatican Council began to discuss mission, the participants were given a working paper that had
been prepared for them. It spoke about the "apostolic origin
of Mission." The council did not accept this description of
mission as starting with the apostles. The true origin of mission goes far back beyond the apostles to the old covenants
with Moses, Abraham and Sarah, Noah, and Adam and Eve.
It reaches back into the depths of the divine life. It is rooted
and grounded in the heart of every single human being. It
might be hidden, it might be swimming in the dark, but it is
there.

When Jesus prays at the last supper "that they all may be

one," he adds "just as you are in me, and I am in you" (Jn 17:21). Mission does not concern only Jesus Christ; it goes back to the creative and loving process of the three Persons in the Blessed Trinity. Mission describes a life we all share, the purpose of the church, a process in which Jesus played a decisive role here on earth.

> The Mission of the Church is not derived in the first place from humanity's need of salvation; its primary source is in God self, who as Living Love, has an inner necessity to give self. Like Jesus, and in the spirit of Jesus, the Church lives by this divine compulsion. Seen in this way, mission is not so much the Church's task as an expression of her very being, God is self-giving love. The Church is the fruit of this love, and can only be herself when she brings it to expression by what she is, before she embarks on any works or enterprises.
>
> The necessity of mission flows from the very nature of the Church, willed by God to carry out the mission of the Son under the impulsion of the Holy Spirit. . . . *All Christians have within them a dynamism directed towards this end. This dynamism is nothing other than the action of the love of God within them, operating by the Spirit* (emphasis added).[3]

Mission is a process all of us are engaged in when we are faithful to the divine-human dynamism at work in ourselves, being — like him — gatherers, reconcilers, peacemakers, empowerers, and healers, and at the same time, willing to be gathered, reconciled, empowered, and healed ourselves. And this leads to the second part of this book.

For Reflection

1. We usually don't think of the Trinity as Parent, Offspring, and Spirit. Do those titles help shed light on our relation with God and with others? Discuss.

2. There are different forms of baptism: by pouring water over the head or by total immersion in water. Those different forms lead to different explanations. Pouring water over the head leads to the idea of cleansing; baptism by immersion calls up the image of going with Jesus from death to life through the tomb. Which form do you prefer? Why?

3. Baptism is an initiation rite. Though we have initiation rites in our society, it is in older societies that we can find them in all their significance.

   For example, many African societies initiate boys and girls into adult life when they reach the age and the physical maturity to marry. Both boys and girls go through a ceremony—a rite of passage—in which they undergo some bodily hardship to introduce them to the rigor and discipline of adult life. This initiation into adulthood indicates that life as a child is over. One ethnic group circumcises them, another tattoos their faces, a third pierces their ears. Those rites do not make the young people physically able to be mothers or fathers. Their bodily growth has already taken care of that. However, they were not allowed to *function* as such before being initiated. Their initiation formalizes and actualizes their bodily maturity.

   Does presenting baptism as an initiation rite help explain what happens during baptism?

4. In a talk given at Woodstock College in 1966 biblical scholar Raymond Brown is reported to have said, "The Holy Spirit is the presence of Jesus when Jesus is absent." What do you think of that statement?

5. Would the followers of Jesus Christ have engaged in mission even if he had not ordered them explicitly to do so? Explain.

Part II

FANNING THE FLAME

CHAPTER 13

Our Mission: Challenges and Priorities

That all of them, Father, may be one, just as you are in me and I in you.

(John 17:21)

P eople attentive to the Spirit in them don't need Jesus' command in order to engage in his mission. God's loving Spirit will move them. The same impelling force made Abraham and Sarah leave their home and enabled Moses to lead his people. The Spirit inspired the scribes to tell the story of Eve and Adam, the prophets to write their visions, and Mary to accept her child, Jesus. The same dynamism made Jesus live, die, and rise. Those key figures and many others—too many to name or even to count—engaged in a world to which we are now the heirs. Now it is our turn to move on, to gather, and to heal. We know and feel that. We too share the vision of the New Jerusalem. As one of the most forceful statements of the Second Vatican Council tells us:

The joys and the hopes, the grief and the anxieties of the people of this age, especially those who are poor or in any way afflicted, these too are the joys

and hopes, the griefs and anxieties of the followers
of Christ. Indeed, nothing genuinely human fails to
raise an echo in their hearts. For theirs is a community of human beings. United in Christ they are led
by the Holy Spirit, in their journey to the Kingdom
of their Father, and they have welcomed the news of
salvation which is meant for every human being.
That is why this community realizes that it is truly
and intimately linked with the human family and its
history.[1]

FAILING IN MISSION

It is a pity that this text speaks about us in the third person: "United in Christ, *they* are led . . ." It would have been
better to speak about ourselves in the first person: "United
in Christ, *we* are led . . ." The text speaks about us, about
all of us. Who among us has not sighed upon seeing the
many human conflicts in our world? Those clashes change
from place to place and from time to time, yet they can be
found all over the world all the time. At the present time
parts of Europe, Asia, Africa, and South America are
involved in bloody civil war and unrest. The cities in many
Western nations are divided between the poor and the rich.
Drugs, gang wars, and street robberies keep the old and the
young out of the streets and the parks. The youngest and
the oldest—always the most vulnerable in any society—are
repeatedly neglected and abused. Families are disintegrat-
ing. Individuals find it increasingly difficult to maintain their
moral integrity, self-worth, and meaning. The old dream of
Abraham and Sarah, the prophecy of so many prophets, the
readiness of Mary to serve, and Jesus' death and resurrection seem irrelevant. The old song of the good news is
rarely heard and hardly distinguishable in all the noise and
uproar.

Yet the good news is the melody Pope John Paul II sang in a long encyclical on mission entitled *Redemptoris Missio* (*The Redeemer's Mission*), which was published in 1991. The "song line" is something of a lament. The author is clearly upset. *Redemptoris Missio* is the letter of someone who is convinced that he, and the church he is shepherding, are failing. He writes about "an undeniable negative tendency" and about the fact that "specific missionary activity is waning." Anyone aware of the actual situation would have written in that tone. We *are* failing. Explaining to himself—and his readers—where we fall short, the pope alludes, as Jesus did, to that pervasive vision:

> "That they all may be one . . . so that the world may believe that you have sent me" (Jn 17:21).

We neglect to work toward the oneness Jesus prayed for in the last hours before his death and resurrection. But it is our mission to work at answering that prayer. If we help to make the whole of humanity realize that we are one divine/human family, we will be not only the carriers of good news, but we will be a divine blessing to all. If we manage to do that in Jesus' name, all will see him as the one sent by God. It is interesting to note the order in that quotation, which comes in John's gospel straight from the mouth of Jesus. We should work at that "oneness," so that people will believe in Jesus, and not the other way round! We should *first* show what it is all about, and only then drop the name, as Peter did when he worked his first miracle!

REASONS FOR SADNESS

There are several reasons Pope John Paul II is in a special and personal way sensitive to the sadness of our situation. He has traveled the world as no pope ever did before. Those pilgrimages to local churches have confronted him with human division and sin, war and hunger, lack of respect for human rights and discrimination, squalor and injustice, sickness and powerlessness, and the fact that masses of people have never even heard Jesus' name. All over the world he has heard the cries of those lost in their material poverty and of others lost in their riches.

There is another reason why all this deeply affects him. As a young man he lived for years in utter poverty. His father starved to death during the Second World War. He himself was chased away from the university where he was studying, because the Nazi occupiers considered the Poles an inferior race, not fit to study at a university. They were destined only to serve human beings superior to them. He did forced labor in a quarry and later in a dye factory. He knows from bitter personal experience what it means when one's human dignity is not respected and God's message about humanity is disregarded.

John Paul II is clearly upset because we don't work sufficiently at Jesus' priority. But there is another reason. Again, it is a reason any one of us might have found out for himself or herself. It is the difficulty of our task. Humanity comprises a great variety of human beings, peoples, cultures, religions, and ideologies. In this century, with its devastating and lasting world conflicts, we have begun to experience how different and unequally the parts of the earth relate to one another. Anthropologists, sociologists, economists, political scientists, politicians, philosophers, educators, and journalists agree that bringing humanity together asks for a total change of heart and mind—a conversion—from all of us. Convergence will be difficult because of the different approaches we have developed over the ages. The oneness of the vision, *"e pluribus unum"* ("out of many one") is far from realized.

It will find full expression only in the realization of the gospel message of the kingdom of God.

SEEKING THE VISION

Pope John Paul II refers to that fullness with a reference to Abraham and Sarah. He reminds us of the divine/human vision first seen by Abram and Sarai. Yahweh promised this couple that they, and "all the clans" of the earth going their way, would be blessed (Gn 12:3).[2] Pope John Paul II notes that the final homecoming of the human family is God's dream and God's plan, and that it found its full expression in Jesus. "Jesus himself is the good news . . . not just by what he says or does, but by what he is."[3] He expressed God's promised future in his love for everyone, friends and enemies alike, and especially for those religiously, socially, or economically neglected and marginalized.

According to its shepherd, the church falls short. We are not sufficiently engaged in our empowering, healing, reconciling, and peace-making task. We are not gathering in what Jesus himself called the human harvest. We even fail to proclaim the good news to those who have never heard it. If we fail to work at our mission, the realization of our divine/ human oneness, we are no help to the human family. We aren't responding to Jesus' ideal, and our worship is failing. We are not forming the house of the Lord, and we are not building a real home for the human family either. We are in danger of being only a kind of sectarian group shelter. And a shelter for only some is in the end a shelter for no one at all. We risk not helping to fulfill God's dream and humanity's own deepest yearning.

THE PRACTICE OF MISSION

The encyclical is especially dedicated to the proclamation of the good news to those who have never heard it. It is

about the need to go to the unevangelized, a work missionaries or missioners, male and female, clerical and lay, have
been doing all through the history of the Christian community. There is good reason for the pope to address this
issue. The numbers of persons involved in that work is
steadily declining.

John Paul II does not restrict mission to this going out to
the unevangelized. Mission requires more than proclamation. Our mission is not accomplished at the moment that
the kingdom has been announced; it must be put into practice. The letter speaks about the mission and the work of
those baptized *in the world in which they live.* It insists on
the need of ecumenical contacts with other Christian
denominations. It mentions those who once were Christians,
but are no longer, and who have to find again "The Way" —
as the first communities in the Acts of the Apostles often
called their Christian lifestyle.

In everyday life these different tasks and interests go
together. We can't do one without the other. We will only be
able to bring the human family together if we reach out to
those far away. It is the example Jesus gave on his endless
trips to the other side of the lake and to the foreign areas in
his own neighborhood. We have to contact people and talk
to them. We have to *dialogue.* We—and they—have to
respect in the others their roots, their history, their inspiration, and the seeds God sowed in them from all eternity.
This kind of contact will only make sense if our own community is hope-giving, inspiring, and attractive to them.

"AT HOME" IN THE HOUSE OF THE LORD

It is useless to proclaim the kingdom of God if we are
not building it in our own communities. We have to be seen
as people who are at work at the kingdom of God, a reign
of justice, equality, and peace. We must be people who not

only have the signs and symbols of the one body and the one spirit, but who also are seen trying to realize it in our personal and communal lives. We have to welcome the ones we reach in a way that makes them feel at home with us. We are accustomed to do things in our way; they have their ways. Yet they should feel just as "at home" in the house of the Lord as we do. We will be able to learn a lot from each other. We will enrich each other. We will be surrounding Jesus with our personal and communal gifts, just as John foresaw in Revelation (Rv 21:24). Yet creating this common home will have its unavoidable problems.

It would be difficult to organize this "being at home with the Lord and each other" ideal from the center or from above. It can only come from within those communities themselves. They should be able to sit at the feet of the Lord in their own circle.

If we want to be carried by God's love and vision for humanity and creation, if we want to work at the mission Jesus left us, if we want to be faithful to his spirit in us, if we want to continue the journey Abram and Sarai, Mary and Elizabeth, and so many others began, then our priorities are clear. We are engaged in a gathering, empowering, liberating, healing, reconciling, and peace-making process. This process is not the exclusive task of missionaries or any group in the church, but the task of the whole church, of the people of God. Gathering into the kingdom of God asks for proclamation and dialogue, justice and peace, empowerment and liberation, incarnation and inculturation. All those terms sound lofty and abstract, but their reality touches our daily life. They were the warp and the woof of Jesus' life. And they are the interwoven topics of the next chapters.

For Reflection

1. What conclusion would you draw from the following report by a missionary sister in Lebanon?

I was appointed for mission work in Lebanon. I taught
at a local school. One of my tasks was to prepare
children and adults for baptism. I like teaching and
introducing Jesus in that way. It was not the only
thing I had to do. We had no water in the house in
which I lived together with some other sisters. We
took turns fetching water at a tap some miles from
our house. The water supply consisted of that one
tap, standing alongside the road in a field. It ran only
an hour or so in the morning. The timing was uncer-
tain. You had to go there early to be sure to catch it.
At about nine in the morning a lot of people, mainly
women, assembled around the tap. Most of them
were local Muslim women. Being American made me
really stick out in the crowd. We began talking to one
another. One day a woman said: "You are from America aren't you? There is plenty of water there, why are
you here sitting waiting for it?" I explained to her that
it was my love for Jesus and for them that brought
me there. She was intrigued by my answer, and I suddenly understood what "mission by presence" means.

2. "People today put more trust in witnesses than in teach-
   ers" (*Redemptoris Missio*, no. 43). Do you agree?

3. The liturgical committee in a parish is preparing for
   Christmas. One group of parishioners would like to use
   an advent wreath, another group a picture of Our Lady
   of Guadalupe. What do you think? What would you say/
   do?

4. Have you ever proclaimed Jesus? How did you do it? Or,
   why did you choose not to do so?

CHAPTER 14

How to Proclaim and Dialogue

Were not our hearts burning within us while he talked with us on the road, and opened the Scriptures to us?

(Luke 24:32)

A ll of us have been confronted by people who have tried to force their religious convictions on us. They might have been followers of the Reverend Moon, Hare Krishna chanters, Latter Day Saints, Witnesses of Jehovah, or followers of Jesus Christ. They stand on a soapbox on the corner of a street in Nairobi. They approach us in their black suits in front of the Royal Palace in Amsterdam. They sing their hymns in the market at Brixton in London. They raise their prophetic voice on the steps of the Capitol in Washington, D.C. They might sit next to us in a bus or a plane. We meet them at the front door of our house. Their messages are different, but their approach is the same. They have the truth, and we don't. They assure us that they have the answer for us, though they don't ask for our questions. They proclaim their beliefs without fear or hesitation. There is no need, they say, for any dialogue. You believe, or you don't. You belong to the saved ones, or you are lost. Is this the approach for the followers of Jesus? After all, they must have some success, or they wouldn't continue.

When questioned about their approach, they often answer that Jesus commanded them to "go to the ends of the earth, preach and baptize in the name of the Father, the Son and the Holy Spirit." This is indeed an order we received. There is, however, more to our mission than just that order.

RESONATING TO THE VOICE WITHIN

Mary, Jesus' mother, did not obey and submit only because Yahweh spoke to her through an angel. She listened to God speaking to her from outside, of course, but she was also charged with God's Spirit and God's dream within herself. When Jesus tells his disciples in the end of the gospel of Matthew to "Go!"[1] he adds, "I am with you always, until the end of the world" (Mt 28:20). That is the reason they do what they do on their mission. It comes from within themselves; it is Jesus' Spirit in them that they feel compelled to proclaim. From within themselves they know and feel that the human family has to be gathered, that justice and peace should be pursued, that creation has to be respected, and that God's kingdom should be realized.

These inner dynamics are found not only in the disciples of Jesus, but in all human beings. God's breath has been blown into all of us! Pope John Paul II put it in this way:

> In proclaiming Christ to non-Christians, the missionary is convinced that, through the working of the Spirit, there already exists in individuals and peoples an expectation, even if an unconscious one, of knowing the truth about God, about humanity, and about how we are set free from sin and death. The missionary's enthusiasm in proclaiming Christ comes from the conviction that he is responding to that expectation.[2]

The North American bishops implied the same presence of the Spirit in the native peoples of the United States when they wrote:

> The story of the coming of the faith to our hemisphere must begin, then, not with the landing of the first missionaries, but centuries before with the history of the Native American peoples.[3]

A person does not need Jesus to value justice, integrity, peace, and love. The disciples were attracted by Jesus because in Jesus they saw those values *in their fullness*. Meeting Jesus, they suddenly saw who they were destined to be.

Some examples from everyday life may help clarify this notion. Perhaps you remember a time that you wanted to express your love, but you felt a bit shy about it. Maybe you wrote a letter, then tore it up because the words were just not right. Or you picked up the telephone and dialed your beloved, but hung up before the phone was answered. The words simply did not come. Then you found a book, just by chance. A book full of poems. One of them was a love poem that expressed exactly what you wanted to say. Suddenly all your thoughts and feelings fell in place.

Another example is music. Most of us are filled with the beginnings of melodies, rhythms, and beats. They sometimes come out under a shower, or while driving a fast car on a clear day. They remain bits and pieces until suddenly, at a concert, a jazz session, or just listening to the radio it is as if you have heard it before. The saxophone in the jazz band expresses your deepest feelings, or the popular song frees your heart!

As a final example, a scientist might have all kinds of hints and hunches, beginnings of theories, vague models, and intuitions. Then suddenly he or she discovers one new piece of information, sees something in a new light, and it all falls in place.

It is this role Jesus plays in the life of many. He attracts us because there are in all of us ideas and dreams, imaginations and realities, intuitions and inspirations.

JESUS' STORY IS FOR EVERYONE

Jesus is no stranger to anyone. We shouldn't announce him as a stranger when we tell his story to others. In his recent writings Pope John Paul II stressed several times that Jesus Christ is connected with each human individual.[4] It is in this connection that we find the need and the possibility of a dialogue with others.

It is pointless to begin an exchange by saying what *we* believe about Jesus and all he lived, died, and rose for. Others must discover for themselves that Jesus is the Way, the Truth, and the Life. Our role is to open a dialogue in which *we* tell the story of Jesus, open the books about him, so to speak, to help others discover *for themselves* who he is. Jesus himself used this method when he met the travelers on the road to Emmaus the day of his resurrection. He did not tell them who he was; rather, he told his story and left it to them to recognize him.

Evangelization and dialogue go together. When I tell the story of Jesus, I proclaim the good news of the kingdom of God, and the listeners will respond from within their own experience. Then we can dialogue. And when I dialogue with someone on these matters, I hardly can avoid speaking in terms of the good news. Which means that in one way or another I am proclaiming it. God's Spirit in me finds its counterpart in the same Spirit in them.

For some time it has been the custom to call the "others" in our dialogue anonymous Christians. To do that is no help. It creates difficulties in our communication. It seems to appropriate the people we dialogue with. We all know from our own personal experience how awkward it is when others tell us, "I know what you think." No one ever knows that. People have to define themselves. Remember what my African colleague told me about telling a story! We can say, however, that we are both taken up in the same process, that we in our dialogue are pilgrims on the way to our common fulfillment! Our dialogue can begin with the gathering and healing story of Jesus.

MEETING GOD AMONG "OTHERS"

Missionaries often say that they learned more from the people they went to than they taught them. This learning is sometimes called *mission in reverse*. It means that those missionaries would like to let their home churches profit from the riches they found among those they went to. We *all* learn in a dialogue on God and on kingdom of God affairs.

It is thrilling to look at children playing or professional athletes breaking records. It is intriguing to read about human feelings and sentiments or to look at films about them. But it can be more exhilarating to share in the life of God in others. Jesus experienced this himself dialoguing with Samaritans and with the Syro-Phoenician woman, a Roman officer, and so many others. Their faith and insight amazed him. Our contacts with others often will amaze us too. Father Vincent Donovan, a missionary among the Masai in the Great Rift Valley in East Africa, called the book about his experiences there *Christianity Rediscovered*.[5] Father Christian van Nispen, a Jesuit who lives and works in Cairo, Egypt, once said at a meeting of specialists in the Muslim-Christian dialogue that the church discovers Jesus when she reaches out to others, as Jesus himself crosses all borders to reveal himself to others.[6] Practically anyone who seriously shares the faith experiences of "others" discovers God is there. Pope Paul VI opted for this approach when he said:

> The Catholic Church looks further in the distance . . .
> beyond the Christian horizon. For how can she put
> limits to her love if she should make her *own* the love
> of God our Father, *Who rains down His grace on all
> alike* (Mt 5:46) and who loved so the world as to give
> for it His only begotten Son (John 3:16)? *She looks
> then beyond her own domain* and sees those other
> religions which maintain the concept of one God, crea-
> tor, sustainer, sovereign, and transcendent, who wor-
> ship God with sincere acts of piety, and *whose beliefs
> and practice are the founding principles of their
> moral and social life.* . . . She cannot help speaking,
> to assure them of the *esteem the Catholic Church has
> for all there is in them of truth, goodness and of the
> human* (emphasis added).[7]

We should not overlook some common human difficulties in this kind of dialogue. All of us have the tendency to
be jealous of what we have and who we are. When speaking
about something as personal and delicate as our relation to
God and God's relation to us, that jealousy may creep in.
Like young lovers, we tend to think that our relationship is
unique, that no one loves as we do.

We need to keep in mind that *all* of us are gifted in our
own way by the same Father, all of us are created together
in the same Son, all of us are enlivened by the same Spirit.
All of us are equipped from within to organize ourselves better while living and worshiping together here on this planet
Earth. It is together that we are on our way to the New
Jerusalem, our heavenly home in which there are—Jesus
assured us—many rooms (Jn 14:2). And we should thank
God for that information!

FAILURES IN INTERRELIGIOUS DIALOGUE

All through history the human family has been discussing
religious and ideological issues. Interreligious dialogue is

part and parcel of human history, often in very violent forms.

One day I took the metro in Washington, D.C. At the ticket machine someone gave me a pamphlet. I was busy and didn't pay any attention to what it was until I sat down in the train. It read in big print: "Jesus is the Messiah." The person next to me glanced at the text. Then he looked at me and said: "Do you believe that? They murdered us in Christian Europe, you know." This is a typical Jewish reaction to the Christian belief that in Jesus the Messiah appeared here on earth. They comment that Christians must be very naive to believe that the world as it is at the moment is a saved one. This is a reaction we have to take seriously when speaking too triumphantly about Jesus being the answer. We Christians believe that in Jesus the kingdom of God broke through in this world. Equipped with his Spirit we should be better at working at its justice and peace. As long as we haven't ended our task, it is a good thing that the Jews keep the ancient Judaic expectation alive. It helps the church to rethink the relationship between Christianity and Judaism.

A similar unfortunate historical relationship exists among Judaism, Christianity, and Islam. In the seventh century Mohammed hoped that either the Jews or the Christians of his region would be willing to help him in the emancipation of his Arab people. When both religious bodies showed no interest, he reconsidered his position and reasoned that both Jews and Christians were no longer faithful to Abram and Sarai's vision of all nations climbing the mountain of the Lord. Both Christians and Jews, he reasoned, had betrayed that original and foundational revelation. He told his followers to change the direction of their prayer mats toward Mecca, where Abram and Sarai built their house. He argued that he had to rally humanity in a new human/divine *umma* or family because the others had failed.

Karl Marx, a Jew who was baptized as a child, blamed the

Jewish, Christian, and Muslim religious institutions alike for their lack of interest in social justice and human dignity issues. Seeing their belief in God as the reason for this neglect, he wanted to bring "God's" kingdom about here on earth without any belief in God at all. It simply did not work.

... AND SUCCESSES

The Asian religions and Christianity have been influencing and often stimulating each other since contact was made centuries ago. Mohandas Gandhi was not only influenced by the teachings and the life of Jesus, but he in his turn influenced Christians of different denominations like Peter Maurin and Dorothy Day of *The Catholic Worker*, Danilo Dolci in Italy, Jacques Maritain and Lanza del Vasto in France, Cesar Chavez, Thomas Merton, and Martin Luther King, Jr., all of whom traced their vision to the teachings of Jesus. Yet they all acknowledged that it was by meeting the Hindu Gandhi, and not through the teaching of the Christian churches, that they met the nonviolent face of Jesus.[8]

LEARNING FROM "OTHERS"

We are surrounded by believers who do not go to church anymore. It is not that they are not religious. On the contrary. They seem to have outgrown their church communities. They hope to quench their religious thirst and solve their religious problems in what they call New Age Religion. They claim that their former church leaders never told them what they discovered since they left their churches. It was in their contacts with others that they discovered a divine spark within themselves. Either nobody ever told them before, as Christians, about the Spirit who dwells in all of us, or nobody told them in a way they could understand. In our dialogue with them we might learn a lot about ourselves and our own religious needs.

It is in our contacts with all those "others," their old and new beliefs, that we discover the ramifications of the risen humanity, how we belong together and complement each other religiously and spiritually. So much remains hidden in us, so many possibilities and potentialities remain undiscovered if we stand solely on our own. It is as if God sowed his goods in all of us in different ways. We are pieces of God's gigantic jigsaw puzzle, a puzzle Jesus came to bring together. It is in him that we have the full picture. But we have to tell each other our stories in order to find in each other what in its fullness is found in Jesus.

Dialogue should not only be at the heart of our contact with the Spirit in others, it also should be revived in our Christian circle. The reformation churches formed themselves in protest against perceived and real abuses. They meant to amend and correct existing administrative and spiritual mismanagement and imbalances. Some stressed, and sometimes over-stressed beliefs and attitudes that were under-stressed or neglected by others. Still, Christians of the different denominations are historically and dialectically intertwined. While in their devotion and ecclesial set-up some pay especial attention to God as Parent of all, others prefer to stress their personal adhesion to Jesus Christ, God's Son and Offspring. Still others prefer to revel enthusiastically in the presence of God's Spirit within them. We cannot understand ourselves without contacting the others. We should seriously engage our differences, bringing together all that is good and true.

DIALOGUE WITHIN THE CHURCH

The same dynamic is found in the Roman Catholic Church. Since the Second Vatican Council we live in a church that has different approaches to the same mysteries. The Vatican II documents so often give different and complementary definitions of one and the same truth and reality. It is in those tensions between old and new that we find inspiration and life in a true dialogue. Didn't Jesus tell us that the disciples of the kingdom of heaven will bring new treasures as well as old out of his storeroom (Mt 13:52)?

CONDITIONS FOR FRUITFUL DIALOGUE

To make interreligious, interdenominational, and interchurch dialogue successful, or even possible, some conditions have to be fulfilled — conditions that flow from the nature of the exchange. The dialogue must be between what Jesus made vibrate in us and what is resonating with God's Spirit in the others. It is there that we find our contact point and our inspiration to go further in our common journey to our final destination. This means that God's Spirit must be active in all partners. They must be in contact with God's presence in them. A prayerful being present to God is thus presupposed as a first condition.

We read in Luke's description of Jesus' baptism by John that Jesus is at prayer when the Spirit in the form of a dove descends on him and the voice is heard. In the Acts of the Apostles we read that the apostles prayed before any mission or "proclaiming dialogue" was undertaken. It is only from that contact point that a fruitful dialogue can start, and the willingness to really listen to each other can begin. Without that touching point with the Spirit in us, we won't be able to do anything at all. We begin by prayerfully relying on God's presence in us and in them, until we both realize how nice it might be to converse with and about God, revealing to each other the treasure we carry in ourselves. And we discover that treasure in ourselves at the same time, because that is how those faith exchanges work out!

Two other conditions have to be fulfilled. We need a double faithfulness.[9] We have to be faithful to ourselves, and we have to be faithful in listening to the others. As Pope Paul VI writes:

> Fidelity both to the message whose servants we are, and to the people to whom we must transmit it safe and sound is the central axis of Evangelization (no. 4).[10]

Dialogue has often been begun by individuals, or by some representatives of the different religious groups. In the case of the Catholic-Jewish dialogue it has led to considerable results. But it is a task that cannot be left to individuals alone. Faith communities should get involved. Taking up this ministry as a community effort is still called "The Wild Card," but as the author who gave it that name, David A. Bos, wrote, it might well go down as a new chapter in the history of mission.[11]

ADDITIONAL AREAS FOR DIALOGUE

As we live together in a world that on the whole is far from realizing the kingdom, and consequently far from ideal, there are many other concerns we have in common. One insight all religious believers and all non-religious thinking human beings alike express is the need to do something about this world socially, economically, politically, and environmentally. This calls for an additional dialogue, one that can be shared even by those who do not choose to join our interreligious dialogue. For them this will be the test of our religious sincerity. If, as followers of Jesus, we confess to believe in a God who is the Parent of all, who sent his Offspring into this world, and who together with that Offspring sends the Spirit into everyone, how can we not be busy with clearing those social and ecological issues? His companions from Emmaus did not recognize Jesus while he was opening the scriptures to them. Afterward they told each other that their hearts had been burning during that explanation. Yet they had not recognized him at the time. They discovered who he was at table, when he took their bread and broke it for them, sharing it in the way they had heard he did at his last supper before his death. Which leads us into the heart of the next chapter.

For Reflection

1. Have you ever prayed with non-Catholics? with non-Christians? Form a delegation in your parish or community to visit a neighboring non-Catholic community or to visit a synagogue, mosque, or temple. (Ask before whether you will be welcome.) Invite the community to one of your services.

2. Comment on the following quotations:

   The history of Judaism did not end with the destruction of Jerusalem, but rather went on to develop a religious tradition (Vatican City, 1975).[12]

   Our common spiritual heritage is considerable. Help in better understanding certain aspects of the Church's life can be gained by taking an inventory of that heritage, but also by taking into account the faith and religious life of the Jewish people as professed and lived now as well (Pope John Paul II, 1982).[13]

   There is the affirmation about Christ and his saving event as central to the economy of salvation — an affirmation which is essential to the Catholic Faith (Section 1, #7). This does not mean that the Jews as a people cannot and should not draw salvific gifts from their own traditions. Of course, they can and should do so (Jorge Mejia, 1985).[14]

3. How do you react to the following opinion?

With the remarks of Paul VI at the opening of the second session of the Second Vatican Council Paul VI began the movement from talking *about* other religions, and talking *to* other religions, to dialogue *with* other religions and with these other religions *about itself*. Pope Paul sought to move the Church in the direction of appreciating and learning from other religions, while simultaneously offering her own spiritual treasures to them.[15]

4. This chapter stressed the need for prayer as a condition for fruitful interreligious dialogue. Can you explain why? Would a meditation on the Our Father be a help in this context? Why?

CHAPTER 15

The Why and How of Justice, Peace, and Creational Integrity

*See what this godly sorrow has produced in
you: what earnestness, what eagerness to clear
yourselves, what indignation, what alarm, what
longing, what concern, what readiness to see
justice done.*

(2 Corinthians 7:11)

I t was early in the evening. It was dark outside in Nairobi, Kenya, East Africa; it is always dark by seven in the evening. The only noises were the traffic in the distance and the crickets nearby. It had been a busy day at the office of the university chapel. Many visitors had come to ask for help, help that often was not available. I was tired and relieved that the office was closed. I entered the presbytery. Someone must have been waiting, because immediately afterward there was a knock at the front door. I opened the door, and a man asked for some food. I said, "Sorry, I can't help you. You are too late. The office is closed," and locked the door in his face. There was another knock at the door. I pretended not to hear it. The knocking continued. I finally opened the door. The same man was there, holding a piece of paper in his hand.

It was old, so often folded up that it almost fell apart. He gave it to me, and he said, "Please, read it. You have to help me. I am your brother!" I then saw that the paper he held out to me was his baptismal certificate.

Two parishes in Washington, D.C., an Episcopal one and a Catholic one, decided to celebrate Pentecost together one year. Both parishes served a variety of ethnic groups: white and Afro-American English-speaking parishioners; Central American and Latin American Spanish-speaking parishioners; French-speaking Haitians; Portuguese-speaking Brazilians; and Vietnamese-speaking parishioners. They all had their own hymn books, their own symbols, their own music, and their own prayers. Meetings were organized to arrange for the celebration. The interdenominational hurdles were ecumenically overcome without too much difficulty. The cultural arrangements (what languages? which hymns? what kind of decorations?) were more complicated, but they also were finally arranged. After the liturgical services (identical worship solemnities in both church buildings) a big potluck dinner with traditional food, drinks, music, dancing, and singing would close the celebration. The program promised to be a real treat from all points of view.

In one of the last meetings the group became aware of one final hurdle. Some of the richer people in the parishes employed the poorer ones. The social relationship between those two groups was far from ideal. The workers were underpaid because they were illegal immigrants. Their working conditions were substandard. It would be difficult to sit at the same table after the liturgical ceremony and pick up the unjust working relationships on Monday. In fact, they decided, it would be impossible. The celebration did not take place. The time was not yet ripe to extend what was possible in the church buildings to the everyday life of the market square and the labor market. The organizing committee regretfully decided to postpone the festival and to work at making it—politically and socially—possible in the future.

AN ACTIVITY WITH POLITICAL MEANING

Proclaiming from Jesus' Spirit in us that all humanity forms one body is at the same time a statement on how our world should be organized. It is a social, economic, and even political statement. When the eucharist is celebrated in a spiritually awake community, the experience will by itself lead to a felt need to extend the sharing around the altar to concrete actions of justice in society.

Being baptized and baptizing in the name of a God who is the Parent to all of humanity and creation, in whose Word we are all created, and whose Spirit contains the life of the whole of the human family and creation, is an activity with political meaning. Any church from which actions of justice and peace-making do not begin to flow is betraying the Spirit of the God it prays to. Such a community is not faithful to the Spirit that brought it together. It is here that the dialogue with others, and with fellow human beings who are nonbelievers, gets a new, practical dimension. In practically all cases it is quite a struggle to realize in our world our new sensitivity to the absolute value of each individual human person. This value does not depend on baptism, but for the Christian believer finds its formalization and its sacramental expression in that sacrament of initiation. All those who accept with us the *Universal Declaration of Human Rights* are our partners in this struggle. We find our motives in the religious inspiration of the gospel touching our inner spirit; others find it in their own beliefs and convictions, thanks to the divine Spirit — consciously or subconsciously — present in them.

This does not mean that we will know how to vote in an election. How to realize politically the justice and the equality we want to obtain is not something we can read directly from Jesus' life. We know better *what* we want, and even better what we *don't* want in these issues of human rights, than we know *how* to realize and obtain it. No political party seems to have the human/divine covenantal project of the kingdom of God as its program. That is why no church should identify itself with any of those parties. We should, however, be in favor of the policy that comes nearest to the ideal, helping it at the same time to get nearer! In other words, we should be politically engaged. The organization of justice and peace belongs to our mission task. How to do it provokes much discussion.

THE EARLY COMMUNITIES

The first Christian communities faced the same problems. They went to the Temple, had their eucharistic get-togethers afterward, and in no time decided that they had to do something about their social and economic relationships. They organized an inter-ethnic food distribution system and began a new economic set-up among themselves. Luke tells the story in the Acts of the Apostles. He describes different ways in which communities took care that "there were no needy persons among them" (Acts 4:34). In one case they kept their own property, but shared with those in need (Acts 4:32). In another case they sold what they had, brought the proceeds to the apostles, who then distributed it according to the different needs (Acts 4:34-35). There were even more fundamental justice issues at stake. Paul and Peter discussed vehemently whether non-Jews had to become Jews before being admitted to the new communities. This is an issue that arises in new ways again and again in our own communities: Must the "others" become like us before we accept them? This question will be discussed in the next chapter.

UNCOMFORTABLE IMPLICATIONS

The praying of the Our Father, the singing of Mary's Magnificat, the reciting of the prophets, the reading of the gospels, Paul's letters about our oneness in Christ and the forgiving of the human past, and the book of Revelation all have political implications. No wonder that discussion is often fierce — and sometimes leads to the rejection of God's plans for the human family. Too many of us get upset when we hear about Christian projects for the transformation of society. Our discomfort betrays us. We know, from deep down within, what would happen if we relate our worship to the ideals of justice, empowerment, liberation, conscientization, education, and the fostering of human equality. Some of us are — consciously or subconsciously — afraid that we would have to live with implications we are not eager to confront. The more we profit from the actual corrupt and sinful situation in the world, the more afraid we might be. Yet, as Belgian theologian Edward Schillebeeckx wrote:

> The nature and the duty of the Christian faith and thus also the official church is to further truth and justice in the world in the way of a spiritual power, critical and ethical, a power which has as its mission keeping alive in the heart of humanity the will to form human society in a *polis*, a city, a dwelling-place in which it is good for everyone to live, something which it is good to live for.[1]

This goodness is recognizable; it was revealed in Abram and Sarai as present as the ideal and dream in the human heart. It is God's own project, which reaches from within us together in this world out to beyond this world for all time to come. This vision, as presence, broke through in its fullness in the person of Jesus.

LIFE IN THE SPIRIT

When the good news about Jesus activates a human community for the first time, the reaction is at its freshest. It

was so in Jerusalem; it is the case nowadays. A newly baptized adult is almost always more fervent than those who
have been baptized for years and years. When the vibrations
of Jesus touch a human community for the first time, great
things happen. In the older Christian communities the Spirit
too often has been interpreted, canonically regulated, and in
a sense almost domesticated. It is in the young churches
that the Spirit's work is most visible.

I remember a meeting of forty lay workers and some
priests in the last week of June 1983 at Kanamai Conference Center near Mombassa in Kenya. They represented
the Christian Development Education Service. During the
meeting the diocesan development education programmers
reported on their activities in the small Christian parish
communities. The list of those church development projects
was long and revealing. It was not so much a list of retreats
or Bible study classes or pastoral seminars or prayer
groups. It was a list that ran from water projects to the
building of one-room houses for the disabled, from intensive agriculture projects to literacy programs, from manage-
ment and leadership courses for women to demonstrations
on the use of semi-arid land, from tree planting to teaching
better cooking methods. And all this was done inter-ethni-
cally! Almost all of them complained that many priests, in
some regions more than 75 percent, had difficulties working
with the groups, because they did not think the projects
"spiritual" enough. But the communities were all sure that it
was what the Spirit moved them to do. I remember how
one of them burst out: "But it is what they did in the Acts of
the Apostles in Jerusalem!"[2]

We should not, however, make light of the work of the
Holy Spirit in older communities. The Spirit continually
inspires those who are willing to listen; a praying community
cannot escape the Spirit's impulses. A good example in the
United States, similar to the one just mentioned in Kenya, is
the Campaign for Human Development, the official develop-

ment program of the United States Catholic Conference.[3] It helps bridge economic, social, and ethnic differences through a well-tested program that helps different groups — sometimes in the same parish, sometimes in the same locality or region — to help in one another's growth and development.

Thousands of justice and peace networks cover the United States from parish to parish, often networking with the rest of the world. They empower refugees and battered women, abused children and dumped senior citizens, and those who write themselves off as valuable members of society because they have been written off by others. They organize "bread and fish" for the homeless and poor. They help to twin inner-city parishes with those more affluent.

Some join Amnesty International as a Christian community and open their doors to all kinds of people who come together to support each other in the rebuilding of their self-esteem and freedom. Others join the Advent Tree of Compassion, the September Hunger Month Observance, and the October Respect for Life Celebration. They visit the sick and give free legal advice for those who need it. They organize convocations and retreats on the social message in the Bible. They mediate in conflicts to avoid the hassle, the antagonism, and the cost of legal procedures. They monitor the legislative processes of advocacy for the poor and powerless in their states and national assemblies with their sophisticated electronic networks and bulletin boards. Participants in some of those networks, like the Sanctuary movement, no longer define themselves as nationals of one country, but as citizens of the kingdom of God. They try to exercise greater control over the evils in their society by using tools such as "Social Analysis,"[4] developed by the Center of Concern. They are in contact with Christians and others struggling for justice, peace, and environmental integrity in all parts of the world.

AT THE CENTER OF LIFE

The Spirit of God is alive and well in millions of ways, although its fire has to be kindled in many more human beings and the communities they form. It has to be aroused not only in activities and responses such as the ones we just mentioned, but in the very center of our life. Gathering the nations, healing and empowering, realizing justice and making peace were not extras in the lives of Jesus and Mary. Mary did not become the mother of God in her free time or as a volunteer. It was her life. Our mission and task are not an extra either, as religion and piety often are for those who only think of them on Sunday or at Christmas or Easter. Our mission and task are not for "amateurs." They should fill our personal, family, and community life; they should be the heart of our educational and professional activities.

SEEKING THE VISION

The vision seen by Abram and Sarai—and put into words in so many stories and parables, sounds and tongues in the Jewish and Christian Scriptures—does not speak only of a "saved" and "liberated" human family where all will be brothers and sisters, all friends; where no master-servant relationships will exist; where pain and tears will be wiped away and forgotten. The vision imaged also a lasting city, where God will be with us forever and ever; where all nations and individuals will share their national and personal splendor to the joy of all. They even saw in that New Jerusalem a bright sky, crystal clear living water, and fruit and green leaf-bearing healing trees. They saw, like John did in his visions later, an undamaged "new heaven and new earth" (Rv 21:1). This vision is of the heaven and the earth we all carry as our destiny in the deepest of our beings. It is this vision we realize at the peak points of our lives — in love-making, in shared beauty and joy, during a festival or dance, in a choir, a concert or successful team work, in prayer and ecstasy. We invoke a oneness with the whole of inorganic and organic nature when we commemorate Jesus' life, death, and resurrection with bread *"given by the earth"* and wine, *"the fruit of the vine,"* forming Jesus Christ's body and blood for and with us.

Every believer, of whatever conviction, faces a world that needs healing. The fact that we know things are not as they should be is another indication of the Spirit we carry in our-selves. We are falling apart; injustice is rampant; the power-ful are exploiting the weak; some have and consume almost all the world's produce while others are starving. Drugs and drink are destroying too many, disease threatens all of us, human services fall short. Ecological disasters are imminent, rivers are polluted, the air is unbreathable, forests disappear, the ozone layer is breaking up, soil erosion and overgrazing destroy the land, the military eats capital that should be used to feed, heal, and educate. The ravages and dangers are so serious that only the deepest motivation can rescue us. That deepest motivation is in us; it is God's Spirit self that makes us reach out to our fulfillment, with God's love in our hearts and full of hope

> not in an indeterminate or undirected way, but in a very definite direction . . . concern for a better society for all men and women, above all for the outcast and marginalized, those who are devastated; pastoral con-cern for communication as an unceasing social and cultural criticism where injustice is evident; concern for the human body, for human psychological and socio-logical health; concern too for the natural human envi-ronment; concern for the wholeness of Christian faith, hope and love; concern for meaningful prayer and for

a meaningful sacrament; and finally concern for the individual pastorate, above all towards the lonely, and those who "no longer hope." Christian spirituality derives both its power and its joy from this eschatological hope in which Christians do all this.[5]

Interreligious dialogue is necessary for all the reasons we mentioned in the preceding chapter. Interreligious action is necessary if we want to save our world and humanity. The World Council of Churches and the Catholic Church formed a joint working group to grapple with these issues in 1965, a cooperation that should be extended to all other religions. A first sign of such a collaboration was realized in Assisi in 1987, when Pope John Paul II invited practically the whole religious world to come together to pray for peace and wholeness.

What cannot be realized as yet at a world scale is often possible at a local level. We need action in solidarity to overcome the dangers that threaten the human family and its environment. All of us should be able to feel at home on this planet.

For Reflection

1. "What does the Lord require of you? Act justly and walk steadfastly" (Mic 6:8). Meditate on this old prophetic saying, thinking of the justice and peace issues in your life. Share your story.

2. Is there a relation between your baptism, the eucharist, and being involved in local and national politics? Discuss.

3. How do you react to the following statement from Walter J. Burghardt, S.J.:

   The distance between the rich and the poor continues to widen. One out of every five children in our country is growing up below the poverty line — one out of every three black children. Yet, I still hear devout Catholics insisting that the poor are lazy, that anyone who wants to work can find it, that the single parent with small children should eschew the welfare check and get into the job market with the rest of us. Thirty-seven million Americans have no access to health care; untold thousands of the homeless cram our shelters or huddle over street grates; the elderly rummage through garbage cans for the food we cast away so lightly. Yet, I still hear Catholics complaining that their hard-earned money is being rerouted to wastrels, to those who have no future, who are a drain on the rest of us.[6]

4. Discuss Paul VI's statement:

Evangelization would not be complete if it did not take into account the unceasing interplay of the Gospel and of man/woman's concrete life, both personal and social.[7]

5. After having worked for years in an impoverished inner-city community, a lay leader in the parish had to leave. At his farewell he was thanked by the community for having given them hope. Comment.

CHAPTER 16

About Feeling at Home:
Inculturation

My Father will love him and we will come to
him and make our home with him.

(John 14:23)

I nculturation is a new word. The most complete English dictionary, the Oxford English Dictionary, does not even mention it in its latest (1991) edition. Yet many theologians use the word. Pope John Paul II has used it several times to express the need to help people welcome Jesus in their own culture and to make them feel "at home" in the church.

REFRESHING AN OLD CONCEPT

The word inculturation might be new, but the idea and the practice are not. When Paul announced the good news in Athens, he began by looking around the city to get some information about its inhabitants. He must have visited a library, because he quotes two of the local poets. The quotation he used from the Greek poet Epimenides, "For in him we live and move and have our being," the church still uses in one of its Sunday preface prayers celebrating the eucharist. Paul was not very successful, but he tried to make his audience feel "at home" in what he was telling them. So the idea and the practice are far from new, but they have been so overlooked that to refresh this approach we needed to coin that new word, *inculturation*.

In the pluralistic world in which we live, travel, and work, most of us know from experience that our home culture is different from the culture of many of the people we meet. When I invited Africans to my table in East Africa, the table was laid in the Western way, a knife, a fork, and a spoon next to each plate. My visitors would use that cutlery without comment. But, when I invited them to make themselves at home, they wouldn't use the cutlery. Before we began to eat, they would ask where they could wash their hands. They would wash them, dry them carefully, and return to table to eat with their hands. Once I asked them for the reason. At first they were a bit embarrassed to tell me. Finally they explained that eating with the hands is more hygienic than eating with "those iron tools." Who was the last one to eat from them? Had they been well washed? Who had washed them? They could be absolutely sure of the cleanliness of their own hands. While I, with my Western mentality, thought that eating with a fork and a knife was more hygienic than eating with my hands, they thought the opposite. So I learned why in East African restaurants the first thing the waiters and waitresses do is to present a big bowl, some soap powder, and a jug of water to let the customers wash their hands.

CULTURE SHOCK

Being polite in one culture can be impolite, even shocking, in another culture. Asking "How is your wife?" is polite in Anglo-Saxon circles; it is offensive in other contexts. Tilt-

ing your plate the wrong way when finishing the last spoon-
ful of soup can be highly offensive. The same word might
have different meanings, even when you speak about Jesus.
Africans who hear that Jesus came to bring us "life to the
full," often call him, as a consequence, their "ancestor" —
something unlikely to occur to a Western Christian. African
traditional marriages are in general organized in a way different from those Westerners are familiar with. For them, it
is a matter between two families, not so much a contract
between two individuals. Child bearing also plays a different
role than it does in the West.

All these differences cause difficulties when cultures
meet. Christian communities have had such problems from
the very beginning. Peter and Paul debated whether non-
Jewish Christians had to be circumcised, because they
themselves as Jews had been circumcised. They discussed
what kind of meat people were allowed to eat, how it had to
be slaughtered, and with whom they were allowed to sit at
table. Often the issues themselves had hardly any real
importance, but these details helped people feel at home —
or not.

MOVING TOWARD THE NEW JERUSALEM

In the final outcome, in the New Jerusalem, everyone will
feel at home. Organizing and preparing the kingdom of God
in this world has to take that desire into account. For years
we used unleavened hosts that were baked in Holland and
wine grown and bottled in France during the eucharist in
the heart of Africa. It was sometimes difficult to convince
Africans that those hosts were real food. It was difficult to
explain to them why the wine, which they had no difficulty
in recognizing as drink, had to come in those fancy bottles
or barrels from Europe. When Jesus celebrated with his
friends at the last supper he did so in a context they knew,

with food they ate, and drink they were accustomed to. It was a typical Middle East Jewish meal; bread and grape wine are Middle East cultural elements. But when we celebrate the same meal in his memory somewhere in the African Highlands, or in an American or European city, the food used is foreign to us. Not only Africans, but Westerners too have to explain to our children that the host is bread.

The food we eat and the wine we drink during those meals are not the only differences. In some African cultures it is customary for women and men to eat separately. The men eat together; the women eat together with the children. Sometimes it is the custom to eat in silence. Celebrating the eucharist is done by men, women, and children together, and many words are spoken and hymns sung. Many African Christians would love to use their own food to express their unity with Jesus and through him with each other. Many are happy that the inequality that culturally existed between women and men begins to be overcome in their celebration of the eucharist, through being together with their common oldest family member and age-mate Jesus Christ in the home of God. Vincent Donovan reports that,

> Masai men had never eaten in the presence of women. In their minds, the status and condition of women were such that the very presence of women at the time of eating was enough to pollute the food that was present. How then was Eucharist possible? In their minds it was not. If ever there was a need for Eucharist as salvific sign of unity, it was here. I reminded them that besides the law of love which I had preached to them and they had accepted, I had never tried to interpret for them how they must work out that law in their homes and in their lives, and in their treatment of their daughters and wives and female neighbors. . . . But

here, in the Eucharist we are at the heart of the
unchanging gospel that I was passing on to them.
They were free to accept that gospel or reject it, but if
they accepted it, they were accepting the truth that in
the Eucharist, which is to say "in Christ, there is neither slave nor free, neither Jew nor Greek, neither
male nor female." They did accept it, but it was surely
a traumatic moment for them, as individuals and as a
people, that first time when I blessed the cup, or
gourd in this case, and passed it on to the woman sitting next to me, told her to drink from it, and then
pass it on to the man sitting next to her. I don't
remember any pastoral moment in which the "sign of
unity" was so real for me. And I was not surprised
some time later when a group of teenage girls told me
privately, that the *"ilomon sidai"* (good news), that I
talked about so constantly, was really good news for
them.[1]

This example shows that being invited to the house of
God, the conscious or subconscious ultimate hope and
desire of every human being, is not only something cross-
cultural using African cultural elements, but it is also something that corrects and amends a culture. It brings people
together in the name of Jesus in a way they were never
together before. Didn't we say that Jesus came to gather
and heal the scattered children of God?

The same Masai in their turn corrected Father Donovan
from within their cultural setup on this same point of
togetherness. When he had come to the end of his evangelization and was going to give the final preparation for baptism, he told the group of neophytes that he congratulated
them. Then he added that one of them, an old man who
had been herding his cattle too often during instruction
time, and an old woman, who according to him scarcely
believed, could not be baptized. At that point an old man,
Ndangoya, interrupted him:

"Padri, why are you trying to break us up and separate us? During this whole year that you have been teaching us, we have talked about these things when you were not there, at night around the fire. Yes, there have been lazy ones in our community, but they have been helped by those who are intelligent. Yes, there are the ones with little faith in this village, but they have been helped by those with much faith. Would you turn out and drive off the lazy ones and the ones with little faith and the stupid ones? From the first day I have spoken for these people. And I speak for them now. Now, on this day a year later, I can declare for them and for all this community, that we have reached the step in our lives where we can say: *'We believe.'* "[2]

Donovan adds: *"We believe.* Communal faith. Until that day I had never heard of such a concept." And then he wonders whether he did hear of it but had overlooked it completely. Don't we ask questions at the baptism of a baby that cannot be answered by the child, but are answered by its community? The Masai definitely clarified something for Donovan that day.

Father Donovan clarified things for them as well. He told the story of Jesus under a full moon in Great Rift Valley. An old warrior stood up and said, "I know what you are telling us, that those others — and he pointed to the other side of the hills in the distance, where their traditional enemies lived — belong together with us to the same family." Some accepted this new challenge; others did not. They all understood that it would mean a whole change of life.

JESUS' SONG OF UNITY

Scholars at the Department of Philosophy and Religious Studies in Nairobi, Kenya, did some research on the psy-

chology of conversion, as they called it. The gospel story
that influenced most "converts" to make their step was the
one of the Good Samaritan. The story recounts how a man
from one ethnic group, a Samaritan, opened his heart and
his purse to a victim who belonged to another ethnic group,
a Jew. When they heard that story, when Jesus sang that
song to them, his listeners started to burn from within. They
discovered in themselves what they always had hoped for:
to be loved together by God and to be invited to God's
home. When they heard Jesus sing his song, they heard it
coming from within themselves! That melody is indeed in all
of us! Pope Paul VI said it well to Africans in Kampala,
Uganda:

> It will require an incubation of the Christian "mystery"
> in the genius of your people in order that its native
> voice more clearly and frankly may then be raised har-
> moniously in the chorus of the other voices in the uni-
> versal church.[3]

We have to organize ourselves in such a way that newcomers feel at home with us; they have to take care that we
find ourselves at home with them. We have to sing the
Jesus song hidden in our hearts and minds together! It is
the same kind of interplay we found in our dialogue and our
work at justice, peace, and a clean environment. We have to
be faithful to ourselves and to them. They have to be faithful
to themselves and to us. It seems a difficult, almost impossible task. John Paul II warns that it will be a slow process,
but it is a process that is called for by the divine impulse in
us, homing in on Jesus organizing with us the "great camp
meeting in the Promised Land."

THE ATTRACTION OF JESUS

When this process is well entered in a good dialogue,
everyone feels at ease and at home. If we discover in the

words of the other our deepest self, how could those words be strange to us? Bernard Bassett, S.J., once marveled that so many people were and are attracted by Jesus. It was not his money, because he had none. It was not his background, which was the simplest possible. His appearance was probably very ordinary. It was not his academic learning; he simply did not have it. He was not a politician. He made no nationalistic speeches. Was it his miracles? Bassett notes that at first sight this might be the answer. He then decides it is not. He explains that at critical moments Jesus failed to hold a crowd. It was not his learning, not his looks, not his miracles, but the ease with which others could be themselves in his company. Nicodemus, Zacchaeus, Levi, the Roman officer, the adulterous woman, the Samaritan woman, Martha, Mary, the twelve, and so many others. All of us can feel at home with him, because he responds to the "red-hot point of consciousness."[4] His approach assures us of our personal and everlasting value; loving us in that way he promises us fullness of life. He makes us feel at home, because that is what love does. It takes away all fear. It allows us to be ourselves. We are destined to be at home with one another, a home where we celebrate each other and ourselves, bringing together our splendor and giftedness—the home of the vision first glimpsed by Abram and Sarai.

THE SCOPE OF INCULTURATION

Inculturation is an issue in our contact with people from far-away countries and neighbors who live in ways foreign to us. It is also an issue in our own local context. That is apparent to anyone who studies the faces of people who are in church for a funeral or marriage. We see people who are not accustomed to a church building; the uneasy pews; the raised altar; the clothes worn by the celebrants; the language spoken; the symbols used; the stress laid on blood and sacrifice. Perhaps the impression is given that some people hardly count, and that others are not only more important but basically different.

We notice it when we try to explain to teenagers the traditional approach to Jesus suffering for them; when we speak about a God who got upset about the sinfulness of this world, condemned it, and was only willing to look at it again after Jesus would have shed his blood in expiation for us. Here, too, we face the inculturation issue. Teenagers, and people of all ages, are often unable to place this kind of God. The story about Jesus has to be told in a way that remains faithful to it but also is understandable in modern culture. His story is a truth that is needed by all, but it should be communicated in a relevant manner, touching the "red-hot point" of modern consciousness—a consciousness that is often aware of our need to change, to be together, to respect human rights, to heal, to make peace, to respect the environment, and to build a more human city. This is a consciousness that reaches back to that early vision of Abraham and Sarah. For the fulfillment of such a dream, many have been willing to put their lives on the line, as Jesus did. It is a universal hope for a world of peace and wholeness, a hope teenagers and seniors alike are well able to understand.

"AT HOME" IN COMMUNITY

It is very difficult to feel at home in a hotel room. The layout, the decorations, and the furniture—in fact everything—are imposed on you from above. Whether a person comes from India, Africa, Europe, or the North Pole, whether he or she is old or young, all get the same kind of room. Feeling at home cannot come from above. It can only come from the grassroots. To make others (and ourselves) feel at home or inculturated in the church asks for another model of church than the one we are accustomed to. The new model was foreseen by the Second Vatican Council, when it described the church as the People of God before mentioning the ministries needed to keep those communities in contact with one another.[5] The People of God in their small communities — in all their variety — are the core and substance of the church. The good news finds its roots in such communities, and nowhere else.

These communities form together the body of Christ, another image (and reality) that indicates how much we should be able to feel at home, as much at home as in our own skin. It also means that these communities need ministries and organizational patterns to keep in contact and communion. That is why there were "over-seers" (*episkopoi*, or bishops). They are meant to keep the necessary contacts to foster a process in which the whole of the world will be knit together, just as a body of a new human being is formed in the womb of its mother.

This model is not clerical. It has confidence in the capacity of Christian communities themselves to discern the Spirit and to realize the gospel at the grassroots level. Pope John Paul II speaks of this reality when he mentions the differences among the four gospels,

> . . . a pluralism which reflects different experiences and situations within the first Christian communities. It is also the result of the driving force of the Spirit self, it encourages us to pay heed to the variety of missionary charisms and to the diversity of circumstances and peoples. . . . The four gospels therefore bear witness to a certain pluralism within the fundamental unity of the same mission.[6]

Jesus lived his life and told his story in a way that made others discover themselves within their own persons and within their own communities. It also made them discover how closely they are linked and how organically bound together. It is the story about the branch and the vine: "I am the vine, you are the branches" (Jn 5:5). It is interesting to note how he speaks of us as branches, not as individual leaves, but as bundles of leaves, families of leaves and flowers, branches. That is how the story should be told, and also how it should be lived. We flourish not only in the circle of our own community, our children and grandchildren, but also with all the others around us. If we listen to the Spirit in us asking us to work at justice and peace, at the gathering of the nations and the healing of the world, we will reach out to all those around us. We do so not to impose ourselves, but to exchange our spiritual experiences; to find out how God and God's Spirit is reflected in thousands of ways in all cultures; to express that we all belong together. And then fear may give way to love (cf. 1 Jn 4:18), and we will be on our way to a fulfillment and salvation more varied, colorful, and at the same time more harmonious than we ever expected in our wildest dreams. We sometimes find glimpses of this age-old vision when we are culturally together in prayer, celebration, and feast. It is a good reason to come together in those ways as often as we can!

The Christian community is the community where everyone should feel at home. It is only in such "home" communities that we can find the safety and security we need to feel at ease, to be happy, and to grow to fulfillment. It is only when these communities are interconnected that all of us, gathering together and at peace with one another, can heal, prosper, and strive after our final destiny, can follow the vision of our forebears. Even then a lot of things still have to happen, which leads us to our final chapter on our mission.

For Reflection

1. "To understand the others, we must not annex them, but rather make ourselves their guests" (Louis Massignon). Discuss.

2. "A cat thrown in water will be able to tell more about that water than a fish swimming in it." Do you agree?

3. Read in all four gospels one event in the life of Jesus, for example, his agony in the garden of Gethsemane, or the reasons he gives for his death on the cross. How do they compare?

4. Would your parish community be willing to organize a transcultural festival?

5. Are you reaching out to those who do not belong to your own circle? Do you ever help others think about those who are not here? How can you do so?

CHAPTER 17

How to Organize and Manage Our Mission

For the people in this world are more shrewd in dealing with their own kind than are the people of the light.

(Luke 16:8)

 et us begin with a fairy tale. It is a tale children tell. And it is a story we sometimes tell our children. It is in a way what is told in any fairy tale with a happy ending. This is the story:

Something had happened to the world, or rather, to the human family inhabiting it. Everybody was filled with love, mutual understanding, and good will. Nobody could explain how it had happened. Was it because of the natural disasters that had ravaged the world—floods, volcanoes, earthquakes? Was it because of the human disasters—the violence and race riots that had hit the streets and whole communities? Was it because of all the conventions that had taken place, or because of all the meditations that had put people in touch with themselves and the presence of the divine in them? Was it because many people had been hum-

ming together the same song? Nobody knew. Yet a
change had taken place. Evil was gone, the abusive
foster parents had died, the dragons had been killed,
the fierce giant and the evil witch had changed their
ways, and all were ready to live happily forever and
ever.

HAPPILY EVER AFTER

The stuff of fairy tales indeed. Yet, let us imagine that
tomorrow morning all people in the world come into contact with the light of God in themselves; that they all wake
up full of God's love for themselves, each other, and the
whole of the world. Would that change of heart change the
world? No, it wouldn't. It would only be a beginning. The
world would still have to be changed in its structures.
Justice and peace would still have to be established. We
would have to forgive the past and to become reconciled
with one another. We would need conventions, seminars,
workshops, symposiums, and meetings to work out new
arrangements and networks. We would have to change the
educational and health systems, the use and distribution of
resources, transportation, communication, environmental
policies, agriculture, industry, and the arts. Good will on its
own does not guarantee a political system that does justice.
That system would have to be invented, tested, amended,
and developed. The good will would help in doing it, but the
City of God would still have to be built. The celebration of
being together would still have to be organized.

That good will does not exist. Or better, it does, but it is
still hidden, tucked away in our hearts and minds. How
many of us, people of the Book, who call ourselves Jews,
Christians, or Muslims, are aware and live the dynamism
that made Abram and Sarai leave their old life and seek a
vision they barely glimpsed? How many Christians live the

dynamism that made Mary accept her role, and Jesus live, die, and rise? Our first *mission* task is to discover and advertise that dynamism in ourselves and in one another.

CONVERSION FROM WITHIN

To do so demands a turn-around, a change of heart, a giving-in to God's love in us. It means lending our ears to God, listening "to the cries of the poor." It means conversion, not an easy thing. When Jesus became aware of the Holy Spirit in his life, and when he heard the voice saying, "This is my beloved son" at his baptism by John (Mt 3:17), he went for forty days to the desert, where he was tempted not to give in to God's call. It is the temptation we find in the lives of those who do heroic things for justice or peace, but also in the lives of those who dedicate themselves to less ostentatious kingdom of God issues. All of us are tempted to say, "I know that this is what I must do now, though I would prefer to do something else and take it easy." Jesus did not give in to that temptation, though it was with him all his life. He decided to make God's call the project of the rest of his life.

SEEKING SUPPORT

It is difficult to resist temptation alone. Nobody who ever succeeded in following God's vision and promise did so alone. Too many thresholds have to be passed, too much fear overcome, too many obstacles cleared, too many addictions mastered, too much resistance and confusion overcome. The first thing Mary does after her self-giving yes is to go to Elizabeth. It is when Elizabeth affirms and supports her that she sings out her hope and expectations. The first thing Jesus does on his first walk along the lake side is to look for company, going so far as inviting people he accidentally met. He could take that risk, because he knew that his dream was the stuff their dreams were made of. Looking for company is also the last thing he does before being arrested, asking the same companions not to leave him alone in his anguish. It is together with his friends that he engages himself to the kingdom of God, washing their feet, breaking his bread, sharing his wine, and revealing to them his and their own dynamism and Spirit.

How far have we made this dynamism and Spirit of his our own? We accepted it formally as present in us at our baptism. That was, however, only the beginning. Many of us don't come any further, just as many are quite willing to celebrate Jesus' birth at Christmas without wanting to go all the way with him for the rest of the liturgical year. During the same initiation rite we were also anointed priest, prophet, and king, which determines our whole personal and social existence. How far is that true in the reality of our life? How many of us put ourselves at the service of God's kingdom?

A WEAKNESS TO OVERCOME

I am thinking of a nurse in a large hospital in the United States, well-trained and highly efficient. She does a good job, is kind and pleasant to her patients. Yet she is dissatisfied with her way of life. After praying and attending retreats she comes to the conclusion that she would like to do something directly for the reign of God here on earth.

She contacts a mission organization that is willing to send her out as an associate. She follows the training program and goes overseas to work in a hospital. She remains there for three years, the limit allowed by the organization that sent her. Now she is back in the same hospital from which she left.

The strange thing about her story is that in her mind and that of the church community she belongs to she only seemed to be working for the reign of God while "volunteering." It was only in the context of a religious, clerical position that she was able to integrate her profession into her view of the reign of God. Once back in her original parish community, she feels things are again just as they were before she left.[1]

This story points to a weakness in our Christian approach, a weakness that affects much volunteerism not only in the church but in the society at large. People set aside "volunteer" time as a kind of self-corrective for a situation in which they have—in a way—banned the Spirit of Jesus from their daily professional and personal lives. This promotes a kind of Sunday Christianity decried by a clerical institution that often has caused it by giving the impression that the spiritual domain was its exclusive own.

THE TOTAL VISION

The dynamism of Jesus' Spirit reaches into our hearts and minds, but it is often far from being the heart and soul of our existence. It was not like that for Abraham and Sarah, for Mary and Joseph, for Jesus. They related to each other, to God, and to their community in view of their vision and hope in God's promise. They begot and educated their offspring taking into consideration the realization of that vision. It filled their whole family and professional life. As we noted before, Mary was not Jesus' mother in her spare time. The vision of the kingdom of God must fill the whole of our existence. Its realization is the core of our lives, the reason of our existence. The mission of realizing the vision is ours; it is the mission of the People of God:

It is clear that from the very origins of Christianity, the
laity — as individuals, families and entire communities —
shared in spreading the faith. . . . The need for all the
faithful to share in this responsibility is not merely a
matter of making the apostolate more effective; it is a
right and duty based in their baptismal dignity,
whereby "the faithful participate for their part in the
threefold mission of Christ as priest, prophet and
king." Therefore "they are bound by the general obligation, and they have the right, whether as individuals
or in associations, to strive so that the divine message
of salvation may be known and accepted by all people
throughout the world. This obligation is all the more
insistent in circumstances in which only through them
people are able to hear the gospel and know Christ"
. . . they especially are called "to seek the kingdom of
God by engaging in temporal affairs and ordering
these in accordance with the will of God."[2]

It is our task to realize humanity's deepest aspirations put
in us by God our creator and lover. We are called by God's
Spirit in us to realize the kingdom of God. That is our task,
whatever our sex, age, marriage status, profession, or skill.
It is not a question of volunteering as a doctor in a clinic for
homeless people for some hours during the weekend; or as
a lawyer spending some hours giving free legal advice to
people who would not be able to pay for it; or as a parish-
ioner cutting the grass around the church building without
asking for payment. It is in our work and our family life that
God's Spirit should be our heart and our soul. The way wife
and husband love each other and relate to their children;
the way children relate to their parents and to their future;
the way professionals and workers render their professional
services and are politically engaged; the way the pope, bishops, priests, and deacons organize their pastoral and sacramental ministry, all relates to this mission and task in the

world. Healing, nursing, producing food, transporting, trading, educating, doing research, banking, investing, managing, servicing, organizing, associating, preaching, and worshiping, all should be seen in the light of that most divine of human visions: the final destination of the whole of the human/divine family. It is because of our universal engagement in this task that we should be attracting others by witnessing to our vision in our approach to life. We should open the dialogue with them in view of our common goals of a just and peaceful world.

HEALING AND GATHERING IN COMMUNITY

All over the world Christian communities are beginning to reorganize themselves into communities with educational, medical, self-help, and development projects, beneficial to themselves and to the wider world. The older male and female religious congregations and societies — which often started as lay movements but almost always got clericalized! — are beginning to share their charisms, residences, and tasks with lay people, families, and sometimes whole Christian communities. Outsiders join communities of contemplative congregations while continuing to live their professional lives as doctors, lawyers, car mechanics, or waitresses.

New associations and societies group professionals together to make it possible for them to organize their lives and their professionalism more integrally in a kingdom of God context. Some family groups organize their worship, family, and leisure time together. Sometimes they only pray jointly and share their faith experiences. In other cases they bring the money they earn together to make it possible for all of them to be available for professional services to all those in need, rich and poor, at the same time.

Entire parishes are reorganizing themselves to reappropriate the healing and gathering tasks they never should have lost. Parish communities are twinning with Christian communities elsewhere. The rich befriend the poor; the poor befriend the rich. In parishes all over the world new groups are forming that come together for tasks set in view of renewal, prayer, justice, peace, racial harmony, environmental wholeness, and a better and more loving society. In Latin and Central America those groups are called Basic Christian Communities, in Africa Small Christian Communities, in North America and Canada they have all kinds of names.

Theologian Gregory Baum has spoken about "the explosion of spirituality . . . a new experience of God . . . a renewal of fidelity to the gospel . . . a development that has great spiritual authority in the churches."[3] Such development has not escaped the attention of Pope John Paul II:

> These are groups of Christians who, at the level of the family, or in a similarly restricted setting, come together for prayer, Scripture reading, Catechesis and discussion on human and ecclesial problems with a view to a common commitment. These communities are a sign of vitality within the church, an instrument of formation and Evangelization and a solid starting point for a new society based on a "civilization of love."[4]

A NEW SENSE OF MISSION

The revisioning and redivision of our task seems gigantic. It is, but the work of reorganization has started. Mission is no longer seen as relevant only to a group of religious male and female missionaries. Still, people especially trained and kept free by communities to contact "others" are needed. These contacts should not only be made "overseas," a term that refers to a time that is past. "Others" are in new ways present to us not only far away, but also around the corner of the street in our own residential areas, towns, and cities. All over the world, people have been emigrating, immigrating, and migrating. We are getting more and more mixed in one gigantic network. Electronic connections offer new possibilities for communication. Racial division and ethnic violence, definitely reported more frequently than ever before, are experienced by all as scandalous disasters. The tragedy of division and failure, of neglect and marginalization, are ever more keenly felt.

Television and junk mail pieces make the global village all too apparent. If you give to one international charity (e.g. Bread for the World), soon you will get mailings reminding you of: world hunger (a near billion malnourished in the world); refugees (millions displaced in El Salvador, Afghanistan, Ethiopia, Sudan, occupied Israel, now also in Jordan and Saudi Arabia); prisons (we build more, rehabilitate fewer inmates and prisoners are, perhaps, those most without voice); the reality of AIDS (growing world-wide and in our country); substance abuse issues in the developed and developing world; prisoners of conscience (Amnesty International deals with 5,000 world-wide); solidarity movements with El Salvador, Guatemala, Haiti, the labor movement; the peace movement, never dead, takes on new life today. Again only those deaf to the news and documentaries, will be unaware of consumerism, world debt, the arms trade world-wide, the corruption of drug and drug trafficking, not only here but in Colombia, Bolivia, and Thailand.[5]

Problems and issues hang together. Concentrating on one brings out all the others. Sickness and consumerism, AIDS and drugs, poverty and sexual abuse, homelessness and the national debt—it is all interrelated. The astronauts saw it looking at our planet from space: we form one organic unit. The whole of humanity is slowly waking up to this interconnectedness. It is humanity's response to God's vision and God's dream, hidden as our vision and our dream in all of us.

In the church we can embrace the whole world and at the same time contact each local community by thinking globally and acting locally. Willing to live God's love for the human family and the whole of creation, we in the church are capable of gathering the scattered children of God. We as Christians cannot do this on our own. We only can do it in dialogue and cooperation with all the others.

Being capable of doing something does not mean actually doing it. It is in the tension between these two that our mission asks for local initiatives and contacts among local communities. The church should be, and to a certain extent already is, a living network that connects individuals, families, and communities in a way different from anything else in the world. Its way, the way of love, is the only way to solve the problems of a world becoming more and more aware of its sinful shortcomings and managerial problems. It is the way to fulfill the dream and the vision of God, hiding as the treasure and the pearl in the hearts and minds of all of us, the dream of being together as one family in the house of God. Living that dream in the reality of his life and waking others up to join in its fulfillment brought Jesus Christ among us. It made Abram and Sarai leave Ur and Haran, the prophets sing, and Mary and Elizabeth joyfully welcome their children.

For Reflection

1. Discuss how marriage and children relate to our mission. Is it understandable that some would choose not to marry in view of our mission? Discuss.

2. The Canadian Episcopal Conference suggested the following work plan to its Christian communities. Do you think you would be able to apply it to your context?

Our pastoral methodology involves a number of steps: a) to be present and listen to the experiences of the poor, the marginalized, the oppressed in our society; b) to develop a critical analysis of the economic, political and social structures which cause human suffering; c) to make judgments in the light of the Gospel principles concerning social values and priorities; d) to stimulate creative thought and action regarding alternative models for social and economic development; and e) to act in solidarity with popular groups in their struggle to transform society.[6]

3. Is there any effort in your parish to keep the lines of communication open with the rest of the Christian world?

4. Do you have anyone in your parish working as a missionary? How do you relate to that person when he or she returns for leave?

5. Is your liturgy organized in a way "that does justice"? Who is present and who is absent in terms of class, race, lifestyle? Who are in the processions? What about the handicapped—are they ever invited to be lectors, ushers, eucharistic ministers? Is the language sexist? Do the general intercessions broaden the vision of the local community, making all conscious of God's children?[7]

CHAPTER 18

Victory and Celebration

And God will wipe away every tear from their eyes.

(Revelation 7:17)

N ow it is time to sum up. Jesus did this at the end of his life. He did it in different ways. Just before starting the last chapter of his earthly life he took the last piece of bread from the table, broke it, and passed it around with the last of the wine. While doing this he said to them, "This is my body, this is my blood." Eating that bread and drinking that wine they formed his body.

He summed it all up in another way at his ascension. He told his disciples that the Almighty, who had empowered him, had done the same to them. They would do what he did—gathering, overcoming the terrors of the past, healing, and peace-making. He added that they would gradually understand their mission better, and that they would be able to do greater things even than he had done. He assured them that he would be with them always.

The Second Vatican Council brought out this truth as it had never been brought out before, except in the practice of the very beginning of the church. All of us share from within ourselves God's love and God's urge to gather the whole of

146

humanity and the whole of creation. Being taken up in the divine process is not reserved to some or to a special group. It is present in the whole of humankind. Those baptized accept it formally as the reason of our existence. We agree formally to have the nerve, the spirit, and the very feelings of Jesus. We are all taken up in the process that found its fulfillment in him. The mission others more or less reserved for themselves, and which we often gladly left to them, is ours. Being a follower of Jesus means more than living a good personal life and joining in a weekend worship; it determines our whole individual, family, social, and professional life. Some of us will be trained to reach out to those far from us. Those professional and specialized missionaries are needed and should be helped. But they cannot replace our own mission of gathering, reconciling, establishing justice, and making peace. It is a daunting task indeed, but at the same time a meaningful and hope-giving one. It is the *only* meaningful and hope-giving program and spirituality for our day and age.

THE STRENGTH OF THE VISION

We all know of people who are so convinced of one or another mission that they have no time for anything else. Jesus was not like that. He goes to a wedding party and provides wine. He takes his rest periods, his weekends, and holidays. He enjoys a good meal in the house of his friends Martha, Mary, and Lazarus. He had to be serious about his mission, and he is. He even put his life on the line, something most of us are not asked to do.

How did Jesus find such perfect balance for his life? He could live fully because he was sure of the victory and of the final outcome. He encompassed the history of the vision.

When Mary met Elizabeth, she not only sang, she must have danced. She sang a song like the far echo of the song we finally will sing together when we sing and dance within the city of God and the heart of the Trinity forever and ever.

The fulfillment of the vision breaks through in every expression of human love. The love of and for our friends, brides and grooms, our children, our parents, our community, and even those far away are the first signals of what in the final instance will be, when God is all in all, and we together in God. Our last dance will not be an end but the beginning of something lasting forever and ever, a dance in which the music, the dance, the folklore festivals, the street feasts, even our better parties, picnics, holidays, outings, fairs, and ceremonies only vibrate in the slightest resonance. They are only an echo of things to come, a surface ripple of what is already going on deep within and at the center.

In the book of Revelation the difficulties that face us are described in apocalyptic detail. We fight with dragons and monsters, worse than in any fairy tale or in our wildest nightmares. John could write in that way because the issue is in no doubt. Children don't mind the stench, the awful colors, the sliminess, the teeth, the claws, the smoke out of the nostrils, and all kinds of other horrible things in tales of monsters, as long as they are sure that those monstrosities are going to be killed or tamed in the end. There is more to the description in the book of Revelation than this kind of fictitious horror, but there too the battle is won.

> The Book of Revelation may be gory, surrealistic, unnerving, even terrifying. But it contains not a single note of despair. Those still in the clutches of the Dragon may not yet experience it, but the decisive battle has already been won. The early church celebrated victory in the midst of calamity. The struggle continues, but the issue is no longer in doubt. The far-off strains of a victory song already reaches our ears, and we are invited to join the chorus. This is the rock on which we stand: the absolute certainty of the triumph of God in the world.

That is why the celebration of the divine victory does not take place at the end of the Book of Revelation, after the struggle is over. Rather it breaks out all along the way (Rev 1:4-8, 17-18; 4:8-11; 5:5, 9-14; 7:117; 8:1-5; 11:15-19; 12:7-12; 14:1-8, 13; 15:2-4; 16:5-7; 19:1-9).[1]

GOD WILL DANCE

This final victory breaks through not only at the moment of our celebrations, though it does then. It is with us not only when we break his bread and share his wine, though it really is there. The reign of God shines through every time people live and die for the sake of human dignity and a just and peaceful world. We all know stories about these break-throughs, about victims who not only affirmed their own human dignity but also that of those who victimized them.

The end will be—as the Prophet Zephaniah wrote—that God will dance.

> The Lord your God is with you. He will take great delight in you, he will quiet you with his love, he will rejoice over you with dancing and singing (Zeph 3:17).

We are still out of step, but the dancing has begun. It is what the three in the Blessed Trinity have been doing from all eternity. We are invited in to their circle. They could have forced their dancing step on us, but instead they invited us. They sent Jesus to us to be our Lord of the dance.

> He dances in front of us,
> he dances before us,
> he dances around us
> in the improvised tent
> we call church

where we have to get in step,
with him,
but also with all our sisters and brothers
together with the whole of creation,
>one step to the right,
>one step to the left,
>one step forward,
>one step backward,

looking up at the tent lines,
and to the sky
through a hole in the roof,
down to the earth,
out of the tent opening
to the far off sky of a new city.
>Tables are set up,
>name tags distributed,
>committees formed,
>bread is broken,
>wine is shared,
>now and then there is a hush
>as if all are in prayer,
>and then the rehearsals veer off again
>>one step to the right,
>>one step to the left,
>>one step forward,
>>one step backward,

groups are formed,
circles opened,
blessings shared,
oil and water
splashed around
anointings and baptisms,
>a trumpet blast,
>the sound of instruments tuned,
>directives are given,
>maps laid out,

and marked are the roads
leading to our destiny
the home of God self.
Remaining ourselves,
but more and more together
in ever growing ecstasy,
    we are taken up in the swirling movement,
    of the dance
    that is already moving around and ahead,
        one step to the right,
        one step to the left,
        one step forward,
        one step backward,
we are still trying
to catch His rhythm,
and the words of the song,
He sings and pipes
in our midst.
    Others are joining,
    balancing gifts on the top of their heads,
    playing their drums and trumpets,
    adding to a cacophony,
    that sounds more and more
    like a symphony
    the longer it lasts.
It is almost dawn,
the rucksacks are packed,
the children awake,
ready to dance
into the dawn of a new day,
    and we,
    we are on our way!

For Reflection

1. Discuss how you as a person, as a family member, and as a worker can structure a mission spirituality.

2. Which obstacles hinder you? In clay, paints, colors, or words express the power that most holds you back.

3. Do you ever celebrate with others the victory of good over evil in your life?

4. Write (separately or in a group) your own perception of the vision of the final outcome of our mission.

Notes

1. MEETING JESUS OF NAZARETH

1. *Decree on the Church's Missionary Activity* (*Ad Gentes*), no. 3. In *The Documents of the Second Vatican Council*, ed. Walter M. Abbott, S.J. (New York: America Press, 1966).

2. AROUSED BY JESUS

1. William Herr, *In Search of Christian Wisdom* (Chicago: Thomas More Press, 1991), adapted.

10. RECONCILING PEACE-MAKER

1. Corrie ten Boom, *The Hiding Place* (Old Tappan, New Jersey: Fleming H. Revell Co., 1981), p. 238.
2. Doris Donnelly, *Putting Forgiveness into Practice* (Allen, Texas: Argus Communications, 1982), p. 3.

11. SIGNS, SYMBOLS, AND REALITY

1. Justin J. Kelly, "Absence into Presence, A Theology of Imagination," Warren Lecture Series in Catholic Studies, University of Tulsa, 1991, p. 3.
2. Samuel Taylor Coleridge, *Animae Poetae, From the Notebooks*, ed. E. H. Coleridge (Boston: Houghton Mifflin, 1989). Quoted in Kelly, p. 15.

12. INITIATION, SPIRIT, AND MISSION

1. Julius Nyerere, quoted in P. Scharper and J. Eagleson, eds., *The Radical Bible* (Maryknoll, New York: Orbis Books, 1972), p. 13.

2. *Decree on the Church's Missionary Activity (Ad Gentes)*, nos. 3, 4. In Abbott.

3. Henri Teissier, Archbishop of Algiers, *La Mission de l'Eglise* (Paris: Editions Desclée, 1985), p. 38.

13. OUR MISSION: CHALLENGES AND PRIORITIES

1. *Gaudium et Spes*, 1. In Abbott.

2. John Paul II, *Redemptoris Missio (On the Permanent Validity of the Church's Missionary Mandate)*, *Origins* (31 January 1991), no. 1.

3. Ibid. no. 13.

14. HOW TO PROCLAIM AND DIALOGUE

1. The order "Go!" as such is not found in the text, though it is implied and found in practically all translations. There are two sections in Matthew's final text. First, the apostles come together at the meeting point indicated by Jesus: "Then the eleven disciples went to Galilee, to the mountain where Jesus had told them to go. When they saw him, they worshiped him; but some doubted." Then, in a second section, Jesus takes the initiative: "Then Jesus came to them and said, 'All authority in heaven and on earth has been given to me.' " The verb that follows is a participle meaning "making disciples." They will do this because Jesus' power and authority are with them. See, for example, D. A. Carson, *The Expositor's Bible Commentary, Matthew* (Grand Rapids, Michigan: Zondervan, 1984), p. 596.

2. John Paul II, *Redemptoris Missio*, no. 45.

3. *Heritage and Hope: Evangelization in the United States*, Pastoral Letter on the Fifth Centenary of the Evangelization in the Americas (Washington, D.C.: United States National Conference of Catholic Bishops, 1990).

4. John Paul II, *Redemptoris Missio*, no. 4: "For each one is included in the mystery of redemption and with each one Christ has united himself forever through this mystery."

5. V. J. Donovan, *Christianity Rediscovered*, 8th ed. (Maryknoll, New York: Orbis Books, 1990).

6. Christian van Nispen, *Journées Romaines* (August 6-September 6, 1991). Cf. G. Evers, *Conferentie in Rome over Jezus Christus in de dialoog met de Islam, Tijdschrift voor Theologie*, vol. 32, no. 1 (1991), pp. 83-84.

7. Pope Paul VI, Inaugural address to the second session of the Second Vatican Council, September 29, 1963. Cf. Z. Thundy, et al., *Religions in Dialogue: East and West Meet* (Lanham, Maryland: University Press of America, 1985), p. 149.

8. Robert Ellsberg, ed., *Gandhi on Christianity* (Maryknoll, New York: Orbis Books, 1991), p. ix.

9. See K. Cragg, *The Christ and the Faiths* (Philadelphia: Westminster Press, 1987).

10. Paul VI, *Evangelii Nuntiandi*, Introduction, 1975.

11. David A. Bos, "Community Ministries: The Wild Card in Ecumenical Relations and Social Ministry," *Journal of Ecumenical Studies* 24, 4 (1988): 592-98.

12. *Guidelines and Suggestions for Implementing the Conciliar Declaration, Nostra Aetate*, no. 4 (Vatican City: Vatican Commission for Religious Relations with the Jews, 1975).

13. Pope John Paul II, quoted in E. J. Fisher, "Interpreting *Nostra Aetate* Through Post Conciliar Teaching," *International Bulletin for Mission Research*, vol. 9, no. 4 (October 1985), p. 162.

14. Jorge Mejia, quoted in Fisher, p. 163.

15. Thundy, et al., p. 149.

15. THE WHY AND HOW OF JUSTICE, PEACE, AND CREATIONAL INTEGRITY

1. Edward Schillebeeckx, *Jesus in Our Western Culture: Mysticism, Ethics, and Politics* (London: SCM, 1987), p. 78.

2. Quoted in J. G. Donders, *Non-Bourgeois Theology: An African Experience of Jesus* (Maryknoll, New York: Orbis Books, 1985), pp. 159-60.

3. Campaign for Human Development, USCC, 3211 4th Street N.E., Washington, D.C. 20017-1194.

4. J. Holland and P. Henriot, *Social Analysis: Linking Faith and Justice* (Maryknoll, New York: Orbis Books, 1988).

5. Schillebeeckx, p. 30.

6. Walter J. Burghardt, S.J., *A Faith That Does Justice: Challenge of the Nineties to the Christian Community*, Warren Lecture Series, no. 18, The University of Tulsa (1991), p. 6.

7. Paul VI, *Evangelii Nuntiandi*, no. 29.

16. ABOUT FEELING AT HOME: INCULTURATION

1. Donovan, p. 121.

2. Ibid. p. 92.

3. Paul VI, address to participants in the Symposium of African Bishops at Kampala, 31 July 1969, 2: AAS 61 (1969), p. 577.

4. B. Bassett, S.J., *How to Be Really With It: Guide to the Good Life* (New York: Doubleday Image Book, 1971), p. 141.

5. *Lumen Gentium*, chaps. 2, 3.

6. John Paul II, *Redemptoris Missio*, no. 23.

17. HOW TO ORGANIZE AND MANAGE OUR MISSION

1. See J. G. Donders, *Risen Life: Healing a Broken World* (Maryknoll, New York: Orbis Books, 1990), p. 28.

2. John Paul II, *Redemptoris Missio*, no. 51.

3. Gregory Baum, quoted by J. A. Coleman, "The Priest's Spirituality as a Mirror of the Global and Socially Concerned Church," keynote speech to the Conference of Religious Superiors of Men, 1991, p. 10.

4. John Paul II, *Redemptoris Missio*, no. 71.

5. Coleman, pp. 4-5.

6. Canadian Episcopal Conference, "Ethical Reflections on the Economic Crisis," 1983.

7. See J. Empereur, *The Liturgy That Does Justice* (Collegeville, Minnesota: Liturgical Press, 1990).

18. VICTORY AND CELEBRATION

1. Walter Wink, "Victory Songs and Fish Fries," *Sojourners*, vol. 21, no. 4 (May 1992), pp. 28-29.